I0462309

Professional, Caring Book Editor ebookeditingpro.co

Book Cover Design by ebooklaunch.com

First printing, 2019.

Connect with Anthony Chaine

www.asalesleader.com

www.linkedin/in/AnthonyChaine

CONTENTS

ACKNOWLEDGEMENTS

My deepest gratitude goes to my clients who believed in my sales training and philosophy. I'm always inspired, whether I'm in the trenches or side-by-side training new hires, existing teams or managers, because you live it and I'm here to serve you, make your life easier and more productive.

To my loving and supportive wife, Naomi: You are my rock, you have been there every step of the way, you listened and pushed me when doubt and procrastination tried to take hold of me.

Finally, I thank my friends and peers whom I learned from, shared my experiences with, and got inspired by. You mean the world to me.

PREFACE

It has taken me over ten years to gather the courage to write a book like this one. I started writing to give back to society and help salespeople understand that professional selling is the most rewarding career one can have. I also started writing because I was frustrated by the constant pitiful internal corporate rivalry and games that damage people's morale, damage the organizational culture, and destroy revenue.

I stumbled into the sales profession over twenty years ago after a few years as a bar restaurant owner. Since then, I've worked for multiple sales organizations, ranging from small boutique retailers to large national and global companies. I worked in numerous industries, from hospitality to retail, advertising to communication, banking to mortgages, payment to software. I experienced and enjoyed selling business-to-business, business-to-consumer, and human-to-human.

After years in sales management, heading multiple sales organizations and educating salespeople in the art and science of selling smart. I decided to share my knowledge, experiences, and concerns about some operational, emotional, and rivalry dysfunctionalities that plague our industry.

To complete this book, I have interviewed and assembled top-notch advice from several sales professionals. I gathered stories and insight from several sales managers, directors, VPs and CEOs who understand and get the complexity of the world of selling!

I'm fanatical about salespeople success, and I firmly believe that when salespeople succeed in helping their customers grow their businesses, companies benefit and economies expand.

My passion and greatest joy is to see salespeople and sales organizations thrive under any economic or geopolitical situation. Success is a formula that can be replicated, but it starts with the implementation of the right thinking, empowering employees and managers to do what's right all the time.

I hope that you will find value in the lessons in this book, whether you are trying to change your business culture, increase revenue, lead better, or improve your sales process. This book has a good dose of reality that businesses suffer from; some are obvious, yet most organizations continue to ignore them, while some are less obvious but widely rampant in most large organizations.

To contact Anthony, find out more about his sales and management training programs, or get his eBooks, articles, and video educational series, visit www.asalesleader.com.

INTRODUCTION

The sales manager job has never been harder. In 1980, a study conducted inside Xerox Corporation revealed that it would require 29 hours for a sales manager to complete all his daily sales and administrative work. Administrative tasks alone require more than two-thirds of the sales manager working hours. Sales management is all about providing team guidance, coaching, setting sales quotas, and salespeople goals. This is in addition to drafting sales strategies and tactics, assigning sales territories based on the sales rep capacity, analyzing sales data, and making changes based on market demand which are all part of a sales manager's duties. Traditional selling belief is sales is a numbers game: the more contact you have with new prospects, the higher the probability of selling your products/services. However, modern selling beliefs are quite different.

Sales Evolution

Historically, in most industries, top salespeople were promoted to sales managers. The transition didn't require a whole new set of skills, but rather the transformation of existing skills. The transformation of skills can be much more difficult than acquiring a new skill, which was often not well understood by new sales managers and their bosses.

The job of the sales manager is much more complicated than that of the salesperson. The sales manager acts as leader, coach, supervisor, *and* manager. The sales manager's job is to empower his salespeople by equipping them with the right training and tools to achieve personal and company goals. Good sales management requires proper planning and organizational skills, along with hiring the right people for the right job, then training, coaching and motivating them to crush goals.

While sales managers and company trainers get involved to different degrees in salespeople training, sales managers rarely receive any training or coaching at all; most sales managers learn by trial and error; they live by the law of "sink or swim. "

Sales training often lacks depth and revolves around the principle of "always be closing" and selling by promoting a product's functionality and benefits. The customer buying cycle starts at the point of perceived need, and the salesperson sales cycle begins the moment you spot a prospect.

The process is simple. Marketing plays a role in triggering customer curiosity via smart adds, social media, or traditional advertising.

The customer triggers the process by contacting the sales organization for product information, quotes, or a request-for-information.

Back in the 1980s, the salesperson's competitive advantage was the information and knowledge he held in his sales binders in the form of product visuals, product lists, statistics, white papers, testimonials, and price lists. Sales were highly transactional and linear in their nature. The salesperson was encouraged to overcome objections by showing more facts, studies, statistics, and testimonials.

Print media salespeople were trained to overcome objections by producing documents that reflect specific data and statistics that minimize customer fear and anxiety. For every complaint, they had a statistical, survey, or study document that proves that traditional advertising works.

The conversation between the buyer and seller was more of a monologue than a dialogue; the salesperson and the sales manager did most of the talking while the customer listened. While these approaches sound quaint and naive at best now, they were viewed as the best in class then. Xerox sales force was admired, as it seemed ahead of its time in term of professionalism, quality of training, and polished knowledge.

The sales profession has evolved since then. Sales is a science and an art form. By science, I mean, it's a tested knowledge that has a clear pattern we can recognize and replicate. The application of its models and concepts are based on fundamentals that can improve the skills of individuals and group practitioners. The art perspective reflects human communication, interaction, and persuasion skills.

Sales Management evolution

As a previous senior-vice-president, sales director and first-line manager, I experienced first-hand the positive impact that a great sales manager can have on an individual salesperson or a team. A great sales manager can turn a mediocre team into a winner, while a poor sales manager can quickly turn a superstar team into a disaster. Good sales managers are critical to the success of any organization. Many sales managers struggle to survive on their own, in a system of sink or swim.

Sales management has changed dramatically since the 1980s. A Harvard study, conducted in 2006 as an annual survey targeting primarily chief operation officers (COOs), revealed that across industries, the selling context has evolved dramatically. Today's customers are much more demanding than in the past, and the effort required by the sales organization to win these customers is much more complicated than earlier: especially in a business environment where most organization product-line breadth, product complexity, and market reach is larger than ever before.

Sales Force productivity

Salespeople learning curve continues to stretch; it takes on average six to nine months for the average salesperson to reach full productivity. The average salesperson quota has increased by 15%-20% every year. Meanwhile, due to cost reductions, most sales organizations have reduced the number of sales support personnel to a skeleton level, making the sales reps and the sales managers' jobs much harder.

Today's sales reps must be creative, smart, and hardworking to meet assigned quotas and stay relevant in an unforgiving world driving by pure productivity.

Creating a competitive edge is becoming a growing challenge for salespeople and companies. Today's advanced innovations can get emulated and improved upon by competitors in a relatively short period. Customers are increasingly more educated today with greater access to information on the web, and access to other companies' products specifications, prices, and customers' experiences and reviews.

Salespeople Challenges

Salespeople are finding their job increasingly more challenging than in the past. Online data information ease of access has rendered the salesperson input almost obsolete. Customers armed with information can shop around knowing they can easily find a similar product elsewhere at a lower cost.

Besides, the sales cycle has become twice as long in business-to-business because most buying decisions go through multiple layers of approval to minimize risk and the probability of failure. Many sales buyers have been burned in the past by unethical sales reps, who failed to deliver on their promises and where the product didn't live up to its hype.

It's common that a B2B sales rep must convince multi-level layers of approvers individually to sign off on the deal. Each approver could become an obstacle requiring additional time, resources, and creative strategies to win them over, causing additional delays to close the deal.

Customers are ultimately in control of the sales process, and they feel they can dictate the terms, negotiate the price to the bare minimum, and fire the vendor the moment they feel manipulated.

Sales organizations are under tremendous pressure exerted by lower sales revenue, decreased margin, higher sales cost, greater employee attrition rates, lengthier employee ramp-up process, and longer sales cycles. Consequently, many sales organizations resort to reducing or eliminating their field sales reps and replacing them with telemarketers and e-commerce platforms to reduce cost and increase revenue.

Methodology Approach

These are all the systems, tools, methods, and techniques that can create a framework and a predictable path to generate sales. CRM systems have radically changed the way we sell, store, manipulate data, and predict future sales.

The first generation of CRMs in 1990 was perceived as a time waster, and it met with tremendous resistance from salespeople. The second and third generation of CRMs changed that perception based on the tangible analytic benefits it provided to the sales organization, its management, and salespeople.

Nowadays, I cannot imagine any sales organization that can do without some form of CRM. Imagine how a sales leader would measure the sales activities of his team, like forecasting opportunities within the sales funnel that will close within a specific time frame. The usage of a CRM to organize and systemize the sales process is becoming the norm.

Many sales organizations had embraced new technologies to make sales prospecting much more predictable and effective. Some of the technology used today are:

- route mapping
- data enhancement
- one-click dialer
- predictive analytics
- marketing automation
- content marketing
- big data
- robotics
- artificial intelligence
- social engagement

Customers are more demanding than ever, and salespeople need access to intelligence data to draft a plan of engagement that meets customers' demands.

Pipeline Management

It's almost impossible to fathom a sales manager today who doesn't rely on some form of pipeline management software to predict and forecast sales cycle progress. Today's pipeline modeling systems are highly sophisticated and intuitive. The growth of artificial intelligence and machine learning has enhanced the accuracy of sales forecasts and sales prediction. Senior executives rely on their line managers' forecast to draft their projections. Pipeline provides quantitative sales metrics that allow the sales manager to measure, control, understand, coach and tweak behaviors that can affect sales results.

PART I: SALES MANAGEMENT

"The difference between a successful sales organization and others is not a lack of resources, not a lack of innovation, not a lack of talent, but rather a lack of shared true purpose and misalignment among cross-functional teams." – Anthony Chaine

"Coming together is a beginning, staying together is progress, and working together is success." — Henry Ford

"Technology is a useful servant but a dangerous master"— Christian Lous Lange

CHAPTER ONE: MARKETING AND SALES SYNERGY

The company missed its quarterly revenue quota for the second time in a row, and a heated conversation ensued between the head of sales (CRO) and the head of marketing (CMO).

CRO: The quality of leads continues to deteriorate, and despite our best efforts, our sales reps are losing the field battle. The marketing material is archaic and uninspiring, and we haven't had any new promotional materials or compelling digital marketing campaigns in the last 12 months. Our telesales folks say the quality of leads provided is subpar. We have a mediocre presence on most popular social media platforms, and we have no brand leverage in comparison with our competitors.

CMO: I believe your sales folks need training. Most of your sales reps don't have a good grasp of the product they are selling and have a hard time positioning our value propositions to their prospects. Many are not following up with their leads in a timely fashion, often dismissing quality leads without thorough qualification, and without ever attempting to revisit their lost opportunities. Besides, many of them lack closing skills ability and blame marketing for their inadequacies. I suggest you focus on developing their skills to an adequate level to leverage our marketing campaigns. My team is continuously engaging potential customers in creating brand awareness and spurring desire and long-term commitment through artful and strategic storytelling. I recognize that we are lacking manpower and financial resources to become a dominant marketing household name on social media, but we're doing our best to work creatively despite our tight budget.

The above conversation, loaded with ego and emotions, is common; many salespeople do not understand the role of marketing, while marketers do not understand the complexity behind sales. Rather than working in tandem and as a force of one, they often tear and blame the other for their collective failures.

Sales often looks at marketing as a support function rather than a partner that drives revenue. Smart companies know that marketing's primary role is to attract, retain, and grow revenue from existing and new customers. Marketing performs product and market research to evaluate demand and appeal, prepare and package business solutions, communicate brand value, and maintain and expand customer relationships.

Despite having different functions, sales and marketing share similar responsibilities and duties concerning customer engagement and satisfaction, revenue generation, organizational growth, and brand positioning. When marketing and sales work together in complete synergy, companies achieve faster growth, better productivity, higher profit margin, greater employee job satisfaction, and higher customer retention.

According to a study done by Salesforce, when the marketing group and sales group have a disconnected relationship, it affects companies' revenue negatively and triggers productivity inefficiencies, costing companies globally almost a trillion dollars per year. Despite the interdependence and the similar nature of the functionality of these two groups, sales and marketing act more as rivals than partners. Missed targets and failed programs turn into blame matches with neither party taking responsibility, thus, turning what could be a tremendous lucrative partnership into a perennial conflict between two groups whose best option is to work together to thrive.

A study conducted by insidessales.com where 696 companies participated in the evaluation of their sales reps' 'lead response behavior' revealed that sales reps took on average 39 hours before attempting to respond for the first time to a newly-submitted web lead. Furthermore, according to lead response management research conducted in 2007, a sales rep is 100 times more likely to contact a new sales lead, and 21 times more to advance that sales lead into the sales funnel, if approached within the first five minutes of lead submittal.

Interdependence Requires Harmony

Marketing and sales are separate functions within most organizations, and they don't always work in harmony together. Marketing often blames the sales force for its poor execution of an otherwise brilliant marketing rollout strategy. The sales team will blame the marketing department for being out of touch with customers' demands, poor-quality leads, outdated marketing materials, and lack of awareness of competitors' superior offers.

Marketing will blame sales for their inability to follow up and close good qualified leads and lack of understanding of products sold. Plus, sales is way too focused on individual customer demands, rather than looking at the whole market and taking into consideration future trends that may affect the industry. In short, these two groups tend to undervalue their contributions rather than build on them to create team synergy.

When marketing and sales are not aligned, revenue and employee morale suffer. Conversely, when they work well together, we see significant improvement on key performance indicators ranging from shorter sales cycle, lower cost of sales, faster conversion rate, better market data sharing, higher employee morale, and greater customer satisfaction.

A *Harvard Business Review* study revealed that companies that contacted potential customers within an hour of receiving the lead were seven times more likely to connect with a decision maker than those who waited two hours or more, and 60 times more likely than those who attempted after 24 hours. Web leads have a short life span; response time matters.

This study highlights the fact that marketing efforts (generating leads) work best when sales teams (close the deal) work with a sense of urgency and purpose.

Why the Friction?

There are two significant reasons why marketing and sales struggle to work together.

Economic reason: Senior management allocates a yearly budget to the marketing and sales department. The marketing departments spend its budget on pricing, promotion, and product. The marketing group sets the pricing in a specific way that will allow it to meet its revenue goals, and sets pricing guidelines and instructs the sales group to sell the price as opposed to lowering the price to makes more sales. Salespeople, facing market reality and intense competition, often recourse to reducing the price as an incentive to meet customer demands, facilitate negotiations, shorten the sales cycle, and speed up the decision-making process. The marketing group has the power to set pricing guidelines. However, the sales team ultimately decides on the selling price.

The vice president of sales often reaches out to either the senior vice president of finance or the CFO for pricing consideration and exceptions when the requests are below marketing specific guidelines. This ability to override marketing pricing guidelines often creates friction among these groups.

Promotion cost: Marketing groups spend money creating ads and promotions on different social media platforms, billboards, and television advertising to generate customer awareness, create interest, build preferences, and invoke a desire for the product. The vice president of sales often feels that television ads and billboard advertising rarely produce value, and when they do, they often cannot be measured. A better investment would be increasing the size and quality of the sales force, and its impact is usually measurable and immediate.

Product: Most product releases come with some level of needed improvement. Salespeople's job is to sell the product as it is rather than how it should be. Salespeople often sell a promised outcome to their customers, and they are expected to deliver on it. Customers get irritated when the product lacks some needed features, has a poor design, or fails to achieve the outcome that was guaranteed by the sales rep. Dealing with angry customers, major escalations, buyer's remorse, and having one's personal reputation tarnished is often a subject of great frustration for salespeople. Salespeople's worldview is often shaped by the needs of its customer, while the broad appeal shapes marketing's worldview.

Budget Contention

Budget issues are always contentious. Marketing requires considerable economic powers to buy space to promote the company brand and its business solutions value. Most of its impact is intangible and long-term, while an investment in the sales group can generate a tangible, short-run effect on the company bottom line. Salespeople view their marketing counterpart as bureaucrats sitting behind a desk, surfing social media, and using predictive analytics to gauge marketing project performances. Salespeople see themselves as doing the hard lifting, field prospecting, presenting, overcoming obstacles, building relationships with their customers while testing and evaluating the product appeal and areas of deficiencies. It is easy to see why these two distinct groups have difficulty working together toward a common goal.

Purpose Driven Compensation Plan

Part of the reason why marketing and sales act as rivals rather than partners lies in their planned compensation structure. The sales organization should design compensation plan incentives that align marketing and sales toward the achievement of specific goals that enhance productivity. The company goal achievement is the ultimate goal. Therefore, these incentives must be a laser focus on the products that the company wants to sell.

Salespeople are driven by their sales quota to achieve bonuses and keep their job. They are masters at working the sales compensation plan and become extremely analytical when it comes to maximizing their ability to make money by taking advantage of any loopholes in the compensation plan.

Compensation plans that are non-performance driven are horrible because they diminish competitiveness, lower production, and spur complacency.

Comp plans that promote individual over-performance are excellent for morale as they compensate the individual according to productivity, rather than being part of a team that performs well.

A good comp plan should allow top performers to make ridiculous money, to ignite other sales reps to increase their performance intensity to over-achieve. The comp plan should be as simple as possible. If you work hard and are super committed to over-produce, the company will pay you extraordinary well. Sales reps who barely get by should not be allowed to stay around these hungry, committed super producers. Underperformance tolerance should be banned.

On the flip side, the company must find a way that allows marketing folks and sales folks to get compensated for working together as a united force to meet or exceed company objectives.

You would probably agree that paying more for newly acquired customers is worth more than paying for maintaining an existing customer. Now, don't get me wrong here. Keeping and growing your existing customer base is vital. However, sales effectiveness is the ability of the organization to capture new dollars. Paying higher commissions for new sales should be encouraged. Sales hunters (business development sales reps) should be compensated differently than sales farmers (account managers). Part of the reason that sales organizations struggle to acquire new business is because the comp plan doesn't motivate sales reps to push hard to acquire the business.

Salespeople are often compelled to lower the selling price on their products to meet quota, while the marketing group would lament that the sales group is not selling effectively and shying away from selling higher margin products bundles.

Salespeople are paid a commission immediately upon selling, installing, and activating a business solution. Marketing folks enjoy a higher salary and discretionary bonus when the group meets company goals. The marketing budget is allocated to specific company programs, not necessarily to people, and to complicate the matter more, some of these program impacts take an enormous amount of time to generate value, and even then, it's hard to measure their effectiveness.

It is easier to measure the success of sales by the number of closes. However, it may take a marketing campaign more than six months to start seeing any measurable results, and it's even harder to begin quantifying a marketing campaign impact.

Marketing is all about influence. But it's tough to measure the latter, e. g., a sales rep closing a lead provided by an existing client. While word-of-mouth is the best referral type, the signing customer may have done some research on the products by reading company reviews, online marketing material, and blog posts to make the right choice. In this case, sales will get credit but not marketing. Marketing and sales are vital forces that complement one another and should work closely together for the greater good because they cannot survive separately.

Scalable good marketing strategy and execution can provide the necessary support to help sales attain its objectives. Marketing creates customer awareness, initiates desire, customizes native content, and sends important communication that moves customers to action. Several studies have demonstrated that marketing and sales interactions within many significant corporations are minimal at best and often awkward. Sales marketers' responsibility is to craft messages that the buyer can identify with and say, yep, that's me.

Most corporations have separate goals for marketing and sales, rather than one common collective goal. Instead of having team performance goals, these company should have division performance goals; all units of production should work to accomplish one goal—company revenue objectives. After all, the company is one unit of output; all its departments rise and fall together.

Factors Contributing to the Discord Between Marketing and Sales

1. *Poor communication.* The irony is that sales and marketing's significant strength is communication skills. These groups often fail miserably to conduct a productive dialogue and establish an inter-departmental communication model that promotes understanding and trust.

2. *Budget.* Allocated financial resources are always limited in nature and scope. The marketing group needs money to finance its programs. Sales needs money to hire and train new and existing salespeople, and it also requires a budget to incentivize

and reward salespeople for exceptional performances. Marketing and sales executives' big egos and entitlement create friction, resentment, and group dissatisfaction.

3. *Professional views conflict.* Most salespeople feel that the marketing group is too broadly focused and often ignore local customer wants and desires. Conversely, marketing people perceive salespeople as having myopic views as they focus on individual customer wants rather than border market.

4. *Professional differences.* Marketers tend to be analytical, factual, methodical, and strategic in their approach to achieve specific goals. While salespeople are primarily focused on building long-term relationships, engaging new and existing customers while closing deals. The marketing group and sales group priorities and approaches, while similar in some areas, are broadly distinct, leaving room for misinterpretation, misunderstanding, and occasional cultural clashes.

5. *Pipeline misalignment.* The marketing group's job is to build a growing, large pipeline of qualified leads. Salespeople's job is to close as many opportunities as fast as possible to meet their quota and achieve their bonuses. Salespeople often complain about the poor quality of leads or shortage of lead flow. Marketing group often blame salespeople for poor follow-up, slow reaction to reach on leads, and dismissal of qualified leads within less than two attempts.

6. *Strategic misalignment.* According to a *Marketo* study, "at least 1 trillion dollars is lost annually due to misaligned sales and marketing strategies." Mismanagement of leads often slows the process down, creates time waste, redundancies, process inefficiencies, and loss of opportunity.

Cross-Functional Team Alignment Leads to Growth

Most functional units within companies (finance, marketing, sales, legal) work toward the accomplishment of their own goals. This strategy often focuses on team and division wins rather than the whole organizational success. Internal divisional competition is well and good, if every division works in harmony with other business units to advance the company toward the attainment of its collective goals.

For example, you cannot have a car run well when its engine cylinders run in different sequences. The power of the engine depends on the synchronicity of its collective parts.

The same principle applies to corporations. All functional teams should work as one force that moves forward to achieve corporate growth by meeting their business objectives while aiding other cross-functional teams in attaining theirs as well.

Amazon CEO Jeff Bezos and CTO Werner Vogels have implemented a method called 'The Institutional Yes'.

This idea generation system allows an employee to present to their manager any good idea deemed worthy of evaluation. The manager's default answer should be a YES, and if the manager decides to say no, then they're required to write a two-page thesis explaining why it's a bad idea. By doing so, Amazon has created an environment where more ideas are being tested and implemented throughout the whole organization.

Genuine company success requires the strength of all its essential divisions; a lack of harmony or weakness of some of its parts can lead to a failure of the whole system, just like a deadlift champion would exercise several muscle groups at the same time, e. g., back, glutes and legs. A champion knows everything matters: good form, movement, hip-width ratio. Any flaw can result in failure and potential injury.

Company internal departments are interdependent of one another, e. g., a sale that requires a price exception and a contract modification to happen will need marketing permission, finance approval, and legal assistance. Without the collaboration of these departments, the sale will never become a reality.

Marketing and Sales Conflict Stages

Given the economic and cultural conflicts described above, it's reasonable to expect dissatisfaction and mistrust among these groups. Now, it's easy to believe that the nature of the issue is way too broad and complex for a quick resolution. In reality, these conflicts are human-made and can be resolved with dialogue and alignment of purpose. When the relationship between marketing and sales matures and they align behind everyday goals, growth happens quickly.

- **Entrepreneurial stage.** The company is at its infancy, and there is no defined strategy on how these two groups should work together. Each group works according to its agenda. Most communications revolve around reactive issue resolutions rather than proactive cooperation. Collective goals are not defined and mistrust abounds among these two groups.

- **Get-along stage.** Sales and marketing understand they should work together civilly to create opportunities and minimize conflict. The marketing team and the sales team focus on what they do best and start working together to promote the company with partners, during special events, and trade shows. Trust and relationship start building gradually.

- **Partnership stage.** Sales and marketing are focused on their distinct business, but have a complete understanding that both parties depend on one another to grow and achieve goals. Both groups agree to use similar work terminology to facilitate communication and speed up progress and results. Marketers start being involved in large accounts, leveraging field reps' customer relationships to conduct surveys and collect feedback and get more involved in the general education of the sales force on how to leverage marketing to acquire more substantial and complex accounts.

- **Fusion Stage.** This is the ultimate stage where the boundaries between sales and marketing become almost invisible. Both groups actively share ideas, insight, opportunities, and systems that gauge customers spend trends, loyalty and reward programs. This stage reflects the ideal state where marketing and sales act as one force, that work together to improve the company brand by providing the ultimate customer experience every time.

- **Risk Mitigation.** Imagine you board a flight, and as soon as you're settled in your seat, you overhear two flight attendants' conversation behind you. "You should know that the pilot had attempted suicide several times in the past, and his co-pilot has just spent a week in the hospital for experiencing major episodes of depression." How safe would you feel getting to your destination? What kind of stress and fear would you experience, knowing these two critical individuals have suicidal tendencies or mental/emotional issues? It would be natural to worry about your safety in these conditions; knowing that your life is in the hands of two mentally unstable individuals is a scary fact. Yet, if you had never heard the conversation, you would be just fine.

Sales and marketing self-sabotaging and undermining each other's value and credibility is counterproductive and harmful. One will never insult a customer by implying they are unrealistic, dishonest or lazy. Yet, sales and marketing often berate one another, demean each other's effort and contribution, just like two siblings who cannot live apart but cannot stand being close.

These self-sabotages can get resolved with conscious effort from both groups to refrain from judgment through a heightened state of awareness and education. Problems and misunderstandings can only be solved once recognized and addressed with the best interest of the company in mind, not self-interest.

How to solve this dilemma?

- Uncover the root of the problem that leads to marketing and sales misalignment and friction.
- Quantify and educate both parties on the economic and moral impact of the problem.
- Design and implement a path of communication and collaboration that is tied to a reward system or an incentive to change to achieve a fusion stage.

Synergy is at its optimum when clarity, understanding, and commitment are aligned to achieve mutual objectives. The integration of marketing and sales can be a winning formula; they are equally important, and they must work in tandem for better company future.

CHAPTER 1: SUMMARY

- Marketing and sales should work as a force of one. Departmental politics and personal rivalry should be identified, discussed, and eliminated to create the necessary synergy to meet goals and surpass the competition.

- Marketing and sales work interdependence requires harmony to achieve mutual objectives.
- Sales executives should generate a compensation plan that recognizes and rewards efforts and exceptional performances that contribute to the ultimate goal—company objectives.
- Aligning cross-functional teams to work as a force of one to deliver on the company goal will lead to revenue growth and employee satisfaction.

CHAPTER TWO: TECHNOLOGY IMPACT ON SALES ORGANIZATION

Technology runs our lives these days. We become so dependent on the technology around us, ranging from smartphones and tablets to laptops and computers, that we cannot seem to function without it. Not long ago, customers had to drive to different stores to compare prices and research a product or services. Researching a company required one to go to the library to compile information. Search engines changed the way we think, search, and analyze data. Finding information got easier and data control power shifted from the hands of companies and salespeople to the end-user. With each technological upgrade, complexity and ambiguity increase. We went from a slow dial-up internet connection (AOL message, you got mail) to faster internet connections, from Rolodexes with customers' names to Salesforce CRM, from VHS tapes to digital downloads, from hard storage capability to cloud-based services like Dropbox and Google drive, from a physical workplace to a virtual workplace.

We can only speculate that the current technology will continue to evolve at a much faster pace than before; we are continually seeing emerging technologies and new smart trends. The exponential evolution of technology is blurring the lines between the physical and virtual world. The internet of things (IoT) is turning home appliances, electronics, and cars into smart technologies that can communicate with us and remind us of tasks and events. Smart cities are already here, intelligent consumers are ready, but businesses need to get smarter fast to survive and thrive toward a better future.

Sales Organization Evolution

The new sales organizations will need to adapt to an ever-evolving technological ecosystem that runs most companies' logistics. Moor's law is accelerating the fundamentals of technology growth. In most industries, the development cycle for products and services grows shorter by the day. Yesterday, leading sales organizations in film photography like Kodak are part of the past. The exponential growth of core technologies, the virtualizing of one industry after another, and the automatization by software have created a new fast-changing world, where historically insulated, stable sectors are at risk of financial insolvency today. New, fast evolving software is leading industries of all sorts. Cloud computing and the app store ecosystems are transforming industries, and consumer behaviors are getting less predictable and much more challenging.

Products are launched earlier, often in their beta stages of gathering vital data and adding changes and modification based on market feedback. Changes and product updates are done quickly, usually followed by the release of a product version 2. 0. Product development cycles moved from years to months and weeks. The market becomes a testing ground, and products early adopters play a considerable part in helping the company improve its products testing via quick feedback and insight on how to improve functionality. Competitors are studying and learning from first-in-market errors and are sharing their development and product improvement with trusted development networks.

The shelf life of a newly designed product is shrinking dramatically as well. Thanks to applied reverse-engineering, the moment a product hits the market, several similar products follow within weeks or months to capitalize on the second wave of buyers that are price-conscious.

While the sales team is selling the latest version of a product, there are often at least two newer versions that are at different stages of realization being tested for potential quick release.

Leaner New Digital Market Entrant

Industries that have dominated the space in the past, due to the high barrier of entry, are being overtaken by new entrants with smart software solutions and new ideas. We have seen significant industries in computing, 3D printing, biotech, and fine-tech being transformed by new smaller emerging players that were historically viewed as disruptors doomed to fail. The evolution of the internet and technology has eliminated huge barriers of entry, narrowed the difference gap, and allowed global entry from unexpected places to compete with local businesses.

The line between industries specialization is blurred, long-standing boundaries that define a specific business or industry are dissolving, allowing the creation of new ecosystems. One example is how Amazon moved from selling books to selling everything under the sun; by acquiring Wholefood corporation, it becomes a giant retailer. You may remember in 2011, IBM Watson computer system won Jeopardy contests, but it is used now to detect and diagnose medical conditions and to draft patient-care-plans. IBM Watson is also being used to study market trends, predict customer needs, and even generate leads.

New market entrants are becoming today's giants sweeping everyone in their path and creating “mega winners”, such as Facebook, Google, and Amazon. However, even these giants are being affected by the same technological phenomenon that created them. Many will be replaced by newer emerging players that do not exist today. Business competitiveness is shifting from its conventional competitive methods to the predictive assessment of future challenges and opportunities to survive.

Sales Force-Displacement

The internet has played a significant role in facilitating the creation of virtual businesses that generate referrals and sell products and services without the need for a sales force. Amazon, eBay, and Craigslist are a few examples of these companies. Today an app or a website with good content can generate traffic and sales.

The idea of scale selling any products without a field sales force or telesales was inconceivable twenty years ago. The print advertising industry has been devastated, and many newspapers went out of business because they couldn't compete with free online classified ads as opposed to paid newspaper ads.

Large companies like Apple have outstanding digital marketing campaigns, a huge network of enthusiasts, bloggers, and social influencers that promote the company products for free across multiple digital landscapes. Social media platforms such as Facebook, Instagram, Snapchat and YouTube are changing marketing approaches and consumer behaviors. Huge swaths of market shares are won and lost because of perceived values and brand influence. The future of sales and marketing is changing fast, and the cost to reach and influence customers is dropping rapidly. This is happening across industries and across time zones.

Net Promoter Score Value

Customer loyalty is vital to the survival and growth of any business. That is why many large corporations pay close attention to their Net Promoter Score (NPS), which is a system that measures the loyalty metric that exists between providers and consumers. *Harvard Business*

Review expounded on the importance of NPS in an article written in 2003 titled "One Number You Need to Grow". The NPS was introduced by Fred Reichheld (NPS varies from a -100 to +100). He explained that an NPS higher than zero is considered good, an NPS of +50 is excellent, and NPS of +100 means everybody is a promoter. An NPS of -100 means that everyone is a detractor.

There is a direct correlation between overall client experience with the brand and NPS scoring. The NPS is based on a simple question. How likely is it that you would recommend our company, product, or service to a friend or a colleague?

Companies that enjoy high NPS like Apple have higher client satisfaction, great peer-to-peer feedback, free promotion, and low sales cost.

Several companies enjoy high NPS score. See examples below.

1. USAA—Insurance = 80%
2. USAA—Banking = 78%
3. Costco = 78%
4. Apple—Laptop = 76%
5. Amazon = 69%
6. Southeast Airlines = 66%

Technology creates opportunity and abundance, but it surely destabilizes major industries that thought they were safe in the past. Many major taxi companies, that owned medallions worth hundreds of thousand dollars in the past and were securing stable passive income from leasing these medallions to taxi companies, found themselves with worthless medallions because of Uber's business model. Uber went quickly from being perceived as a disruptor, to a game changer, to a global domineering industry force.

Uber's ability to scale its fleet quickly, empower its customers with a better ride, smart social interaction, and safe payment choices made a huge difference in the transportation business. Additional, Uber leveraged extremely well peer-to-peer promotion strategy making it the preferred transportation system for city dwellers.

Airbnb used the abundance of supply of residential rooms to create a supply that today exceeds the largest hotel chains in the world. The marginal cost of adding a room digitally to the Airbnb system is virtually zero. However, that is not the case for an established hotel chain, hence, giving a considerable upside to Airbnb. Again, Uber and Airbnb NPS is very high, allowing them to acquire new customers for virtually no cost.

Many significant advertisers are shifting today from billboards and TV content to Facebook, Instagram, and YouTube as they realized that their customer base has moved to a younger generation that consumes news and information using social media rather than traditional television and newspapers mediums.

Selling Dynamics Have Shifted

Sales have been affected and will continue to transform and adapt to meet new customer demand. Marketing has morphed from an ad-based to a socially interactive medium that caters unique content to fit its consumer base context. Obscure products that were impossible to get off the ground in the past can virally sell via smart, targeted social networks that cater to risk takers and early adopters. Startups with good marketing strategies are becoming game-changers.

Large competitors' strategies that revolve around lowering prices to drive a new competitor out of business no longer work. People are looking to buy from organizations that are value-driven and socially motivated.

We have seen many startups that promote their product along with their social responsibility. People love to buy products they need, but they prefer to buy from a company that contributes some of their buying dollars toward a social charity that helps someone or something to achieve a more dignified life.

For example, Tom.com gives as a charity a pair of shoes for every pair sold. Boxlunch.com gives away a meal for every $10 you spend and theelephantspants.com clothing company donates 10 percent of its proceeds to the African Wildlife Foundation to help fight elephant poaching.

These are companies that promote social causes while doing business with caring loyal customers. It's a form of charity that preserves human dignity and pride.

Expertise and Innovation

Beware, sales experts with decades of experience in the field may slow progress. Experts tend to focus on reasons not to take a risk. Experts often draw their thought process from personal and collective experiences. However, experiences are part of the past, while innovation is all about the future, things that have yet to happen, to be created, tested and tried.

A fresh perspective is often needed to uncover new patterns that an industry expert may not be able to see. Not long ago, it was unthinkable to imagine that computers could drive cars, trains, and space ships.

Tesla is primarily a computer with wheels, and these electric cars are becoming widely accepted by a more significant segment of sophisticated consumer who care about comfort and the environment. The future will require collaboration between the industry experts and the new creative minds. Better results will require advanced creativity, technological innovation, and alignment with consumer demand.

Nowadays, with information overload, customers must rely again on a salesperson to simplify their decision-making process. The relationship between the salesperson and the customer must be transparent, based on trust and harmony.

Multiple studies have shown that only 10% of the sales force have in-depth knowledge about the product/services they are selling. Fifty percent of the salespeople surveyed demonstrated average technical expertise on their core products, and only 20% of the salespeople surveyed showed a good understanding of the company's newly launched products. These numbers are indeed not very encouraging, and that's part of the reason why salespeople are not perceived as real experts in their field.

Size No Longer Matter

For decades, bigger companies leveraged their scale and size to win more significant market shares. Profitable, large companies were the darling of Wall Street, which triggered CEOs' egos to seek further aggrandizement by acquiring additional companies and market shares. Salespeople were leveraging their company brand name and market dominance to impress customers and win business. Smart start-ups catch up quickly by leveraging their boutique-friendly customized solution, exceptional customer care, and lower overhead.

To stay competitive, these larger organizations start sacrificing profit margin to win on sales volume against more creative, nimble smaller competitors. Despite their smaller size, many of these organizations begin specializing in specific industry verticals, making them indispensable to some businesses and eclipsing the competitive advantage of scale and size their larger competitors possess.

Netflix has used a similar strategy that forced Blockbuster to go out of business. Netflix sold convenience and speed of delivery, and

Blockbuster focused on the physical retail experience, while underestimating customer preferences evolution.

Technology is a force that is changing the market, transforming industries and destroying old business models. What has worked in the past may not necessarily work in the future as technology continues to develop at a faster speed. Consumers' buying behaviors often meet quickly and even exceed current trends in innovation speed. However, salespeople are resisting change and lagging in multiple areas. To stay relevant, sales professionals and sales organizations will need to hit the reset button often, to allow quick mental reboot and install new thinking and new business models that evolve according to customers' demands. While salespeople can learn and adapt fast to new requirements, they have limitations. Salespeople of the future must become growth specialists rather than generalists to stay relevant.

Specialization will become the way to create depth of knowledge and expertise to meet customer demand. A cardiologist and an OB/GYN are medical doctors, but each has their specialty. A woman who needs to manage her pregnancy, labor, and delivery will need an OB/GYN to handle her health. Similarly, the cardiologist is someone who can handle your cardiovascular system. While these two doctors may have a general idea of the other's expertise, each one will focus primarily on what they knows best. Future selling will need to become specialty-based rather generality-based. Special knowledge and expertise will be key to value selling.

Millennials Salespeople and Technology

Millennial salespeople love autonomy, flexibility, and the fluidity of the process. The new millennial sales generation is digitally wired, independent, resistant to authority, and linear top-down style management. Millennials operate well within horizontal structures that permit exploration of new ideas, encourage creativity, and innovation.

This group of salespeople loves when a sales manager provides clear objective, steps back and allows people to work to create the intended results.

Millennials accept and love challenges, but reject excessive management control and suffocating behaviors.

Let me elaborate; millennials know they are smart, able to resolve complex issues, and love to overcome difficult obstacles. They understand the power of networking and tapping into all available resources to get things done. A controlling manager will suffocate this group to the point of paralysis and will demotivate creativity and innovation. Millennials thrive in an open and transparent environment that promotes meritocracy and rewards people according to their contributions. Many companies that employ millennials, like Zappos and Facebook, have seen incredible market share gains, more considerable market appeal and greater consumer trust. Zappos management trusts its employees to deliver customer excellence according to the fundamental precepts that drive their culture.

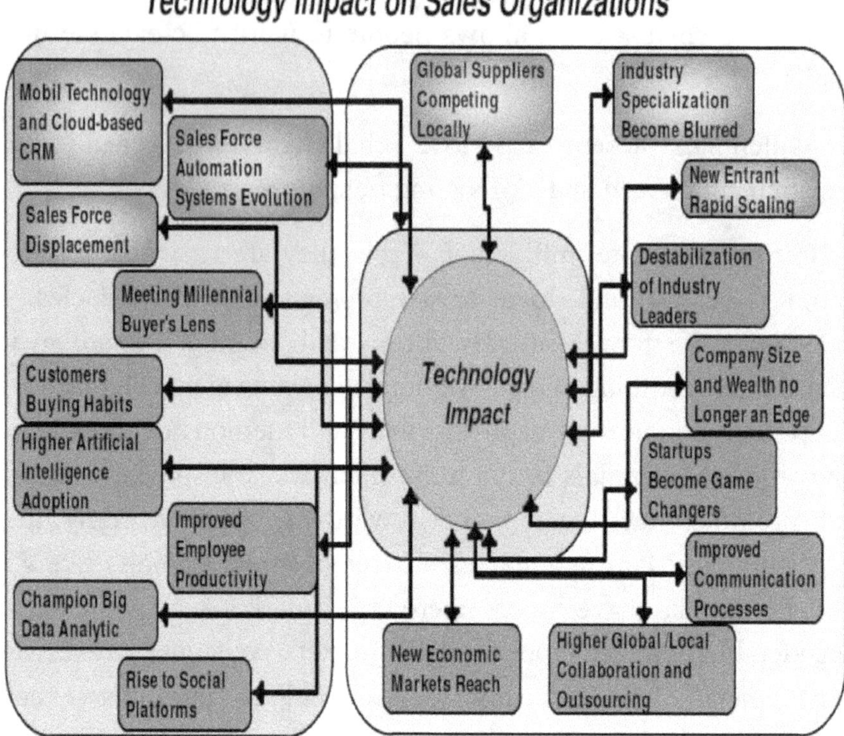

CHAPTER 2: SUMMARY

- Sales technology and the internet advent will continue to transform customers' buying behaviors forcing sales organizations to adapt quickly and continue to stay relevant and survive.
- Local markets that were shielded from competition in the past will experience a flood of new small entrants that serve a digital, growing customer base, along with large global companies that will compete locally via e-commerce.
- Startups with smart marketing strategies will become game changers. Digital marketing and social platforms will displace a

lot of businesses and industries that were deemed safe in the past.

- Business legacy and size no longer matter: what counts is the business' ability to meet customer needs using their preferred way of communication and delivery.
- Millennials will become the new sales force. Baby boomer sales managers will need to accept and adopt the way millennials, think, communicate and work to achieve goals.

CHAPTER THREE: THE SALES MANAGER JOB

The sales manager's main responsibility is to ensure that every salesperson on the team is focused on the vital core KPI rather than the many urgent generalities. Lean organizations concentrate on new business development, customer retention, and expansion. These critical KPIs generate the necessary revenue, without which sales organizations cannot survive, thrive, or prosper. Most organizations lose customers for a variety of reasons, and it's imperative to replace these losses with equal or better opportunities to stay in business. However, it's easier said than done!

Organizational survival and prosperity requires nurturing, converting new opportunities into new customers while retaining your client base, growing it and expanding it via cross-sales and upsell methods. That is why it's crucial to recruit continuously, train, structure, align, deploy and provide incentives to sales reps to spur production. Sales managers should provide ongoing support to ensure that salespeople, working mainly in an unsupervised field environment, operate as a cohesive force toward meeting corporate goals. The sales management process is complicated because it deals with multiple variables that consistently shift directions. Even selling your products to similar customer's base within similar geographies will require different methods and approaches. Sales in one specific territory may create results above expectation while a similar territory results may be inadequate.

The sales managers ensure that the sales process is followed and assist with coaching and training their sales reps on the following sales processes:

1. Prospecting. Company generated self-generated leads represent the lifeblood of any organization.
2. Setting the appointment.
3. Qualifying leads.
4. Making the presentation.
5. Handling objections.
6. Closing the sale.
7. Getting referrals.

Sales managers work with their sales reps to draft a plan that details specific actions that will lead to achieving goals. Sales reps' progress is evaluated regularly against pre-set goals, and corrective feedback is shared continuously to avoid falling behind. Additional monthly and quarterly progress reviews are established to assess the sales rep year-to-date standings.

During these feedback meetings, the sales manager assesses the salesperson skills and capabilities as well as required behaviors and activities that drive results.

Common performance capabilities that require regular evaluation:

- Product knowledge.
- Customer knowledge.
- Market and demographic knowledge.
- Selling aptitude.

- Analytical skills.
- Territory management skills.
- Industry knowledge.
- Expertise mastery.
- Learning capabilities.
- Planning and research ability.
- Customer retention, satisfaction, conversion rate, repeat business portfolio growth, customer feedback, and dissatisfaction level.

Sales Manager Impact

A medical company tracked performance of its newly hired people for a period of 24 months. The purpose was to find out the level of impact that a great sales manager has over their team versus an average sales manager. The study found that the salespeople reporting to a great sales manager performed better on most critical metrics. Furthermore, these salespeople acquired more in-depth knowledge of products and service, knew better how to handle obstacles, had a higher level of confidence, believed strongly on the value of sold products, and felt like they made a difference with every client they interacted with. Additionally, they closed 60% more deals than their peers; they were satisfied with the job and were willing to refer friends to the company. These salespeople reporting to top sales managers performed much better than the salespeople reporting to an average sales manager.

The study also concluded that these sales managers focused on the following activity had the most impact.

- Spent double the time training and coaching recruits during their onboarding period, followed with above average field time to help the new sales rep to get accustomed to the company way while building internal confidence to master customer objections.

- Spent an additional 30 minute per day educating new hires on company systems, tasks and goals requirements as well as internal relationships building to overcome hurdles.
- Arranged for mentorship and shadowing with experienced salespeople as well new hires that exuded initiatives and potential.

Salesperson Daily Responsibilities

- Prospecting and identifying potential customers
- Generate leads, identify decision makers and purchase influencers
- Create awareness around company products
- Provide prospects with information and insight
- Explain business solution advantages
- Qualify customers
- Evaluate client needs
- Listen for cues
- Negotiate and persuade
- Close deals
- Ensure product delivery and installs
- Address critical issues
- Follow up with customers, cross-sale and up-sale based on need

The above list represents some of the salesperson's responsibilities in addition to time allocated to training, conference calls, administrative work, pairing with business partners, field time and so forth. Salespeople are busy creatures.

Sales manager expectations

Quarterly and Monthly

The sales manager should conduct quarterly and monthly business reviews with each sales rep to measure and coach on how they are progressing against the pre-set plan.

Bi-annually

The sales manager should perform a mid-year review with each sales rep and document the conversation, while drafting an agreed upon plan of action. The prescribed corporate guidelines outlined by human resources should be followed to minimize liability and risk.

Annually

The sales manager should discuss progress against "rep model" quota performance and conduct an evaluation of income against corporate compensation plan. It's vital to ensure that the sales rep is making enough progress on the job and is financially satisfied to stay at the position.

In addition, the sales manager should have a thorough conversation with each sales rep and lay out their vision and expectancy plan for the year. It would help to start with a sales rep best case earning scenario and assist the sales rep in understanding how their earning goals translates into corporate revenue objectives.

As a sales manager, you should create a customized earning plan for each sales rep, according to their true potential, competencies and strengths. Keep in mind that this activity should involve the sales rep market potential and the personal commitment needed to achieve the goal. This exercise with follow-up should help the sales rep become more effective and more efficient at hitting targets. Additionally, it's vital to incorporate a developing mentor program for the sales rep career development and other aspirations around sales leadership to allow for upward mobility based on desire, motivation, and potential.

Sales Manager Responsibility

The sales manager's schedule tends to be even busier. (Field Time 70%, Administrative work 10%, Performance Inspection 15%, Recruiting 5%). Consider the following list.

- Coach salespeople on and off the field
- Monitor sales reps' behaviors and performance
- Monitor how your sales reps spend their time
- How are your sales reps creating value?
- How do your sales reps interact with their peers, clients, and partners?

- How is your sales reps' morale?
- Get to know their competencies and deficiencies and draft a plan to remedy gaps.
- Review the health of your team pipeline and revenue KPIs
- Review your sales reps ability to work with their internal departments such as human resources, finance, marketing, product management/ deployment, customer service/ order management, sale operation, legal and partners.

Also, as a sales manager you will needs to manage the following.

- Lead flow generation and distribution
- Sales cycle
- Close rate
- Sales process ROI
- Territory alignment
- Customer management strategies
- Sales management effectiveness
- People management (hiring, coaching, and on-boarding of new hires)
- Escalation resolution

You got the picture; the sales manager has the most challenging job in any organization. The sales manager must be able to manage simultaneously and effectively in the following areas: customers, business, and people. These areas are equally important and challenging.

The ability to focus on these three areas with the same level of attention is tough and complicated.

- *Customers.* The sales manager's role is two-fold. Strategic and tactical. Strategic area means ensuring that the sales reps' account management and territory engagement is carried out according to the company's strategic plans. While, the tactical area refers to the sales manager time with his sales reps aiding to close business deals and resolving customer's issues and complaints.
- *People.* The sales manager's role is extensive and complex. They are responsible for the entire lifecycle of the salesperson, from selecting and recruiting a new hire to developing the person into a full-productivity level. The sales manager spends the bulk of time in the field training and coaching sales reps to attain higher performance level. The manager is responsible for implementing and reaching the organization quota.
- *Business.* The sales manager acts as the voice of his sales reps and the liaison with the company senior management. The sales manager is often responsible for creating business forecasts and relevant financial reports that provide an overview of senior sales managers to make their decisions.

The sales manager's job is to balance these competing business priorities while keeping team harmony. The sales manager creates results through people, by managing activities, processes, and budgets. The sales manager's role is to lead people to achieve their full potential by focusing on the events and behavior that create results, which requires continuous coaching and training of the sales reps.

Sales Manager Motivational Role

Sales management success is everybody's business. As a great sales manager, you will need to motivate your team in addition to:

- Show the way
- Inspire your troops
- Challenge everyone to reach higher goals
- Enable your team to thrive by eliminating obstacles
- Keep everyone emotionally involved to accomplish personal and company goals

Many sales organizations marshal huge sales kickoff meetings, provide amazing trips to exotic destinations, and incentivize their salespeople with generous commissions bonus. These incentives may generate a short uptick in productivity but often fizzle quickly. Long-term motivation requires a continuous, daily dose from the sales manager. A good sales manager makes the team motivation a priority. They set stretch goals, leverage their team trust, and keep everyone focused and engaged on their critical objectives. They use collective creativity to keep an environment that supports fun, recognition, celebration, and hard work.

The irony is many sales executives often think that sales managers ought to succeed on their motivational role despite all the obstacles generated by the company's negligence and lack of focus. Even the most egregious mistakes committed by the executive's management team get transcended down in term of ownership to the sales manager and the sales force. It's easier to reprimand and blame incompetence on lower-ranking managers than point fingers at the wrong strategies implemented by higher-ranking sales executives who have power and stronger ego.

Sales Management by Trial and Error

I still recall my senior vice-president call. "You have been promoted to our coveted sales director position. Going forward, you will be responsible for leading your team to achieve their sales goals. I understand that it has been historically an underperforming team. However, we believe that you can turn this team around quickly. You will be responsible for your team performance and profits and losses." As a young manager, I was happy to be promoted, but I was concerned about the challenges ahead of me. Thoughts like this were racing in my head: What kind of sales leadership training would I be getting? What type of coaching, assistance, and guidance would I be given? Who is going to explain to me the first thing I should be doing? I had a million questions, but I couldn't utter a word to avoid sounding stupid.

A quick call to my new colleagues revealed that the company had no traditional training or coaching program for managers. I found it to be puzzling; how is it possible this is a Fortune 100 company, yet they don't provide any management or leadership training for managers? Curious, I asked a friendly vice president of sales: "Did the company provide you with any training upon your promotion?"

"Senior management expects you to learn on the job through trial and error, by asking your peers, and by field osmosis. Once a year, the organization will have a two-day leaders' training on general leadership skills, but that's about it." Those were his exact words. I was stunned and disheartened, to say the least.

Another sales manager explained to me that senior executives and human resources teams pour money into training salespeople, year after year, to trigger higher performance. However, most of these trainings had little to no results, because they never invested in the preparation of the sales managers who can drive meaningful behavioral changes.

Management by Osmosis

As a sales manager, you ought to self-educate continuously because you will need to lead, manage, and coach your sales reps to meet their goals. I was promoted under the assumption that based on my past performances, I ought to know how to manage, motivate, coach, and inspire my team.

I was a top individual producer, and now my responsibility was to make a top producer out of every individual in my team. A quick assessment of the team talent and capability revealed that I was in serious trouble. My team needed a complete overhaul; my top performer was 40% behind his quota. I couldn't terminate everyone at the same time, and I had to work extremely hard to rebuild priorities and focus. I put in an insane number of hours and spent numerous nights and weekends with my willing sales warriors, forming a merit-based sales culture and a solid foundation required to attain success. My dad taught me the value of hard work. I was a rookie sales manager, and I was on a mission to show my boss that I could outwork, outthink, and outdo the performance of most sales managers in the company. It took me a year of insane work to turn the team around. I had a plan, and I was committed to making it work. I became the force behind the team progress; I was supporting everyone, I was in the trenches daily with the team, pushing and pulling and helping the team any way I could. I spent countless hours on the phone planning and discussing all topics. Our conversations ranged from current escalation, sales tactics to overcoming objections, pricing, and marketing initiatives. I was working non-stop. I was exhausted but excited to lead my first team. I had to prove my worth, and I was willing to pay any price to achieve it. I became the heart that pumps energy into the team. Salespeople's cohesiveness improved, morale was up, team retention improved, and results followed.

The pace I adopted was too fast and too intense. I was no longer in control of my time or actions; I became managed by my daily events and felt that I lost control. My strong salespeople needed my support, while my average producers became too dependent on me. They required constant support, and I realized by being a rookie manager I allowed myself to become the first destination for all answers. My underperforming salespeople needed me to provide them with moral support and assist with closing complex deals. I know that some underperforming employees needed to go, but I couldn't replace them fast enough due to lack of talent and the fact that the senior management had to manage employee retention to minimize financial and reputational impact.

Senior management required sales managers to spend four to five days in the field, yet when I was in the field, I was constantly interrupted and asked to provide financial reports that required office time and meticulous preparation. Also, it was common that human resource folks called in asking for specific information on specific cases. Additionally, I received a barrage of calls from my salespeople asking for updates on deals stuck with the underwriting group. Between sales calls, I had to fire a deluge of rushed emails and text reminders to several cross-functional team leaders pleading to get a decision on multiple pending requests. Anxiety built when I feel that despite my best efforts, I could only go as fast as these cross-functional teams' bottlenecks allowed.

The sales manager job is hard and incredibly frustrating sometimes. It may be a financially rewarding and exhilarating job, but sometimes, it feels like a job from hell. I often went home very late and stayed until 2 am and woke up at 5 am, including the weekends, to catch up on critical issues. I often doubted myself, my sanity, my competency, and the sustainability of workload.

Exhausted and frustrated, I asked my colleagues for input and direction, but it seems that everyone was in the same or worse position. We were all overworked, frustrated, lagging in terms of self-education and acquisition of new vital skills, and powerless to make any changes beyond what the existing system offered. As a sales manager, our role was not clearly defined, our responsibilities were too broad, and our internal support was horrible. The company expected us to impact our salespeople's mindsets and behavior to meet or exceed quota, but without proper training and coaching, most sales managers struggled to achieve their quotas.

Just Another Day

"Anthony, do you know how many customer calls I received today asking me about an account that I have no access to, especially while I'm in the field? Eight so far in the last couple hours. Not sure what's happening, but it needs to stop. Customer service reps cannot transfer their issue to field sales reps and circumvent their responsibility. Please, intervene and make it stop," said Tony, one of my top sales reps.

"I will handle it," I answered, before I looked at my computer screen. Several urgent matters needed immediate attention, and my boss had just sent for additional reports that would require at least three hours' work, as it was needed by 8:00 am the next day. A large business partner was threatening to pull the plug on the relationship unless we immediately addressed the current challenges at hand. Part of the agreement with this large partner was to assign an adequate number of field reps to handle the occasional surge of new customers. We didn't have enough workforce to handle remote areas, and senior management was not willing to hire additional reps. I was told to keep this decision confidential and try to buy time. I could maybe justify a one-to-two-month delay, but not a whole year. It was a failed strategy. We took on more responsibilities than we could handle, and we were not honest about it. Come to think of it, many of my colleagues were dealing with frustrated partners who realized that we could not live up to our promises. It's easy to promise but hard to deliver.

More phone calls came in, and several sales reps had multiple issues that required quick escalation and resolution; it was just one of these days. However, this was an average day in the life of a sales manager. I was wondering; maybe it was the industry I was in. Was the fintech industry any worse than banking, manufacturing, medical devices, software, or financial services?

If they were all the same, we didn't stand a chance. How could a sales leader be effective while buried in all this crap?

Back to Selling Basics

Sometimes our leaders forget that selling happens primarily when you are facing a buyer. Customer facing time is the most precious time as value is exchanged and relationships are built. Rather than increasing customer facing time, it seems that most corporations are increasingly forcing their sales managers and salespeople to perform tasks that decrease revenue generation time.

A boxer trains for months or even years on techniques that make him look aggressive while making his opponent feel nervous and even scared. The boxer learns how to box, walk, brawl, punch hard, but what matters the most is to win the bout either by a knockout, technical knockout, or by unanimous decision. At no time does the boxer management team advise the boxer to steer away from his focus from winning the bout. All that matters is the total focus on one opponent to win.

Sales organization's primary reason for existing is to build sales leaders who are willing and able to sell their product in quantities large enough and fast enough to generate profit to sustain the company growth while creating value for the customer and building trusted relationships with their employees and customers.

If the goal of sales leaders is to achieve results through their people, then the sales organization ought to eliminate all distractions that inhibit sales performances. If sales and revenue are the backbone of any organization, why allow these interferences hinder the company's ability to sell more, more frequently at a higher margin?

CHAPTER 3: SUMMARY

- The sales manager job is multifaceted, complex and extremely demanding. A good sales manager will strive to manage team demand, execute management requirements, and customer requests while maintaining internal harmony with cross-functional teams and influential external partners.
- The sales manager will need to continuously learn and upgrade their knowledge and expertise to pass it on to their team. Great teams are built on the backs of great managers.
- The demand for the sales manager can be incredibly intense. The sales manager will need to stay calm under pressure and continue to serve their constituent to the best of their ability despite the stress and the urgency of competing matters.
- A sales manager who is not meeting the organization goals will experience shorter job tenure and a higher probability of suffering career derailment and reputation loss.

CHAPTER FOUR: SALES MANAGER'S ROLE IN REVENUE GENERATION

For companies to exist, they need to generate revenue. Sales growth often triggers investor interest, while declining sales growth suggests that the company's products and services may have less appeal to a buying audience.

To grow sales, investments will need to be allocated to the sales force training, coaching, retention, motivation and incentive plans.

The role of the sales manager is vital to ensure that the investment made on the salespeople translates into increased sales. In a business-to-business environment, a well-trained, disciplined, and organized sales force can significantly enhance the company position in the market, create awareness, generate revenue, and win increased market share.

Most for-profit organizations focus on revenue generation as it matters to the company, its shareholders, employees, and its clients. Company executives focus on critical financial metrics that are reflected in the company financial statements and annual reports. Some of these critical metrics that are reflected on these documents are: revenue growth, percent share of the market, gross profit and customer satisfaction ratings. These business metrics reflect the current state of company affairs. It shows whether the company is growing or shrinking, whether it's making a profit, winning against its competitors, and its customers' satisfaction score.

Corporate business results reflect the financial health of the corporation, its market share within the industry, and the satisfaction factor indicating how its employees and clients perceive the company.

Revenue Drives Everything

Sales success is measured by revenue; the survival of most organizations depends on it. It's the metric that fuels people's ambitions, desires, and ego. CEOs jump on the opportunity to label themselves as strategic revenue creators. The head of sales are glorified for driving revenue up and terminated when they fail to deliver on it. Sales managers' bonuses and promotions depend on it, salespeople pride and compensation depend on it as well. Failure to generate sufficient revenue and profit for an extended period will mean corporate and business demise.

Revenue varies according to the company size, industry, business longevity, the product sold, and sales cycle. A large company like Apple may be looking toward a yearly revenue margin in the tune of billions of dollars, while smaller companies may be thrilled with just having enough cash flow to survive another quarter. Without question, revenue means the survival or demise of any business. Therefore, it should be the focus of every organization, but that's not always the case. Let's break it down.

Revenue is created by selling products or services to customers. The more products and services are sold, the higher the income. Revenue depends on the market demand of these products and services; marketing helps create awareness and demand for the company's products. Great marketing generates customer awareness, captures prospects' attention, and ignites their curiosity to act. Customers' questions and interest become part of the pipeline funnel that is managed by sales professionals.

Sales Pipelines

A healthy sales pipeline means potential market demand that could be translated into sales and revenue. The pipeline has two purposes. First, it defines the health of the company in terms of product desirability and potential revenue creation. Most corporate executive financial projections are based on potential quarterly sales. The second purpose is to measure sales force effectiveness in creating revenue by closing the business. The sales pipeline is a documented path that measures productivity and the progress necessary to move further down the success path.

Strategic Planning Spur Growth

A fintech company realized that its field salespeople in densely urban areas were neglecting smaller opportunities for more significant opportunities. The company also recognized that small businesses require more hand-holding, forcing the sales reps to drop other priorities to help customers in crisis mode. An internal company study concluded that it took about 23 months to achieve a break-even point with these small accounts. However, the average tenure of these small opportunities was 20 months, resulting in an average loss of $123 per account. The urban sales reps were stretched beyond their capacity to serve these small accounts that resulted in a financial loss.

To remedy this issue, the company contracted an outside telesales force that could handle these small account challenges and were able to upsell and cross-sell additional complementary services, turning this non-profitable business segment to profit. Furthermore, the outside sales reps were now enabled to focus their efforts on more considerable, more profitable opportunities. This change allowed these mid-market sales reps to reduce travel time, reduce travel cost, and increase the number of larger accounts market share.

Another software company that provides a leading management software for hotels and restaurants had difficulty penetrating certain demographic areas. An internal study found out that most employees spoke only English. Meanwhile, the demographic they were trying to serve has more than 130 ethnicities and spoke at least seven main languages. The company hired bilingual sales reps who spoke fluently at a minimum of one of the required languages. Within 24 months, the bilingual new hires were producing 300% more than their average peers who only spoke English. The main differentiating factor was the ability to speak a native language with a certain demographic that valued the language affinity as an attractive factor in doing business with the company.

The vice president of a high-end national retail watch and jewelry company attested that their business suffered immensely when they failed to recognize a new economic and trend wave. He explained that economic growth in some countries increased specific tourist spending overseas. He stated that he lived through several spending waves that were led by the Italians, Russian, Brazilians, Japanese and currently Chinese. Recognizing these economic waves promptly can translate into financial gains and brand promotion. Being prepared and quickly hiring professional salespeople and managers who understand people's cultures, needs, and wants can be very lucrative and can create enthusiastic international followers and customers.

The example above provides some insights on how to spur and manage internal and external opportunities. Finding opportunities for growth will require keen observation, leveraging people's flair differences, and finding specific areas that can be exploited. The opportunity lies within the gap. Seeing the gap will require a study of market, demographics, and psychographics.

Finding the next source of growth is a necessity for business survival. The business opportunity that got you to where you are today will become obsolete tomorrow. One should continually transform and reinvent the company to stay in business, to grow and expand; the company will need to be at the forefront of creativity and innovation to remain relevant to market demand. Technology will always play a significant role, but human ingenuity and creativity will continue to be the best sources of significant growth.

Transparency Create Revenue

For profit, organizations depend on revenue creation to survive, evolve, and grow. Revenue generation is the livelihood of any organization, but the revenue generated must reflect the company integrity, transparency and accuracy. The main reason why companies go out of business is that they cannot raise enough revenue to sustain their business model, they get sucked into devastating corporate scandals, or when the company products are not selling in quantities large enough or fast enough to create the needed cash flow. There is no bottom line without a top line.

Technological advancement has eliminated many barriers; small companies can now have a global reach. Established large companies that enjoyed stability for decades in the past are now forced to deal with multiple newcomers previously regarded as a fad or transitional disruptors.

Square Inc. is a merchant services aggregator founded in 2009 by Jack Dorsey and Jim Mckelvey. When Square Inc. launched as a startup, most large companies within the industry dismissed Square Inc. as a fad. A decade later, this entrepreneurial startup surpassed several well-established companies in terms of sold volume and market share. Square's innovative technology and creative business concept became like an idea-virus that took the market by storm, disrupting the industry and forcing companies to spend enormous resources to catch up.

Square initially went after a market that was deemed nonprofitable and high risk. Square Inc.'s strategy was unique, as it allowed single small entrepreneurs and home-based businesses to take credit cards from their customers. This strategy turned out to be brilliant, because in the past these high-risk small businesses and home-based business run by entrepreneurs were denied that ability or had to pay exorbitant fees to accept customer's credit cards.

Square Inc. was the first company to let entrepreneurs and small businesses to use their phone as a payment method. Their business model was simplicity, transparency, and speed. All major players within the payment system space thought it was just another gimmick by Jack Dorsey and doomed to failure due to the complex nature of the payment industry. Jack Dorsey's system seemed simple, but it was based on a complex algorithm that remove the enigma behind merchant services' hidden fees that legacy companies profited from. Entrepreneurs loved it because it was simple, transparent, and fair.

Multiple legacy companies were using deferent complex pricing schemes to confuse the merchant and maximize their profit. Merchant services statements were so complex that the average merchant gave up trying to understand what he was being charged and for what. There were multiple fees, interchange fees, and discount fees drawn directly from the business checking account, and the merchant had no other choices but to keep the service to keep accepting customers' payments. For years, merchants felt they were trapped, used, and abused by unscrupulous companies that only cared about their profit. A merchant was a cash cow to be used and dismissed when he raised questions. Worse, the processing company often tied the customer to legally-binding terminal leases and long-term contracts that carried penalties disguised as early termination fees.

Jack Dorsey's payment system was predictable and straightforward; As a customer you knew precisely how much you would pay and for what transaction. No gimmicks, no contracts, no early terminations fees, no binding terminal leases, no fees except what you agree upon the first time.

Small business owners and entrepreneurs were thrilled, and the Square concept spread quickly like a virus. Word of mouth and customer satisfaction became a weapon that Square Inc. fully exploited to propel the company to stardom.

The irony here is Square's innovative thinking capitalized on people's satisfaction and self-promotion to gain market shares while most legacy large competitors had to rely on partnership contracts with national and regional banks, software, and hardware vendors to feed them new leads in exchange for a fixed initial payout, in addition to a percentage in future recurring revenue profits.

Square customers became huge advocates for the company. These legions of entrepreneurs and small business owners promoted Square for free and organically faster than companies with substantial advertising budgets.

Revenue Creation and Client Retention

Today's ideas travel the world at the click of a button. Many entrepreneurial start-ups struggle with revenue generation and scaling operations even when endowed with incredibly innovative ideas, products, and concepts. To survive, a company needs to create revenue and profit in quantities large enough to meet its financial obligations and invest in innovation to stay relevant. That continues to be a significant challenge for most business, as customer demands and attention are continually shifting toward novel products and services.

Today, even large companies with established mature products and services struggle with revenue creation as new ideas and concepts keep entering the market and siphoning away profit, customer attention, and loyalty. This market and customer volatility puts a lot of financial pressure on companies to retain their existing customer base, which is lured by the latest innovative products, trends, and fashion.

We agree that a company's survival depends on its ability to retain, grow, and expand its client base. The most successful companies manage to build a cult-like following like what Apple and Tesla have built. Enjoying a technological cutting-edge, and a product that appeals to the market is certainly a competitive advantage that helps retain your loyal client base and grow influence, but loyalty is no longer guaranteed; it requires constant product improvement and innovation. Customers will stay loyal to your brand as long as the company performs above expectation, meets perceived economic thresholds and social demands, and stands for a cause that its clients feel proud to promote. One example is Tesla's vision "to create the most compelling car company of the 21st century by driving the world's transition to electric vehicles".

Today's customers are inundated with options; creating a lasting relationship is a thing of the past. Customer influence is affected by the environment, friends, social media, and personal worldview.

Business has always been hard, but it just got much harder. The old dogma' "survival of the fittest" has been replaced with "survival of the fastest". Business survival requires mental agility, a fluidity of thoughts, social nimbleness, innovative adaptability, and resourcefulness.

Innovate to Meet Market Demand

Continuous innovation is hard to accomplish; most companies fail because of the intense competition that erodes margin to win customers. Lack of technological innovation can lead to products and services stagnation, which makes a company less attractive to follow and patronize. A good example is Yahoo. Years ago, the business ranked number one in the industry. Yahoo owned over 20% of online advertising. However, because of lack of innovation, the company market share spiraled downward. Rather than dominating search engine space, the company focused on media. They opted out of buying Google in 2002 and failed to acquire Facebook in 2006. Today, Yahoo is working hard to stay behind Microsoft, Google, and Facebook.

The best innovative companies create products that meet scalable market demands. If the product solves a specific problem, the first market adaptors start spreading their excitement, thereby creating a new wave of second-generation adopters and loyalist. From that point, the quality of the product along with customer experience will dictate the scalability and the success of the product — the more significant the achievement, the higher the impact on the brand name and revenue.

The higher the demand, the more pressure to invest in sales and marketing to stay relevant in a competitive market. The competition can exert pressure by creating substitutes that will steer away part of the market client base, rising financial stakes, depressing margins, and creating additional options while potentially bettering functionality and lowering cost.

Like all products, the market will reach a certain equilibrium in terms of demand that will be followed by a stage of market saturation. The higher the demand of a product that commands high profit, the fiercer the competition, which will evenly erode profit and depress prices to incite the customers to buy faster.

When the major differentiation factor for a product is the price, it's time to reevaluate your strategy. Price is not a sustainable competitive advantage. Investing in the product to create a significant competitive technological advantage will create new demand, or you can try to pursue a different line of products with less competition.

Adapt, Innovate or Die

Eastman Kodak had a near-monopoly in the high-margin film business. Faced with revenue stagnation, the company ventured into inventing the digital camera in 1975. When the revenue didn't manifest fast enough, it was dropped to focus on the computer printer business. While Kodak was the leader of traditional film business, it failed to reinvent itself, grow revenue, and evolve according to market demands.

Microsoft built the Zune to take on the iPad, but it failed flat because the company created a substitute chaser product rather than an original product people want to acquire. The market wasn't impressed enough to buy the Zune, forcing the company to drop it. I should note that Zune was a great product in many ways; the problem was the consumer perception that saw the product as a substitute to an iPad rather than a unique product that brought unique functionality and technological innovation that dwarfed iPad, forcing the consumer to shift loyalty toward Zune. Microsoft's marketing strategy was a big failure as well, as it failed to create a tribe of believers that promoted their experience with the product on social media and other venues that would have created strong appeal to be part of a group of first adapters and promoters.

History is filled with corporate failures, from small entrepreneurial to large conglomerates. You can trace most product launch failures to lack of product differentiation, poor execution, and flawed strategy.

Revenue Strategy Tactic

When revenue growth slows down, companies often try to reverse trends by pushing the sales force to produce higher results at a much faster pace. Incentives, rewards, and pressure are commonly used as tactics to stimulate the sales force's productivity. Marketing pitches in by creating creative ads and incentives to influence customers' desires to buy the company products. This strategy is often used as a short-term solution. Some companies may opt in for a long-term strategy by focusing their energy working with their research and development teams to develop new and innovative products that may generate new demand while some CEOs may consider the option of acquiring other companies with better capabilities, market share, and competitive advantages.

Business strategies and tactics may differ according to the vision of the leadership team. You probably read about great mergers and acquisitions between companies that failed due to a cultural clash, lack of compatibility, and poor internal dynamics that contribute to talent defection.

Business is a complex system that requires constant balancing of multiple competing forces to maintain harmony, peace, and progress.

Sales Organizations Growth Principles and Pitfalls

Planning to succeed as a sales organization is not extremely hard. The market can be analyzed, the competition can be studied, the internal strategies can be modified, and systems can be upgraded to meet demand. Salespeople beliefs can be influenced and enhanced to meet company expectations.

In short, everything within an organization can be fixed, but it takes planning, building consensus among leaders, and cooperating to achieve specific corporate goals.

Many sales organizations with superior business solutions, strong brand name, large resources, and talented teams fail because of:

1. Senior management's misguided belief and satisfaction with the status-quo.
2. Mistrust and lack of harmony among cross-functional teams.
3. Deliberately ignoring customer and market demands.

The above issues may sound easy to fix, but they are not. You can fix products and systems issues in relatively a short time by allocating the necessary resources to get it done. However, it's hard to align people behind a specific cause; personal agendas, beliefs, and egos always get in the way to solve big problems. Many sales executives may recognize the problem, but will sabotage the fix. Most failures stem from leaders being disengage from the real problem and keeping the status-quo.

Corporate Reinvention

History has shown multiple companies, in diverse markets and industries that were able to reinvent themselves and create value for their customers. Organizational reinvention is a complex process that requires strategic changes to ensure its success.

- *Clear a strategic, well-defined path.* Senior management should define a strategic path to implement transformative changes, then deliberately and enthusiastically drive it to completion.

- *Management ownership.* Business delivery, implementation, execution, and motivation to ensure cooperation and collaboration among cross-functional teams and people. Leadership should ensure that no one falls behind when things get off track. The leadership role is to paint a clear vision of the company's purpose and individual's objectives to get there in terms of commitment and dedication to serving. Management should drive the mission with a sense of purpose, urgency, and excitement to ensure total adoption throughout the entire organization. Employee buy-in into the company mission is a must because when employees believe in a noble purpose, they will stretch to serve it faithfully.

- *Harness the power of the people.* Fluid communication should be the norm across hierarchy and throughout the entire organization to adopt the best ideas and act swiftly to meet market demand. Marketing views business from an analytical perspective, while sales views it from a customer viewpoint. Sales success often depends on functional departments to facilitate operation, legal, and financial transactions. All cross-functional team should be allowed to contribute and add value to shape the company strategy and meet revenue goals. Cross-sales and upsells teams should drive innovative ways and approaches to provide additional value to the existing client base.

- *Elimination of barriers.* Simplifying the process and improving structure and tactics to ensure revenue sustainability and growth. Goal realization should be a collaborative effort. Victories should be celebrated, and new challenges should be implemented, measured, controlled and evaluated.
- *Forward acceleration should be the norm.* Market domination should be the aim and forward thinking should be a baseline.

Organizational growth, through constant innovation and changes, should be the way entrepreneurial and large organization operates. The pursuit of sustained growth, innovation, financial prosperity, greater market share, and brand recognition is vital. Healthy organizations contribute to the community, and society. Revenue is the lifeblood of all organizations; if it flows at the right velocity, the corporate organism lives and thrives.

Factors that Increase Sales Revenue.

Sales leadership's primary job is to drive existing and new revenue steadily upwards. It's a tough job to affect revenue and sustain growth. Every sales leader believes they know the lever that can influence the desired outcome. These assumptions are derived from personal belief, experiences, education, and risk tolerance.

To increase sales, some sales leaders focus on finding ways to increase lead flow with referral partners, value-added resellers, cold calling, paid to list. Other leaders concentrate on training, coaching, and educating salespeople to improve their closing ratio, grow margins, shorten the sales cycle, improve opportunity convergence, or close high-value opportunities. While the goals are the same, every sales leader wants to achieve better results, though their approaches and methods are often different.

Viable Strategy

You cannot achieve results without a clear, well-defined sales strategy. A strategy is a game plan that allows you to move from the current state to a more desirable future state. It's a method that can be specific, such as achieving operational excellence, creating international growth, or producing worldwide recognition for app innovation. It could be as simple as targeting a particular market need to generate growth. Having a great strategy increases the likelihood of success; having the wrong approach can speed up the business' demise.

A good strategy arms you with the knowledge and awareness of the challenges ahead along with a solid understanding of market needs and client perspectives. Your business strategy will encompass your value proposition, your strategic objectives, goals, actionable items, directional maps, and performance measures that should be attained.

Revenue is a byproduct of good strategy, and the latter provides you with a terrain overview that shows opportunities, traps, and dynamics that may affect the business. A good strategy is also a learning system that allows adaptation and changes based on dynamic feedback and evaluations.

Sound Structure

A sound structure that is based on market requirements and reality is vital to strategy success. The structure is the *skeleton* that holds the entrepreneurial organism together and facilitates the implementation of the company vision, mission, and core values. Business structures are the hardware that allows support of your strategic software (ideas, insight, creativity, requirements to do business). These structures define how you are going to get to your goals, what resources, brain power, control systems, compensations systems, alignment process, operations, and sales enablement is needed to achieve your goals.

Right People

The most challenging area for sales leaders is to find the right salespeople for the job. Finding people is one thing; finding the right people for the job is a colossal task. Revenue growth requires salespeople who are competent, able, willing, persistent, tough-minded, hardworking, creative, intelligent, analytical, passionate, and driven to succeed under the most challenging conditions.

Sales leaders can stimulate salespeople by managing their inner desires, aspirations, and goals. However, finding salespeople who possess this complex web of qualifications is difficult. Most sales growth and business success depends on salespeople's ability to negotiate shrewdly, influence decision makers, and resolve issues creatively while ensuring a seamless delivery on the expected outcome.

Salespeople are continuously challenged to work beyond their comfort zone, and they are asked to project relentless optimism, excitement, create added-value, and plan forward.

Finding the right people is undoubtedly a challenge; however, with the right level of training, coaching, and continuous motivation, an average salesperson can become a great producer. The level of success that a sales organization achieves has a direct correlation with the level of competency and ability of the sales force that constitutes its team.

Aligning each salesperson with the appropriate role and appropriate territories based on their unique competencies, language skills, professionalism, knowledge, and maturity can make a huge difference in terms of affecting positive or negative revenue measures. You cannot expect a sales farmer to produce the sales results that a sales hunter would, nor can you expect a field salesperson who specializes in larger accounts to provide the same level of output as a professional telesales salesperson who targets small accounts.

People's capability and qualifications must be documented and measured to ensure you are placing salespeople in areas of strengths rather than weaknesses. Careful analysis of people's strength and allocation of territories that matches one skill is vital to maximize people's success, improve morale, increase employee satisfaction and retention while growing revenue. Good strategies focus on the art of matching people's strengths with the right available opportunities.

Smart Sales Process

Nothing frustrates customers, salespeople, and sales managers more than a dysfunctional sales process. A fluid sales process where all cross-functional teams work as a collaborative unit of production ensures greater morale, higher productivity, better communication, faster responses, and better performance and collaboration. A suitable process creates a group that promotes a shared vision and mission.

A lousy process creates resistance, bottlenecks, bureaucracy, anxiety, and frustration and generates negative performance and revenue. A sales process is a system of doing things either right or wrong; it's a repetitive emotional journey that can improve to generate better results. A lousy method allows people to start making false assumptions, building bad habits and personal bias, wasting resources, and losing confidence in the management's ability to address these dilapidating issues that slow productivity.

A good sales process is built on facts, empathy, understanding, and good management practices that affect people and organizations. People sell to people. One study found that happy employees are 20% more productive than unhappy employees; when it comes to sales people, happiness factor may even be greater, rising to 37%, the happier the salespeople, the more significant the results. Today's customers are impatient. Improved organizational process and happy, empowered employees can contribute to customer satisfaction and retention. A better sales process promotes a better buying experience, repeat business, and more lucrative cross-sales and upsells.

Sales process requires cooperation among multiple cross-functional teams. Decision processes need to be streamlined and handled with care and urgency. Resources need to be allocated where needed. Congruency and uniformity should dominate the sales process, from the client buying process, to the finance and underwriting process, to hiring and boarding salespeople.

Revenue creation is always going to be a challenge. A targeted effort is required to ensure that the sales delivery process across the cross-functional team is understood and followed with the purpose to stimulate growth.

Process Improvement

- Better efficiency: The company needs to establish standardized processes to improve communication, decision-making speed, and business results. Innovation should be recommended and encouraged, and existing working systems should be continued until the new innovative ways are proven tested and verified to avoid process disruption.
- Mapping: Guidelines and playbooks for employees and managers need to be created and continuously updated to shorten the learning phase, eliminate mistakes and confusions.

System conformity minimizes challenges, speed productivity and provides an action path that ensures continues momentum free of interruptions.

Corporate Sales Vitals

Corporate growth becomes optimal when these vital business forces — business strategy, people and process— work in congruence and harmony to achieve a common purpose.

Business strategy drives the company's vision and mission, its intelligent dynamic mapping that creates a path to success, despite market and environmental changes. Sales talent is the force that fuels the economic health of the sales organization. The sales process is the plasma that allows the delivery and exchange of resources between the sales organization and the market. All these vital elements need to work in congruence and in sync to create a value chain that the sales organism depends on to survive and thrive. Getting these key elements right and managing expectations correctly can predict the overall health of the sales organization.

Sales growth is the result of customer buying and investing in a specific value proposition offered by the company. When strategy, structure, people, and process are aligned the right way, customer patronage increases, employee loyalty grows, mindset improves, client satisfaction increases, and brand loyalty becomes a staple.

Revenue creation is an extension of client satisfaction. The higher the quality of the product and the commitment to serve customer needs, the more significant the revenue generation and the greater the organizational impact.

Sales Manager Role in Revenue Generation

If revenue is king, why do salespeople focus on everything but revenue-driven activities? The answer is simple. Predictable sales results require control over specific behaviors that lead to an outcome. These controllable behaviors must be specific, timely, and repeatable. For example, prospecting, dialing-for-dollars, face-to-face prospect visits, meeting with decision makers, or presenting.

Salespeople often get lost in their day-to-day tasks. These tasks, while part of the job, are not necessary revenue drivers. Additionally, most sales managers are primarily focused on lagging metrics such as win rate, deal volume, and quota achievement. These metrics are the results of past activities and do not allow to correct behaviors in real time.

Your ability to monitor, manage, and coach your sales force in real time in the right practices to achieve quota is critical to:

- Increase revenue generation per salesperson
- Change tactics and strategy to meet company goals
- Correct wrong behaviors and advise on best practices
- Evaluate gaps and draft a winning plan

As a sales manager, you should monitor and provide daily orientation to your team to correct course as necessary and share best practices that improve efficiency and effectiveness. Some ongoing activities may be necessary, such as administrative work. However, this should be limited in terms of time and scope while revenue-driven activities should be the primary focus.

More substantial ticket sales require multiple stages of face-to-face interaction to answer questions, eliminate doubt, provide support, and clarify the process. Targeted revenue-driven activities tend to advance the sales process and win deals while eliminating bad opportunities that are clogging the sales funnel. Not all opportunities create value or revenue. The sales funnel needs to be inspected, cleaned, and refreshed; often, the trash need to be disposed of accordingly.

Burying oneself in company CRM, social media, and emails can hurt your productivity. It's not that these activities are wrong; it's just when managed poorly that they can waste valuable time from value-driven and revenue-driven operations that are necessary to meet your quota. The emphasis should be on the activity that drives economic value.

Know Your Business and Process

Revenue is achieved by following targeted potential customers within a specific sales space. You would expect that salespeople know their target customers and market and know where they stand in the process. The reality is that most salespeople do not have a thorough grasp of the opportunities in their sales funnel. Many have difficulty describing their accomplished progress year-to-date and a good majority hope their customers will make up their mind and say, "Let's do it," or "I'm ready, send me the document for review and signature." While it happens occasionally, it's not a sound selling strategy.

Selling requires the salesperson to know with absolute precision where they stand with every opportunity. You may say that's a tall order. However, the salesperson's job is to ensure that they know where they stand at any given time. Great salespeople never end a conversation with a customer without advancing the sales cycles further toward the close by using collaborative approaches and adding value throughout every interaction with the customer. This approach ensures that the salesperson is aware of the following:

Knows all obstacles and hurdles that need your attention

- Awareness of the steps necessary to move the deal forward.

- Reevaluate and refocus one approach based on needs.
- Rethink strategy and tactics to influence decision makers.
- Repackage and customize a better business solution that will impress the customer and speed closing.

Sales activities need to have a purpose that leads either to revenue growth, customer retention and customer base expansion.

Busyness Pretension

It's common that sales managers and executives manage salespeople activities by the number of hours spent on their screens or the phone troubleshooting customer issues. In these business settings, work is equated with busyness rather than productivity. Salespeople should focus principally on creating revenue and wealth for the company. In sales, most non-essential activities should be handled in downtime, prime time should be all about connecting with customers and prospects to advance the sale or close a deal.

I witnessed a Fortune 500 VP of sales organize every other Tuesday and Thursday a sales blitz for the whole day. Field salespeople had to cold call on businesses in the street of New York. Without a pre-set appointment, most of these salespeople ended up having to introduce themselves to busy business owners, who advised them to set a date before they came by next time or collected a business card for follow up purposes. Within a few weeks, salespeople dreaded these blitzes. They were not working, results were negligible and sporadic at best, yet the same vice president insisted on carrying them on for almost a whole year. It was total insanity. These blitzes were not only a complete waste of time and energy, but they were wasting precious time that could have been used to create revenue by focusing on closing deals in the funnel and prospecting more effectively by making warm calls on qualified leads and acting as a trusted thought leader that consultatively helped businesses achieve their specific outcome.

It was clear that the VP was going the wrong path, rather than brainstorming with his management team and top salespeople to craft a better strategy that would generate revenue and lift salespeople's morale. He stayed the course of mediocrity by pretending to be proactive and resourceful.

High-Pressure Selling Doesn't Work

I have a friend who was in the market to change his company's entire POS system. The salesperson and his manager showed up and provided a demonstration on the features, functionality, and benefit of their digital POS. After consulting with his team, he decided to do further research to ensure their system was the best he could buy—this was a capital investment, and he needed to make the right decision.

During the second meeting, it became apparent there was some level of desperation in making the sale. The sales person and his managers wanted to conclude the transactions. They started hinting about sweetening the deal in exchange for his immediate commitment. He didn't budge and insisted that he needed to shop a little longer to make sure he was making the right decision.

A few days later, a barrage of follow-up calls ensued from the salesperson and his sales manager. The proposed price dropped several times without ask, and multiple methods of trial closes were used to seal the deal. Their system was the best in the market, and my friend would have bought it anyway. However, the company sales methods were not trustworthy. Alarmed with their push to sell, he researched the company's customer service reviews, and he was horrified. Great products! High-pressure sales tactics were a turn-off, but horrible customer service post-sale was a sales killer — no wonder why they struggled.

My friend ended up buying a product that had less functionality, but was backed with excellent price integrity, professional sales methods, and excellent customer service reviews.

In reality, customers buy the whole experience, not just a product or a service, as many salespeople tend to believe. Sales pressure may work sometimes, but it has no place in professional selling, as it ruins good relationships and tarnishes good brands.

For example, Zappos is known for its exceptional customer service that stretches above and beyond the industry norm. Zappos employees use zero sales pressure and an outstanding return policy. Call center employees don't have scripts, and they are not constrained by time. The most extended Zappos call reported being above 10 hours.

Doing right in term of customer service is so essential for Zappos that it offers any of its new hires $3,000 to leave the company post spending four weeks shadowing an experienced employee.

Zappos doesn't have performance reviews; rather, cultural fit assessments that offer suggestions on how to fit better within the company culture.

Raises and promotions are based on passing a mandated skill-based test.

Zappos' biggest strength is its employees, who are trained and challenged to do what's right for the customer, even when the requests are outside the norm.

Leveraging Your People

Corporate sales are often broken, as it stymies initiatives and creativity, by keeping all significant decisions at the level of few executives at the top of the organization. Sales managers are often kept in the dark until they receive directives for execution at the last minute.

Some large organizations employ thousands of salespeople but rarely ask for any advice, insights, ideas or direction from them.

These executives believe they are the brains and the rest of the employees are hands for hire. Rather than tapping into this immense network of human intelligence, it often goes ignored. People can achieve company quotas while adding more value by sharing their idea and thoughts that can generate impactful differentiation.

Executive management often discounts, undervalues, and underestimates existing employees' talent. Many defer to external services provided by the business consultant to understand, evaluate, and resolve significant challenges. Sales consultant can undoubtedly make a positive difference, but it takes time to understand the business the way an employee understands it.

Neglecting this available, savvy, and knowledgeable source of intelligent, caring employee is a mistake that is quite common in the corporate world. Many senior executives either have a poor relationship with their employees or they cannot bring themselves to listen to their subordinates because they feel that they may be perceived as incompetent or unintelligent.

Sales have evolved and continue to do so at an incredible pace. Customers are savvier than ever, and they are aware of industry trends changes and cutting-edge innovations. Many are social media savvy, know industry news, products pricing, brand impact, and company reputation.

Some of these savvy customers know more than the salesperson. The advantage that the salesperson has is the ability to leverage specific differentiators that meet each customer and customer type with the right business solution. Customers buy business solutions along with the ability to access information and innovation that can positively impact their business output and provide access to a knowledgeable, reliable sales professional who can keep them aware of significant industry changes.

Recreation of Success Doesn't Always Translate Well.

A new CEO came on board a Fortune 500 company; he was new to the role. He hired a reputable advisor who became a vice chairman shortly after that. This vice chairman's job was to revamp the sales organization and make it profitable quickly. The company had been profitable in the past, but due to structural and environmental changes, it started losing ground to its competitors, which triggered multiple senior managers' resignations. With each new CEO, things got worse; the board of directors had all their hopes pinned on the latest CEO who had a stellar reputation in the banking industry. The belief was if there was one person who could turn the economic tides around, it was him.

Under pressure and armed with a carte blanche in hand, the new vice chairman hired a head of sales. Except, this head of sales was full of ego and arrogance, and lacked humility. As a result, within eight months, he lost half of the sales leadership team. The vice chairman did quite a lot of damage as well. Vital people left the company in droves to the competition, the vice chairman was demoted, and the head of sales got terminated. The losses of some valuable managers were severe.

New CEOs often bring their "A" team to make dramatic changes that will revamp the company culture, create new revenue, cement and expand existing relationships, and improve the business core.

Despite the hype, only a few experienced CEOs can create impactful changes that can improve a company's bottom line. Many CEOs fail miserably, primarily because of the "A" team mistakes syndrome. The idea that bringing on board people who have generated some level of success in the past can recreate it, again and again, is a dream. While it's possible to recreate a path to success, the probability is dependent on multiple variables that can affect results. I have witnessed several times the new "A" team concept where new significant changes get adopted only to fail, forcing the company to revert to the old models that sustained the company growth in the past.

Every new CEO wants to create meaningful changes that carry their signature. That is the reason for bringing outside talent, to become part of the new team, and new thought process. Hiring segregation often occurs by labeling the current team as incompetent and labeling the new team as competent and better.

The example above, unfortunately, is the norm in many companies. The new leadership tries to erase all accomplishment generated by the old team, labeling them as failures. —until they become the former team that will need to be replaced with a newer "A" team that follows a new CEO. The cycle repeats, similar errors doom many companies that could have learned from the old mistakes, kept methods, systems and experiences that worked and improved upon them through smart innovation and creative technologies.

CHAPTER 4: SUMMARY

- Revenue generation is the core purpose of most sales organizations. Most salespeople cannot self-organize and self-lead to accomplish their corporate objectives in a repeatable fashion. The sales manager often acts as the subconscious of the group, by aligning everyone behind the achievement of company goals.

- Sales managers act as a strategic tactician, coach, coordinator, and motivator to keep everyone motivated and enthusiastic about achieving the personal and company goals.

- Smart leaders don't try to impress their bosses. Instead, they do what's right even when it goes against their interest.
- Intelligent sales leaders tap into everyone's brain power by creating an environment that encourages the sharing of ideas, insight, observation, and external competitive data to improve the company operations and business model.

CHAPTER FIVE: SALES MANAGER'S DUTIES

Sales Manager Stretched Beyond Capacity

There is a certain limit to one's capacity to handle tasks efficiently and on time. Many sales managers are eager and willing to take additional workload to broaden their skills, please the boss, or be a good team player. However, too many other responsibilities can affect one's job.

The sales manager's willingness to help shouldn't be mistaken for availability. Senior management should ensure that their sales managers are focused primarily on the activities and behaviors that drive new customers, opportunities and revenue. Operation duties should be minimized only to what is vital. The job should be razor-focused on sales- and revenue-driven initiatives. There is a massive loss of opportunity when the sales manager's focus is divided and diverted from their economic function.

Large complex corporations, as well as small businesses forced to do more with less, suffer from "lack of focus" syndrome. Sales managers are not available to dive in at will in unrelated tasks and unfinished projects. This disorganized business model often led by senior managers is among the reasons why quotas get missed, margins decrease, and revenue plummets.

Right Head Count Makes a Difference

In a continued effort to cut organizational costs, a software sales company reduced the number of its sales managers from 55 to 22 almost overnight. The management span of control had more than doubled; it went from an average of seven to eight sales reps per manager up to sixteen to twenty sales reps per sales manager.

This initiative saved costs, but it affected the sales managers' efficiency and made coaching sessions an impossibility. These sophisticated business-to-business customers required that the sales rep deliver customized, technically-challenging business solutions. The sales manager's involvement in the entire sales process was vital to both the customer and the salesperson. This increased span of control decision affected the sales managers' ability to assist their sales reps with their customers calls.

Sales manager optimum output requires having to manage the right number of salespeople, while allowing ample time for strategy, preparation, and coaching.

If the sales manager oversees fewer people than what they can handle, then the process may reflect some level of inefficiency. Smaller teams may force the manager to spend more time in lower value administrative tasks or start micromanaging their salespeople's activities instead of empowering and trusting them to do their best.

Alternatively, if a sales manager has a too large span of control, they may become an ineffective sales manager. The sales manager may not have the time to adequately coach and train their team. Hence, their team will reflect different degrees of skills and aptitude mastery. Opportunity win rate will indicate a varied level of success among sales rep, making it harder to accurately forecast future success. Additionally, the sales manager won't have enough time to spend with key clients and partners, nor would they have adequate time to develop sound strategies that will focus on the team's long-term growth.

Sales Manager's Job Responsabilties and Function

The sales manager's main duty is to keep the revenue flowing and achieve corporate goals. Most sales managers find themselves often involved in many projects and tasks that not related to their team productivity. A sales manager's obligation is to develop his salespeople to work in harmony toward achieving company goals by improving customer retention, expansion and growth.

People Management. Most sales leaders spend on average 30% to 60% of their time managing people issues. The time spent on these tasks varies by industry, product complexity, sales cycle, salespeople tenure, knowledge, and experience. Robust support systems enhance customers' experience and allow the sales manager to focus on coaching his people. For example, field trainers can add value to the sales manager initiatives and empower the sales reps to act more independently.

Customer Management. Is comprised of the following activities: prospecting, funnel management, account planning, boarding, and critical customer visits. Most managers tend to spend 20% to 40% of their time removing obstacles that hinders their sales rep's productivity. In addition to managing, cultivating, cementing customer relationships. and exploring future opportunities.

Business Management. This segment comprises administrative duties, forecasting, and budgeting report preparation, managing meetings along with other activities. Most managers spend on average 15% to 30% of their time dealing with business management duties. A manager who has some level of control over the organization's budget and resources may find they are spending additional time managing the business. Some struggling organizations may increase management meetings to address critical issues. A meeting can last anywhere from 15 minutes to a few hours. Most sales managers prefer fewer meetings to free up their time to handle essential KPIs.

Manager Duties and Tasks

Let's explore the broad manager's daily duties and tasks.

People Management.

1. Set targets, performance plans, and objectives for sales reps
2. Meet weekly with salespeople on a one-on-one basis to review progress, performance, and target attainments
3. Provide feedback on field observation, supervise, coach and train
4. Conduct performance reviews and remove obstacles
5. Participate in daily field rides to add value, advance complex sales, and understand primary client's needs
6. Support, counsel, discipline, and terminate underperforming salespeople
7. Develop a scalable process and hold salespeople accountable to its structure
8. Ensure that all salespeople use company CRMs effectively and accurately
9. Hold regular sales training to educate on critical topics and changes
10. Select, recruit, onboard, and train new hires
11. Provide additional peer coverage based on needs

12. Lift morale and ensure that the team works cohesively
13. Embed the company culture and values in the salespeople's daily behaviors

Managing Customers' Needs

- Understand customers' needs and monitor their preferences
- Resolve all escalations on time
- Ensure vendor and partner engagement and satisfaction
- Educate salespeople on how to address customers' requests to ensure new product placement, higher retention, and satisfaction
- Provide price exceptions based on the level of authority
- Advance complex negotiations to win the business
- Liaise company senior management with critical customers' executive management teams

Managing the Business

- Determine and assign quotas based on headcount, territory, and longevity. Project and forecast weekly, monthly, quarterly, and annual revenue
- Develop a strategy to acquire new clients
- Share critical KPIs with sales leadership
- Analyze sales performance and address gaps
- Collaborate with marketing to generate additional opportunities
- Work with cross-functional departments to get deals moving in a timely fashion

- Prepare budget and approve necessary expenses
- Monitor market intel, economic indicators, and industry trends. Share impactful market intelligence with senior executives
- Learn and adopt innovative strategies to ensure continual growth

We will probably agree that most sales organizations, regardless of their size and maturity, don't have a thorough understanding of the sales manager's job beyond the job description written by the HR folks. Most senior managers don't have a solid understanding of how a sales manager spends their time managing different business needs and wants. Most vice presidents will attest that the sales manager's job is the hardest in the entire company and that's often an understatement.

Sales Manager's Time and Tasks

Cost-cutting initiatives have become the norm in most organizations. Hence, most sales managers find themselves spending an enormous amount of time handling urgent low-value and low-priority tasks. These immediate priorities creep in daily and consume time and energy that could be spent on high-value and high-return activities.

Unfortunately, most sales managers find themselves deeply embedded in many required administrative tasks that deprive them from spending time gathering business intelligence to manage market shifts. It takes time to understand local market needs, demographic changes, new trends, and competitive dynamics. A good sales manager needs time to perform customer visits, interview local businesses, to uncover any new customer buying behaviors and develop strategic action plans that incorporates these new dynamics.

The solution: Sales organizations need to allow their sales managers to delegate all low value, time-consuming, redundant tasks to support groups who will do them faster, better, and for a lesser cost.

It doesn't make sense to bury your sales managers in tasks that have nothing to do with improving people skills or generating revenue. Additionally, even the best sales managers have a bandwidth capacity that shouldn't be exceeded. Allocate each sales manager with the right span of control according to his competency, management effectiveness, historic performance, and experience while taking into consideration the team member's tenure, experience, and client portfolio complexity.

CHAPTER 5: SUMMARY

- Sales managers should focus on revenue-driven initiatives. Everything else should be secondary. Stretching your sales managers beyond capacity is a recipe for a company's financial disaster. You cannot divert your sales managers' attention to secondary and tertiary tasks and expect them to deliver on their primary task –revenue generation.
- A sales manager's span of control needs to correlate with one's capacity, experience, tenure, bandwidth tolerance and willingness to handle a larger team. An appropriate compensation plan should reward sales managers handling large teams accordingly. Doing so will create an environment where sales managers will strive to keep performance high despite the size of the team.
- Low-value and low-priority tasks should be allocated to appropriate support group. By freeing the sales manager's calendar, they can focus on high priority, high value functions that create high-value returns for the team, company, and shareholders.

CHAPTER SIX: SALES MANAGER CAUGHT IN OPERATION QUICK SAND

In the U.S. Army, the generals set the strategy and coalesce the group behind the vision by giving specific orders. However, it's the hundreds of platoon leaders who lead the charge during war and peacetime. These lieutenant leaders are the lowest-ranking commissioned officers in the Army. They are often commanding 20 to 50 soldiers made up of two or more squads of soldiers.

We all know the importance of the role of these platoon leaders in managing the troops. They turn average individuals into highly-trained skilled killing machines. Similarly, we know that the sales manager's job is the most critical position in the entire sales organization. The head of sales (general) determines the direction of the organization, but sales managers (platoon leaders) turn average salespeople into a high-powered selling machine. Great sales managers are transformative forces who can elevate under-performing teams to five-star performers, while poor sales managers can quickly destroy even the most resilient teams.

We discussed in previous chapters the role and complexity of the sales manager job. It is a position that must serve several constituencies ranging from organization goals, customer's needs, and employees and partner's requirements.

Additionally, the sales manager must meet company quota obligations. Salespeople's success determines the sales manager's success. A good sales manager manages all aspects of the business by coaching and training his team to focus on revenue generation, while effectively addressing unexpected situations in the field on their own. In the Army, the soldiers often enjoy total flexibility while carrying out their missions. The platoon leader usually spends an enormous amount of time designing contingency plans and altering instructions to meet external threats.

Training and Readiness Tasks

Platoon leaders, just like sales managers, work hard by training, coaching, and conducting drills (roleplays) preparing soldiers for combat and real-life events. The platoon leader designs drills to simulate real combat situations while holding soldiers accountable for performance; failure in the military is not an option as it often means injury or death. A sales manager performs similar drills in the trenches —classrooms and on one-on-one settings — failure is not an option as it means demotion or job termination. Intensive training and coaching sessions are intended to ensure team readiness for field combat.

The military world and the sales world are complex environments; they are fast-paced and tend to evolve unexpectedly fast.

The sales manager must focus on the following task to meet performances objectives:

1. Analyze market trends and opportunities
2. Meet customers' and referral partners' needs
3. Improve sales strategy
4. Manage profitability
5. Maintain a successful culture
6. Improve the quality and competency of current sales talent
7. Build excellent bridges with cross-functional teams

8. Organize, plan, motivate, challenge, and report progress
9. Stimulate and facilitate learning
10. Encourage salespeople to perform at a higher level
11. Recognize and celebrate performance
12. Recommend great individuals for increases, promotions, and bonuses

The list is undoubtedly extensive, and sales management is a hard business. Period. All the above activities require focus, time, effort, and energy. Dedicating time to any of these tasks comes at the expense of diverting the sales manager's focus from his most critical revenue generating tasks.

- Meeting sales goals
- Focus on net new account acquisition
- Coaching to address the performance gap

Corporate reality

Most sales managers spend their days buried on the following activities:

- Responding to a flood of emails
- Attending meetings that sound important (most add little or no value at all)
- Resolving customer issues (most sales organizations have dysfunctional customer service departments — view chapter on corporate NPS score)

- Case prepping and writing to justify moving deals stuck with various cross-functional departments that are often either sales-antagonistic or love to play internal power games
- Fixing unpredictable escalations before they hit their boss' inbox (at a minimum, they feel they must be aware of everything about their team and customers, no matter how inconsequential it is, hence the constant email checking.) Nothing scares a sales manager more than not being aware of any issues that hit the CEO's inbox and are now being down-cascaded for a quick resolution with a feedback report to the upper management.

Managing Chaos

I'm sure you can relate to the above list; it's a dilemma that is crippling corporate productivity. It serves low-performing sales managers well as they can justify their lack of productivity behind these penalizing, debilitating, time- and energy-consuming issues.

However, it taxes primarily top sales managers who want to spend time helping their salespeople in the field. Their focus is to increase their team members net new appointments to drive new revenue while maintaining and expanding the existing book of business. All other non-revenue generating tasks reduce productivity and deprive salespeople of the sales manager's coaching and feedback time during these precious joint-calls and scheduled together-time.

Managing Through Chaos

When productivity is below par, senior managers will question line managers on their work ethics. It's common to hear a sales executive ask his manager, "What are you doing to affect productivity?" This simple question gets most sales managers to rumble in terms of describing all the activities they are doing with their team members to affect sales productivity. Senior managers love to put their sales managers on the spot and listen to their struggles, trying to demonstrate the work and tactics they had put in the process to generate the desired performance.

Activity is the name of the game! Not so fast. Specific, deliberate, targeted activity is what creates the sought-after results. Forced activity creates the pretense of work that yield no meaningful value. Targeted actions, reinforced with evaluative benchmarks, create results and ensure customer satisfaction. You will often hear desperate sales managers pushing their salespeople to go after every opportunity in the sales funnel without distinction. "We need business, call them all, someone is going to say yes," says one sales manager. "If they are not responsive, schedule a drop by to leave some information and try to set up a meeting while you're there," says another sales manager.

Many reputable company's sales departments are managed through disorganized chaos. Too many highs and lows, too many hits and misses, too many lost opportunities, and too many mistakes repeated over and over. Intense pressure forces reactive behaviors to become the default mode.

Remote Sales Management

I met a sales manager who have never spent one field day with his new hires. I understand, vast territories could present a challenge, a large span of control can be a challenge; however, a sales manager who is not willing to spend field time with his team members should not be in sales. I met this salesperson who was struggling in a vast remote territory, which got me concerned. Our conversation went like this:

Me: How long have you been with the company?

Mike: A little more than two years now.

Me: How do you like it here?

Mike: Honestly, I'm doing my best; however, it has been rough.

Me: Why is that? I understand you don't have a sales manager now, correct?

Mike: That's correct. The last sales manager just quit after only four months. However, it doesn't matter, because I never get to see any of them anyway.

Me: What do you mean?

Mike: Two individuals interviewed me over the phone, and a job offer followed, which I accepted. I went to Chicago for one-week training. I was lost, but we were told by sales trainers that we will have full support from our sales manager once we get back home. Once back from the training, I heard that my sales manager was recently fired. The vice-president of sales called me and assigned a salesperson to assist me remotely (the other salesperson was working in Texas, while I covered New Jersey territory) while he looked for a sales manager replacement. The vice-president of sales left the company to join a competitor in the same month of me coming onboard. The assigned salesperson was always busy, and honestly, I felt after two calls that he didn't want to be bothered by a new rookie. The moment the vice-president of sales termination was announced, the salesperson assigned to assist me stopped responding to any of my calls or emails.

Four months later, we had a new sales manager, and he was quickly on my case. He reviewed my numbers and put me immediately into a performance plan without ever understanding my situation or even bothering to listen to my story. He established a 30-minute per week one-on-one session where he was either reprimanding me or telling me that I will be fired, if I don't meet my quota quickly. It didn't take him long, he quit within six months on the job.

In brief, you are the only regional-vice-president of sales I ever met from my first day of hire. Currently, my performance is among the top ten percent in my region, primarily because of my commitment to make it work. I'm a single father with a sick child, and I need health insurance to cover my son and money to pay my rent and keep a roof over our heads. I have no choice but to make it work. I'm self-taught. I hope you are not going to be fired or quit soon. It gets lonely when you are working so hard in a remote area with little or no support at all.

Me: Mike, thanks for your candor. I genuinely appreciate your sharing with me your story. It's sad that a Fortune 500 company must deal with issues like this, rather than striving to be exemplary.

Mike: I'm a former enlisted U.S. Marine. I have seen my share of pain and joy. I have learned to retain a sense of pride even in the most challenging circumstances. Everything that I do is for my family. My son has been diagnosed with cancer, he has made tremendous progress, and I promised to do everything possible to make his life better every day.

I was floored; how could a sales organization and its sales management team ignore their employees' plea for help? I promised myself that I would make sure that I got to know every employee's challenges, learn from it, and help as much as humanly possible.

You would think, how could a Fortune 500 company allow itself to operate in such a dysfunctional way? Several trips around the country tagging these lone-wolf salespeople taught me that Mike's situation was often the norm rather than the exception—an unfortunate reality, but not a singular event. Mike's story was sad, but a powerful reality. There are many salespeople out there whose stories are ignored, dismissed or forgotten in the name of corporate profit.

Salespeople should never be considered as disposable inanimate objects; they are humans with feelings, emotions, and brains capable of creating unlimited corporate wealth. Caring goes a long way.

Senior Management Accountability

I have witnessed salespeople being terminated for poor performance, even though they were never given any type of training or coaching opportunity to help their sales career development. A sales manager can have 50% - 70% yearly turnover without anyone questioning their management style or guiding principles. Sales managers are not held to the same standards as their salespeople. A vast number of sales managers' recourse to micromanaging and bullying rookies and underperformers because they don't know any better. Instead of helping their salespeople, they spend time avoiding tough decisions, shifting blame, failing to listen, stealing credit, herding information, engaging in unethical behavior, and failing to develop their team because they were never trained on how to manage and lead people. Most managers assume the role and are expected to learn through trial and error. The issue with this negligent corporate strategy is that it's not only costly in terms of economics, but it ruins the company corporate brand and business legitimacy.

Senior management assume that whatever blunders the sales manager commits, it's the salesperson job to manage his relationship with his boss to stay employed. Your sales peers will advise you to practice conscious empathy and emotional intelligence to manage working with your crummy sales manager. However, we neglect to take into consideration that the sales manager behavior has the power to act as a productive or distractive force. A well-trained manager can become a positive transformative power that elevates productivity, morale, and people's spirits. A weak sales manager can have a devastating effect on people's morale and productivity.

Poor Leadership

John was assigned to head the new sales division in China. He had been happy with his job in the United States, and he was successful at it. He didn't speak Mandarin or Cantonese and made no efforts to learn Chinese or adapt to Chinese customs. His behaviors alienated several significant customers and he didn't get along well with his new staff members. Additionally, he tried to implement some proven U.S sales strategies in the Chinese market. John want to apply his ideas and did not tolerate any input or challenges from his subordinates. When he missed his corporate goals, he blamed his employees who were disrespectful and did not comply with his instructions. John's division was not meeting deadlines and had cost overruns. To exacerbate the matter further, John needed to deal with several legal regulations, but he was not willing to implement his local legal team advises.

Sales heads stubbornness can be a problem, but it's rare that the boss gets challenged, even when it's a dire situation. It takes two to three years to figure out that a senior manager dogma, belief, or strategy is the root of the problem. It is much harder to point the finger at the head of sales. Replacing a head of sales is hard—it takes, time, energy and money. Hiring a new leader doesn't guarantee success and stellar pedigrees and great past performances do not guarantee a home run either. Most hiring decisions have a probability of failures of 50% or higher. Hiring a great head of sales that manages resources and lead people exceptionally well remains a challenge across industries.

Commonly, additional time and resources get allocated to the head of sales to turn around their own failed strategies. This is because a speedy termination of the head of sales, even when justified, is not only costly but reflects poorly on senior management, who must go through a lengthy process to find a valid replacement. Identifying and hiring a new sales head is a lengthy and risky process. It's easier to terminate a lower ranking sales manager than to terminate the head of sales even in the case of incompetence or negligence.

CHAPTER 6: SUMMARY

- A sales manager performs similar drills to what an army platoon leader does in the trenches, classrooms, and on one-on-one settings. Failure is typically not an alternative as it means demotion or job termination.
- The team is only as good as its leader. The sales leader needs to keep himself at peak performance mentally and physically as they serve as a role model and inspirational figure.
- Specific, deliberate, targeted activity is what creates results. Sales managers often work in chaotic environments. Their job is to lead their team to stay focused on their mission regardless of the nature of obstacles they may face.
- Sales managers who care less about their teams or act unprofessionally should be terminated. It's a privilege to lead a team. Hence, one should treat others as they wish to be treated. Poor leadership should not be tolerated at any level across the organization.

CHAPTER SEVEN: MANAGING UNDERPERFORMERS

Underperformers make the sales manager job more difficult. Good sales managers can turn willing underperformers into good performers, through deliberate, planned effort and strategic initiatives. The sales manager should know the answer to the following questions to facilitate the journey of taking his underperforming sales reps to the performance zone within a period of three to six months.

Things you should look for in determining your sales reps' performance:

1. Is the underperformance due to a will or skill factor?
2. What is the sales rep's strength and weakness?
3. What competencies did they demonstrate so far?
4. Does the sales rep exude the necessary level of desire, motivation, and enthusiasm to do the job?
5. How are their month-to-date and year-to-date performances in comparison with their peers?
6. How is their overall attitude and professionalism?
7. What are their aspirations and goals?
8. How do they spend their selling hours?
9. Are they open to coaching?
10. How do they interact with their peers, partners, and customers?
11. Do they lead with value-selling or product-selling?

12. What is their communication and interaction style?
13. What's their peer, customers, and partner feedback?
14. How savvy are they in using the company systems and tools?
15. How much coaching and training do they need?
16. Are they eager and willing to turn their performance around?

Most managers prefer to ignore hard-to-deal-with underperformers for as long as possible. Many managers believe that teams cannot be made primarily of top-caliber salespeople. Hence, a certain percentage of underperformance is inevitable. Others avoid conflict and tensions that arise when dealing with these underperforming sales reps, especially when the sales manager is not fulfilling their coaching and training duties. Many sales managers prefer to invest their time with solid performers to generate higher ROI and show improvement results corresponding with their efforts.

You are Accountable

Smart sales managers don't avoid tough conversations around poor performances. Instead, they address them head-on with smarts, empathy, sensitivity, care, and bravado. You cannot protect nor allow underperformance; it's a virus that needs to be cured before it spreads and contaminates the whole team. It's necessary and only fair to help your underperforming sales reps get better. If they show up, listen, follow instructions and work hard, you should help them turn around their performance, from poor to good, then from good to great.

Inspect what you expect and validate.

- Your sales reps should explicitly understand what is expected from them.

- Your team members should understand the impact underperformance has on the overall morale of the group.
- Clarify the consequences of underperformances.
- Provide your sales reps with regular training and face-to-face coaching sessions along with meetings focused on honest conversations and planning of next steps.
- Ensure that your sales reps understand their areas of underperformances and collectively draft an action plan that will get them back to the performer's zone.
- Avoid emotional confrontation and approach the situation with empathy. Avoid accusatory approaches, or threatening behaviors; stay calm and collected to connect and build trust.
- Be prepared. Gather facts and don't assume anything. People won't dispute facts; avoid comments such as "You are performing poorly." Rather, say something like, "As you can see, your pipeline has 10 prospects this week, and based on your current conversion rate of 20%, you will need 50 prospects this month to achieve your goals." Be specific during your coaching sessions.
- Emphasize a sense of urgency. Underperforming sales reps need to understand that adopting a sense of urgency to improve their current state is a must. Listen to your sales rep's needs, concerns, and challenges, and help them to resolve existing problems while boosting their morale.
- Schedule weekly face-to-face meetings. It would help if you met your underperforming sales reps once or twice a week to review progress, milestones, success stories, and next steps.

Additionally, you should:

Follow up. Salespeople tend to lose focus, drift away, and sink into desperation when their best efforts are not yielding results. Follow up continuously with your underperforming sales reps, assist in getting them over humps, be their chief motivator. People accomplish miracles under the right leadership. To keep your sales reps focused on their goals, ask:

- What are your short-term goals and aspirations?
- What goals do you want to accomplish within the next 12 months?
- Where do you see your progress 12 months from now on?
- What can I do to help you achieve your goals?
- What challenges are stopping you from accomplishing your objectives?

Sell the big picture. Appeal to your sales reps' pride by demonstrating how their work fits with the company mission. Higher employee engagement yields better results and improves employee morale. The coaching period should remain as needed and until notable progress is accomplished over a reasonable period.

Managers and organizations that protect and accept under-performers in the team are by default contributing to their people's demise. Not addressing this issue will erode the whole organization's performances.

Understandably, top performers love to work with other great performers, however, tolerating low performance often accelerates the exodus of top producers who seek competitive environments where the scrutiny and demand are high along with potential rewards. The success of the team depends on the manager's ability to retain top talent while upgrading existing talent, and eliminating team underperformers.

Sales managers have the duty to do whatever it takes ethically to improve team performance. Successful salespeople tend to be happier doing their job and driving higher customer satisfaction and retention. When dealing with your underperforming sales reps, stick to addressing performance issues and the reasons behind it; it's never about the person. It's all about correcting the wrong behaviors and improving one's ability to perform his job and attain the company's expected objectives.

Mindset Influence Performance KPIs

Start the conversation with a positive, open mindset. Highlight one's positive accomplishments, then gradually move to the subject of performances you need to address. Express how much you believe in the capability of the person and stick to it until their confidence and self-belief kicks in. You are both looking forward to performance improvement; hence you goal is to fulfill your mutual shared purposes.

Identify Underperformance Source

Identify hidden or unspoken underperformance issues by asking open-ended questions and listening to the sales rep without judgment or interruptions. It's always wiser to hear your sales rep's perspective. Your observations and preconceived notions may be entirely different from the salesperson observations and belief. Allowing the sales rep to identify and reflect on their shortcomings may lead to faster and improved outcome.

Do not neglect your underperforming sales reps as they clearly need your help. Underperforming sales rep's poor results give you full right to micromanage their activities to ensure progress. Many underperformers don't realize how far behind they are due to ignorance or denial. Your job is to guide them to understand the seriousness of the situation and draft a collective plan of action that will speed up recovery.

You will need to hold your underperforming sales reps accountable for reaching the milestones you develop together. Success is a collaborative effort that requires a daily discipline that yields results. For example, the sales rep can leverage available technological resources and opportunities to manage current partnerships more efficiently and lead sources to create better qualified opportunities. The sales rep can align his business solutions to meet his customer needs by improving his selling skills and overall capabilities.

Good Management is Like Teaching

Great managers often act like teachers; they care, listen well, help identify problems, write them down, and assist by helping create sound solutions driven by shared agreement and collective insight. Then, follow up to ensure progress, inspect behaviors, give a hand when one is down, guide when one is stuck and give a nudge when one needs encouragement. Sales reps naturally want to succeed, but often don't know how to get to their destination. The sales manager guidance and encouragement help build the sales rep confidence and momentum.

Pay Attention to What Your Salespeople Need

Work in one specific deficient skill at a time until mastery, then move to another. Grade underperformers' skill progress from one to five, with five being the lowest level. As they progress upwards, share the accomplished progress. The aim is to achieve reoccurring lasting progress.

If the sales manager realizes there are simply too many issues, lack of willingness, substantial knowledge gaps, and failure in execution, it may be that the sales rep is not a good fit for the position. In that case, assist the sales rep to find a better transition.

Poor Attitude Should Not Be Tolerated

Underperforming sales reps who are toxic destroy team morale and work harmony. Toxic behavior should be addressed quickly; refusal and lack of compliance should result in swift termination of the offender. It's better to lose a bad apple than corrupt team morale. You are the manager, and it's your responsibility to ensure harmony and performance. Be fair, but decisive. Your team members should understand what you stand for to ensure that the right attitude and behaviors in a professional environment are as essential as performances.

Finally, while dealing with low performers is always a difficult challenge to address, it's still better to handle it the moment it manifests rather than deal with it at a later stage, and there should be no surprises along the way. Often a direct correlation exists between one's performance and one's state of mind. Great sales managers know how to touch people's minds and hearts to create a successful sales cultures that promotes respect, hard work, and individual uniqueness.

CHAPTER 7: SUMMARY

- Good sales managers can turn a disoriented willing underperformer into a solid performer. However, without a total commitment, grit, and willingness to follow guidance, success will be difficult to attain.
- Underperforming sales reps will need to be addressed professionally with smarts, empathy, sensitivity, care, and honesty. Facts and progress metrics should be shared, and an action plan will need to be drafted and agreed upon by both

parties. Then, a follow-up routine will need to be established to hold the sales manager and the salesperson accountable for results.

- A sandwich approach should be applied during each conversation with the salesperson. Start with something positive, discuss your concerns, and finish with something positive and encouraging to lift the underperformer morale. The goal is either improvement or a separation if the salesperson continues to underperform despite your coaching and training efforts.

Understand that salespeople are different, but you should under no circumstances tolerate bad attitude as it destroys team morale in the long run.

CHAPTER EIGHT: SALES MANAGERS' PERSONALITY TYPES

Sales managers come in all shapes, sizes, genders, and most importantly, personality types.

The Peace Maker. This is the manager who acts more of a mediator, always looking for ways to make peace; they are busy trying to solve everyone's problems. They are a control freak and cannot tolerate things to get out of hand. By nature, they are passive and do everything they can to appease their boss. They find their comfort and purpose by micromanaging everyone. They tend to have a high level of tolerance for negativity, and they can live with it. They firmly believe that the truth has many forms, shapes, and shades; hence they hide it by spinning everything. They tolerate incompetence and act gullible, but profoundly believe that the company's goals are unrealistic when missed and somewhat reasonable when attained. Generally, they prefer lower targets than stretch goals, hard work is not one of their virtue.

This type of manager avoids conflict at any cost. They hate being exposed, and they procrastinate as much as possible before making any tough decisions. They prefer to stay off the radar, they are not heroes but rather good mediators. At heart, they are followers, not leaders, despite their authority; they enjoy power in peacetime and prefer not to have it during turbulent times. They are naturally fearful, under pressure they cave quickly, and default to their boss or other stronger colleagues for guidance and assistance.

They often rely on their leading salespeople to make it big for them to share credit. They are good at building internal relationships to get things done for their people. They tend to excel at managing customer relationships and administrative tasks. They are generally not authentic, but are adept at hiding their true intentions.

Their primary objective is to ensure that things run smoothly. They are aware that revenue generation and performance KPIs are essential to keep their job. But that's not their biggest priority, because they are extremely busy putting out fires and making sure that everyone knows the great job they are doing salvaging customers relationships and partnerships. When they miss their quota, they always have a well-prepared justification ranging from extraordinary events to bad luck. Their fingers never point inward because they truly live in a permanent state of denial and feel they're doing everything possible to help their salespeople and the company.

The Motivator. You can count on this type of manager to get things done; they are solid, they know how to rally the troops, and they are decisive and strong-minded. They love to compete and win. They get results, and they deliver on critical metrics. They have strong beliefs. They stand for their team, know they are right; they love recognition, they crave credit, and love to stand out.

The motivator sets precise goals, customizes their communication according to their audience, makes time for their salespeople to coach, listen and guide, recognize achievements, and finds a middle ground solution to pending challenges. The motivator sales manager takes their job seriously, but allows themselves to be criticized and challenged, knowing that their smarts and communication skills will lead them to defend and lead their people toward the outcome they have in mind.

The Boss. They are on a different league; they don't think in terms of competition – they believe in domination. They understand the market dynamics and how to navigate the corporate highways to get things done, with a sense of urgency and precision. The "Boss" type don't tolerate mediocrity in the team. They know how to push people beyond their natural limits, but they are there to pull them out of the quicksand every time. People trust them as they feel they are the reason behind their success. Senior management loves stellar performance, but not so much their cultural fit. The "Boss' type can be hard-headed, and they may carry a confident swagger in their demeanor; they operate north of confidence and south of arrogance. They have presence and authority, and they love it.

They stand up, make their case, and fight for what they believe is right. They have courage and bravado; they believe in pushing forward against all the odds. They know that persistence and strong belief win the fiercest battles, and they have no doubt that leaders are warriors who lead from the front. They win despite the economic downturn because they are creative and have sales reps who act almost like devoted fans. Their team adopt corporate changes faster, knowing that their leader will find a way to guide them through difficult times and market lapses.

The "Boss" is a manager who is all about achieving greatness and creating new leaders that are as good if not better than them. They know how to read faces, emotions, and hearts. They see strengths where others see weakness. They are rebellious by nature; they respect true leadership, not job titles or authority. They exude confidence and walk with a chip on their shoulders, knowing they are among the greats. They know they may not be part of the CXOs group, but they act like leaders at that level, knowing that the five-stars don't make true generals, but the war does. The "Boss" type leaders have a killer instinct and an unbelievable drive to dominate their field colleagues. They rarely get satisfied regardless of the level of success they achieve. They are confident in their capability for extraordinary accomplishments.

You see, repeatedly winning, under complex and sometimes impossible situations, makes you a "Boss" sales manager. It's not about brain power or unique talent, it's more about an instinctive winning drive that allows this breed of leaders to push beyond boundaries and connect with their team on a deeper mental level, creating synergy and subconscious unison where team members are interdependent and connected to the sales manager's mental and spiritual force.

A "Boss" personality is often the source of energy and drive that propels everyone towards the achievement of impossible goals.

The power of a "boss" sales manager goes beyond the visible. The invisible part is the force of team dedication and commitment to pleasing the boss through impeccable discipline and spirit of responsibility to deliver exceptional results and contributions. The boss sales managers cede part of their decision-making to their reports to empower them to learn and grow. Errors are tolerated; blame is discouraged. The team is often part of the decision-making, and everyone owns the outcome.

The "Boss' sales manager ultimately owns the team outcome, and they get the results by confidently leading each member of the team to achieve the impossible.

For example, John is an experienced sales manager with "Boss" characteristics, and he has earned the "Sales manager of the year" award every year since he joined the company. He has corporate courage; he speaks when no one dares to bring up an issue. He is respectful, thoughtful, but fearless. He is admired in silence; many other sales managers believe his audacity stems from his accomplishments. John often gives voice to the voiceless, and he speaks from the heart to generate awareness and communicate the obstacles to his senior management, so he can assist and improve the system. He knows that some senior managers may not like his outspokenness, and he may get penalized for it.

Nonetheless, he believes that if that's the case, then it's a price worth paying. Caring is a heavy burden, but it costs way more not to care. John is a natural leader, and he is a sales manager who runs his division better than most CEO's.

The Bully. This is the most challenging manager of all. They are often intelligent, creative, capable, charming to their superiors, politically savvy, and dedicated to their job with a strong desire to overtop their peers' performances. They love the attention, the raises, promotions, and being the center of attention. Their bosses often praise them, but they are hated by their subordinates as they have a reputation to kiss-up and kick down without hesitation or remorse. They love the fight and can get dirty in an instant. They are calculating machines and excellent strategist; in short, they have all the qualities of a senior executive, which align well with their career ambition.

Their people don't trust them, as the manager has betrayed them often, taken others' credit, and bullied anyone who dares to stand up to them.

This type of managers seems oblivious to their dysfunctional management style, and their subordinates' nervous furtive looks and avoidance don't faze them. They don't feel they're a bully; instead, they feel that their subordinates are merely lazy, incapable, uncommitted, undisciplined, untrustworthy, and jealous and out to get them. That is why they are often sabotaging the manager's hard work and performance by purposefully derailing their initiatives.

The "Bully" type are found everywhere, and many are quite successful because most employees will support their abuse to keep their job. The Bully manager repeatedly uses health-harming behaviors that affect their subordinates' mental health, physical health, and emotional health. They often recourse to yelling, insults, threats, finger pointing and dismissals; and they throw relentless tantrums, steal credit, berate, humiliate, intrude on your privacy, undermine your work, spread falsehoods, withhold vital data, impede your success, ignore subordinate requests as a form of punishment, and promote based on likeability rather than merit.

Personality Matters

The Peace Maker is paycheck-driven, their leadership is driven by their job title. They are often challenged by their team members, and they have difficulty defending their ideas. Pushing forward requires forcing changes, and they tend to hire people who are like them in temperament, attitude, and background. They are often the manager that states, “Thank God, it’s Friday.” They are hanging by a thread, and at their very core, they are hollow, weak and pretenders. Their mission is to survive another week to collect another paycheck, stay hidden, act busy, and get buried under administrative and customers service issues to justify their position and authority. Peace Makers are everywhere, and they represent a good majority of the sales management team at all levels. They work for corporations, governments, states and cities. They are entrepreneurs, vendors, lawyers, doctors, developers, pastors and construction managers. They are easy to spot, but hard to get rid of. They represent the largest pool of management. They are often silent and unhappy managing others.

The Motivator is a competent manager who can deliver results; they are image-conscious. Their reputation matters to them. They know how to address and motivate their team. They love to win, but can tolerate defeat as well. They micromanage and take control quickly when negativity spreads and starts eroding organization morale.

They are transparent, can tolerate mistakes, but despise incompetence and laziness. They strive to meet or exceed goals despite ambiguity and challenges. They love money and recognition but have difficulty taking new paths without a blueprint, as they prefer assurances.

They worry a great deal about making mistakes because they care about their reputation so much. They prefer to execute on a chartered company plan, love to beat their quota, but get lost when deprived of direction. They can manage a tough situation as they possess courage, experience, and brain power. They are a moment leader; they will step up and confront the challenges head-on and will strive to win. They love to surround themselves with active players and watch them execute, knowing their wins will make them happy.

The Boss towers over everyone else. You put them anywhere, and they will come at the top. They are a natural predator, the alpha; they are a calculating machine of success probability, but also a nurturing, docile force. They know how to build a team from scratch and master developing and nurturing talent.

They are the team source of energy and wisdom. They connect their team members to a collaborative matrix that serves as a guiding map.

They focus on the mission at hand and won't stop until they're victorious. They often lead multiple battles at the same time. Without missing a beat, they channel everyone's energy to ensure every task is driven to add value and get one closer to the winning goal.

The boss sales manager's victory celebration cycle is intense but short-lived; the focus is always forward and on to the next victory. They recognize their people's outstanding accomplishments, but remind everyone that the next win is as important as the last. They inspire salespeople to achieve far greater victories than what they have accomplished so far. He keeps everyone focused on their unlimited potential, knowing that people's potential is boundless. For example, you may agree with me that Bill Belichick is an accomplished coach and one of the best in NFL history. Love the patriot or hate them, Bill is a Boss. He applies the "Art of War" principles, knowing that every battle is won before it occurs. He pushes his team to go to exhausting preparation to be able to adjust to any sudden changes without losing sight of the goal.

He sticks with his tried-and-true champions to get things done in a consistent, dependable fashion. He pushes everyone to their limits but gives everything he's got as well. Bill sees his team not just as players, but as warriors in the field carrying substantial off-the-field emotional family and parents' burdens. Moreover, Bill understands that yesterday's victories are history, what matters is today's game and tomorrow's strategy, because that's all one can control.

The boss manager take responsibility for everything, and happily own individuals and team screw-ups. They are willing to get fired to protect a team member when they believe on his innocence. They are all in, and they mean it. They encourage mistakes to learn, knowing that errors of judgment often happen in an uncertain business environment. The boss sales manager understands it, they encourage creativity and corporate courage, knowing that all blame is theirs and all credit should go to the team. Boss sales managers appreciate the recognition, but they don't crave it. They trust their abilities, and they work hard on themselves every day to better themselves. The only way they can help their team is by transferring new knowledge, capabilities, and experiences into the intertwined team mental matrix.

The "Bully" team plea with management and human resources goes unanswered, because they like the bully, get along well with them and feel that the team members simply cannot handle a tough, strict but fair manager that holds everyone accountable for their results.

- According to a 2010 Workplace Bullying Institute Survey, 13.7 million adults reported being constantly bullied at their work place.
- 72% of bullies tend to occupy managerial positions.

- The financial impact of bullies is often reflected by employee excessive turnover, absenteeism and anemic engagement and collaboration

The "Bully" managers tend to have an inflated sense of grandeur or superiority complex, huge ego and heightened sense of entitlement. They tend to listen only to the higher-ups and ignore their subordinates' suggestion. They must have the last word, and everything for them is a challenge, a game where they must be the MVP.

Bullies know they cannot fight everyone, that is why they surround themselves with admirers, until they turn on them to form a new alliance. The "Bully" doesn't have allegiance to anyone but themselves. Bullies know how to read emotions, faces, and unspoken words. They have incredible mental power to push the team to achieve results, not because they want to, but rather that they should as a condition of the job.

Yes, bullies are tough-minded, unfair, and unscrupulous, but they get the job done. How they get it done doesn't matter to them much, but getting it done is all that matters. Their ethics are questionable, as they believe in leadership by fear with their subordinates, minimal cooperation with their peers, and total collaborations with their superiors.

Team members' errors are chastised and reprimanded, and all decision must be approved in advance. They are control freaks, their subordinates fear them, they hold grudges, and know how to fight dirty. If you are not in their corner, you will soon become history, because they will find a way to terminate you.

Whom should you hire?

Peace Makers: They rarely make the president club, unless luck has something to do with it.

Motivators: Can make president club, but accept occasional defeats. They are experienced fighters who know when to pull back to recoup.

Bosses: Make it every year; they are elite fighters who live to win battles. They are perennial goers along with their team elites. They take no credit and give it all to their team.

Peace Makers: Blame the company pricing and competitive pricing strategy for their deal losses.

Motivators: Win against the completion offers, and always find a creative way.

Bosses: Make the competition obsolete; study competitors' strengths and weaknesses and prepare the team to outdo and outperform their strategies and tactics. Competitors often knows these Boss managers and strive to hire them to benefit from their exceptional talent.

Peace Makers: Struggle to make decisions. They would rather defer the tougher decisions to higher authorities to deflect the blame in case the consequences are terrible.

Motivators: Make tough decisions and study all scenarios and implications. They do what's necessary, but no more.

Bosses: They make tough decisions without hesitation. They calculate the risk and probability of failure. They know it's the right thing and get it done, no matter the odds. They trust their gut and instinct that it will work.

Peace Makers: Desperate for wins, cannot wait to use other people's success story to spur internal competition.

Motivators: Leverage mind and spirit to get people to perform and create success stories to show their leadership to executive management. They believe their actions are vital to team success. The team cannot operate without them at the helm.

Bosses: Success stories are the norm, and everyone has one, and they are often shared to improve the winning odds. The boss sales manager needs no credit; the salespeople are merely doing a good job. Success stories are simply the essence of a job done well.

Peace Makers: Have no ability to share internal issues that hinder the team performance. When asked, they curl small, minimize the severity of the problem, but act as they are in control.

Motivators: Tend to speak and grow louder to express their concerns and worries. They are capable sales leaders but often take the initiative only when it becomes necessary. Once they decide, they will drive it fast and forcefully to completion.

Bosses: Will provide well thought-out potential resolutions that will resolve current issues. They are in charge, and they have already been experimenting with a few possible recommendations.

Peace Makers: Pretend to fight for the team. They are a “yes, sir” with their boss.

Motivators: Challenge anything that they are not going to benefit from directly.

Bosses: Educate their superiors to foresee the pros and cons they may not have taken into consideration. Then they will draft a plan to create a path of success while avoiding the field mine. They lead the battle from the front, knowing they have the team support.

The bully has incredible ability to drive performance, by fear or intimidation when necessary to get results. The bully stands tall and defends themselves by any means necessary. They feel that their reputation is online; that is why they take the stand of a fighter to handle anything that comes their way. They have a team but always feel alone. They cannot trust anyone but themselves.

They are a master at pretending they fight for the best interest of the team, but they only care about themselves, their performance, and upward financial and hierarchical gains. They will take credit for everything and dismiss their team members' contributions and sacrifices. They feel their team is nothing without their exceptional talent and work ethics. They believe the team members are lucky to have them, as they teach the team tough-mindedness, discipline, and commitment to excellence.

Who Is Your Manager?

Are you surrounded by Peace Makers, Motivators or Boss sales leaders?

A Peace Makers will struggle to maintain the status quo, they are more of a cheerleader, they know they are weak to average at best, but they will do their best to keep their team operational.

The Motivator is a capable manager who knows what they need to do to keep the team going in the right direction. They will get results, they are motivated by money and recognition. They push hard to get things done, but they crave attention and desire to be in the limelight.

Bosses turn mediocre teams into greatness. They turn subpar products to acceptable, incompetent CEOs to powerhouses, and local business solutions into global solutions. They can turn undesirable companies into a magnet for talent, and adverse circumstances into opportunities. They are the middle movers and shakers that turn average individuals into production machines.

Bullies can maintain status quo performances and even elevate team performances upwards. However, the mental and emotional destruction that the team must endure often outstrip any temporary gains. Rather than strengthening the team, the bully managers weaken it, and rather than attracting talent, they become a magnet that attracts the lower-tier talent no one desires. Salespeople work extremely hard, and they deserve a manager who gives credit, not someone who strips them of their hard-earned accomplishments and crushes personal aspirations because of personal ego and weak character.

Many have experienced working for a bully; they are horrible managers and human beings. However, you should know that bulling is a sign of weakness, mental inferiority, and a consuming anger. Keep your bully manager at work in perspective, know that they are the one with the problem, not you. If the workplace condition becomes intolerable, speak to your boss's boss, or even higher if you deem necessary. Document everything, seek assistance, and file a complaint to protect yourself from retaliation. If necessary, seek outside counseling, or start looking for a different job. Your physical and mental health is vital to the longevity of your career.

You Are a "Boss" Sales Managers if:

1. You don't believe in limits, and you push yourself and others to the maximum every day, knowing that tomorrow you will increase your threshold again. No win is too high to savor for too long, no battle is too great to win, and no fight is worth losing. The past is history, and what matters is the next accomplishment, the next challenge, and the next stretch!
2. Winning against all odds is what matters; the improbable the odds the better. Achieving the impossible is the target.
3. Your goal is to always be above your company's quota requirements. Your goal is to build leaders who can operate, think, push forward uphill in the mud and in the dark with no directives or maps.

4. You know precisely what you want, and you know that your powers have no boundaries, just like the vast powers of your imaginations, creativity, and talent.
5. You never panic. You are always in charge of your mind and actions as well as the minds of everyone else you lead. You stay focused on your goals and purpose.
6. You operate better under extreme pressure. You rely on your creativity and fluidity of thought to analyze complexity and resolve denting challenges.
7. What matter is results, and everything else is secondary.
8. You are not feared, but rather liked and respected for what you stand for in term of ideas, principles, and purpose. Those who report to you respect you, admire you for who you are, and the ideals you represent, knowing that they owe their mental evolution and success to your tutelage.
9. Your peers envy you silently, knowing you dwarf their competency. Your competitor looks forward to learning from you.
10. You trust your team, and they never fail your trust test.
11. You despise mediocrity, you will not tolerate subpar performances, and your team members will go above and beyond to show they are worthy of your coaching lessons.
12. You are willing to work day and night, weekends and holidays, to coach, educate, and help your team get better.
13. You are involved with everyone emotionally, spiritually, and mentally. You are the trusted leader when your team members need counseling, advice, and a dose of honesty.
14. You believe in winning, no matter the odds or challenges.

15. You own the outcome for failures and success. You are a leader that everyone aspires to become.

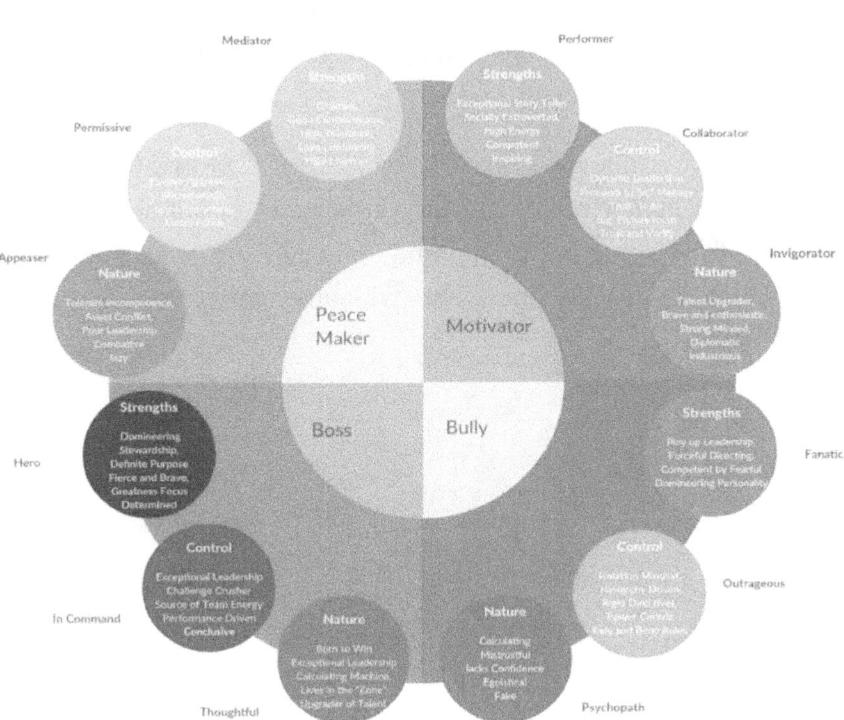

CHAPTER 8: SUMMARY

- Sales managers are leaders who possess different characteristics that drive their thinking, behavior, attitude, relationship building skills, communication, and tolerance level. Some are manipulative and others are straight shooters, some prefer finesse and diplomacy, others prefer brutal candor and tough love.
- Some sales managers are upbeat, inspiring, engaged, and focused, while others are disengaged, disaffected, and dissatisfied. Some are respectful, considerate, and professional,

and others are bullies that verbally abuse, shout, berate, and create a climate of fear and intimidation. The abusive type often ends up having short careers as no one respects what they stand for. Salespeople will remember the leaders that taught them how to evolve and get better, but they will also not forget the leaders that made them feel insecure, small and worried about their jobs.

Whether your manager is a “Peace Maker”, “Motivator”, “Boss”, or “Bully”, what matter most is what you learn from them. You can learn what to do from some managers, and you can learn what not to do from others; both lessons are incredibly valuable when you are managing your team.

CHAPTER NINE: POOR SALES LEADERSHIP EFFECT

Successful sales organizations invest heavily on education, processes, and systems to create an environment that promotes learning and growth. Hiring, training, and retaining great talent requires hiring great sales leaders who lead with purpose.

Strong sales leaders build strong teams and influence individuals. A good sales manager can add value, energy, and strength to the team. A bad sales manager can singlehandedly destroy a good team and damage the organization in ways that can last years. It takes on average a minimum of a year to start realizing the damaging effect of a bad sales manager. The damage may be economic, reputational, ethical, legal, cultural or social.

Damaging Effect of Poor Leaders

A large payment company hired a well-respected sales leader who had over two decades in the banking space. This leader had extensive knowledge and experience managing large sales forces. He had a good record in his industry and was a respected leader. He certainly had a great deal of expertise in human resources and operational matters. Everyone expected him to boost people's morale and increase team performances reasonably quickly. This highly respected leader failed to achieve his corporate goals for three consecutive years. The executive team was concerned and confused, and no one understood why such an accomplished leader with a proven track record could not turn the division performance around.

It became apparent after a while that this manager was adamant in recreating the same results realized in his prior positions by using the same old business strategies that worked in the past. However, these old strategies worked well in different times, under different market environments, and in a different industry. The sales cycle was different, the type of customer and market demands were different, and the sales systems and approaches were different. The sales leader wanted to recreate the same success using the same old methods and formula because that was all he knew. He believed that, with the right level of tweaking, whatever worked well in the past would work again, so he stayed the course. He had the full support of the executive team, and within the end of his first year in the job, he started losing a few good sales reps. Soon, talent turnover started ramping up to an alarming scale.

Replacing lost talent was tough; despite the immense company resources, revenue started taking a nose dive. Panicked, he started putting a lot of pressure on his sales vice presidents to shake things up to make up for lost revenue. Under intense pressure, salespeople's morale sunk to a new low, employee turnover reached a critical point, and faced with an imminent disaster, the board decided to terminate his employment. After his departure, it took the company three additional years to recover from the damages created by his poor leadership.

Good Leader Don't Require Pedigrees

Great leaders are often ordinary people who achieve extraordinary things leading others. Great leaders emerge all over the globe; they represent all age groups, all faiths, and ethnicities. They work for profit and non-profit organizations, public and private, high-tech and low-tech, large and small. They are everywhere, and they do everything.

Some are legends, and others are unknown. Some occupy the corner office, others work the trenches. Some went to Ivy League schools and have incredible pedigrees and accomplishments; others attended unknown schools and possess little or no lineages that boost one's social status.

Leaders are people like you and me. Leadership is erroneously equated with one position, title, organizational authority or scope of responsibility, but that's wrong. Leadership is about what you do and how you do it; it's about your relationship, credibility, passion, belief, and empowerment of others to achieve a collective worthy goal.

Leadership is an internal affair. If you believe with conviction in a cause or purpose and can influence others to follow you to create the outcome you seek, then you are a leader. Your outcome doesn't have to be lofty; it should just leave a positive impat on your people. Real leadership is seizing the moment and doing something that inspires others to emulate you, follow your lead, or act according to your guidance.

Humble Leadership

Every weekend, a man came early morning to a local run-down neighborhood park and started removing trash, broken glass, drug syringes, and other sharp items. It was a rough neighborhood, cops rarely ventured inside, and the same park that served parents and children during the day became a party hub at night. The man kept the same schedule for years. He was polite and kept to himself, and everyone thought he worked for the city as park cleaning stuff. Suddenly, he didn't show up for four consecutive weeks.

The park became dangerously filled with trash and syringes. A few kids got hurt by glass debris that covered the kids' ground playing area. Parents got furious and called the city to protest: *Why did you stop sending cleaning people?* The city representative replied that they had never sent anyone to that park due to budget cuts that occurred years ago. Intrigued, the parents started looking for that mystery man. It took several months, but he finally came back with two helpers. Parents rejoiced, kids were ecstatic, the park was going to be clean again.

A friendly parent approached one of the workers, and started a conversation.

Parent: Do you work for the city?

Worker: No ma'am, I worked for decades for the man over there who has been cleaning this park for years.

Parent: Does he have a cleaning company?

Worker. No, ma'am, he is the CEO of a major corporation, I'm his executive vice president, and the other man is his assistant.

Parent: Are you kidding me? Why would a man of that stature come here every weekend to clean people's trash?

Worker: Well, years ago, his only son died of a heroin overdose in this very park. Rather than visit the area where his son took his last breath, he prefers to clean the park to provide a safer environment for the kids and parents.

Parent: Wow, what a sad story.

Worker: My boss was recently diagnosed with terminal cancer. He was in the hospital for a while and the doctor gave him a couple of months at most.

Parent: My God, thank you for sharing this wonderful man's story with me.

Worker: You are welcome ma'am. He is a very private person and he likes to keep it that way.

After he died, the man donated part of his wealth to renovate the park. That park today is a vibrant, healthy space where families and children take pride in cleaning it and restoring it to look like a little paradise.

The above story illustrates that leadership has everything to do with what one does, rather than one's position or status. Leaders are role models; they are business leaders, community activist, athletes, coaches, religious and political leaders.

They are firemen, nurses, sanitation workers, engineers, doctors, actors, bankers, and everyone in between. Leaders take initiative in handling complex situations, crises, and significant ethical dilemmas. Leaders are coaches and teachers who know how to influence others to trigger meaningful desired changes. Leaders give their best all the time to impact people's engagement and performances.

Good leaders know how to get people to stretch to reach beyond what they thought possible. The gap and impact between ethical leadership and poor leadership is enormous.

Historical Blindness

A newly-minted CEO taking over a struggling bank wanted to shake thing up, so he hired a well-rounded insurance executive who had substantial experience in sales. His purpose was to transform these banking employees from service professionals into sales professionals. Historically, the insurance sales business model is based on aggressive sales methods and approaches. It often relies on pressure and manipulation to speed up the decision-making process. The bank selling methodology is relationship-based and customer-focused, with a low- to no-pressure approach.

Banking is all about nurturing good client relationships. Bankers are not trained as salespeople, nor do they see themselves as such.

Many bankers despise putting any pressure or coercing their clients to do anything that is not in their best interests.

This new sales executive implemented this new sales strategy, expecting everyone to follow it closely. The change happened way too fast; the training was rushed, the pressure to sell the bank products escalated too quickly, and the bankers and their managers had almost no time to adjust to these new requirements. Many bankers were taken by surprise, and things start going downhill fast. Healthy bankers start taking consecutive sick days, and some stated privately that the daily pressure was just too much to bear. Others started complaining that they didn't sign up for this type of treatment, they felt betrayed and pressured beyond reason, and many thought that the trust built with their customer over many years was being destroyed.

The rate of leave of absences and resignation increased dramatically. Several bank branches start having significant issues providing adequate staff coverage during rush hours. The new sales executive was unfazed. He managed to convince the board of directors that this employee behavior should be expected during the initial phase of transformation, and discontent and dissatisfaction would need to be endured to get to the normalcy phase.

Within twelve months, it was clear; the situation went from bad to worse. Customer dissatisfaction increased and employee morale hit rock bottom. Many customers start closing their accounts and moving to more friendlier competitors where they felt wanted, respected, and less harassed.

Shortly after, the board members terminated the head of sales, citing that his way was too aggressive, careless, and lacked empathy.

The terminated sales executive methods had worked within the insurance industry but failed miserably within the bank environment. Sales approaches and techniques that may work in a specific sector may not work in another. A sales executive that is considered a legend within an industry may fail miserably in another.

People Are All You Have

Success in sales requires a close study of the market, industry, people, and market socio-economic forces. Executives cannot manage people whose success they depend on like cattle. Leading people requires finesse, empathy, sensitivity, and open-mindedness. A method that works in an industry under certain conditions with certain people may flop in another.

The bankers resisted change because the sales leader never took the time to explain why the changes were needed and why the bank must become more sales-oriented to survive and compete. While the change was necessary to the bank's survival, its implementation was flawed. This senior executive could have taken his time by engaging all bank employees from top to bottom on why the changes and sacrifices were necessary. He should have detailed his purpose, strategy and implementation process. People resist change when led blindly. When you're armed with a detailed plan showing you your steps ahead, even the most radical transformation becomes a mere evolution. It took the bank several years to undo the damage created by his poor leadership.

Hiring the wrong sales leader can leave a devastating long-lasting financial and mental effect on the organization. It takes time and significant economic resources to replace a sales leader, and it often takes years to restore employee confidence and recover from these losses. Losing talented employees can damage the company's reputation, create a vacuum, and expose the company to financial losses when a competitor swoops in and grabs existing, large, unprotected clients.

Regardless of previous accomplishment, a leader who is not capable or willing to change his methods to affect change will ruin the performance of the entire sales force. It takes time to test a leader's performance, and even the most seasoned sales managers will find it challenging to quickly recognize the signs of poor leadership and the possible damage that one can create, especially when the sales leader has good past records.

Why Do Leaders Fail?

Sales leaders fail because of the following reasons:

- *Poor Direction.* Jumping into action by relying on your prior experiences is often the wrong strategy. As illustrated in the above example, the key is to take the necessary time to understand a business thoroughly; failure to do so will lead to making fatal errors that cost money, time, effort, and repute. The implementation of a sound strategic vision requires a total understanding of the nature of the business.

- *People's talent is what defines superior companies.* Your ability as a sales leader to surround yourself with talented individuals can determine your success or failure. Your ability to attract talented employees, retain them, and create an environment that promotes learning and growth can make your company a talent magnet.

- *Flawless execution.* Even the best sales strategy will fail without proper implementation. Most sales strategies don't fall apart because they are bad strategies, they fail when implemented into action and not followed upon with good communications, progress measurement, and compensation that incentivize the right behavior to drive its execution.

- *Healthy organizational culture.* A sales culture is the environment that unifies, aligns, and motivates every employee to do the best work possible every day. Great sales culture promotes and celebrates people's successes and encourages openness and development. It fosters acceptances and collective focus to create a better working environment and improved society. Toxic organizational culture is like a poison that paralyzes the organism by rotting it slowly from the inside out.

Effective leadership doesn't require a high IQ, raw talent, exceptional past performance, or even experience. Leadership is all about one's willingness to learn from their environment and adapt to meet current and future challenges. It's the passion and devotion to deliberately practice acquiring new knowledge and skills to share with salespeople. It's one's ability to seek and ask for feedback to modify trajectory to meet new demands. It's the leader ability to evoke strong empowering emotions that lead ordinary people to achieve extraordinary accomplishments.

CHAPTER 9: SUMMARY

- Leadership failure is responsible for many sales leaders' career derailments. Poor leadership creates toxic workplaces that prevents progress, misses goals, and destroys employee's morale.

- Poor leadership generates a culture where employees are disengaged and dissatisfied.

- Good leadership requires the flexibility of action, integration of others unique creativity skills, and fluidity of thoughts. Effective leadership has nothing to do with pedigrees, experience, or position.

- Good leadership requires innovative approaches in coaching and reorienting people behaviors to achieve specific, worthy goals.

CHAPTER TEN: PERFORMANCE AND COMPENSATION

Vice president of sales: Your quarterly results came in short again. What happens now?

Tom: Well, I thought I had a solid plan. Two of my top producers who often finish above quota did come up short. The decision makers had a few internal constraints that delayed their buying decisions.

I also had two salespeople who went into a leave of absence, and the rest of the team's production was simply subpar. I honestly feel that sometimes I'm spending too much time with my underperforming salespeople rather than spending more quality time coaching my top sales performers. I understand the heavy focus of senior management to improve the results of our low-performing salespeople.

However, based on my field time and one-on-one training sessions, I feel that at least 30% of these salespeople don't have the will or capability for the job. I'm also worried that I may be losing a couple of my top sales reps to the competition who is aggressively wowing my reps with exciting offers to join their organization. You are aware that I recently lost one of my top performer because we couldn't meet the competitor's offer.

VP: Okay, what's your plan going forward, Tom?

Tom: Honestly, I'm doing my best, but I'm running out of options to achieve my goals.

VP: Perfect, let’s start there. Let's draft a plan that is going to ensure your success, retain your top performers, and better engage your underperforming salespeople. Let's schedule a meeting this week. I’ll take the liberty of inviting a couple of my peers along with a few of your successful colleagues and brainstorm the best path to your team success.

Tom: Glad to hear it, let’s do it.

Goals Are Roadmap to Achieve Results

Goals are targets, and targets can be hit with deliberate practice. In sales, having to achieve quota is often a mandate to keep the job, get recognition, make money, grow within the company, and potentially achieve upward mobility.

Sales are all about meeting goals and achieving results. Failure to meet targets can put one in a stressful situation; no one likes to justify failure to their boss. Knowing your goals is one thing, achieving your goal is entirely another thing.

Salespeople failure to achieve goals may stem from several reasons, including:

1. Goals are too aggressive or unattainable, setting your sales team up for failures.
2. Poor lead generation system, inadequate training on how to acquire quality leads and inadequate funnel management.
3. Sales and marketing misalignment.
4. Sales and cross-functional teams’ disengagement.
5. Poor follow-up and lack of progress tracking measurement CRMs.

6. The sales manager gives order and directives but never coaches his salespeople.

The list above reflects some of the reasons, among dozens, why a salesperson may fail to meet their quota, but many other factors can contribute to this. A good example would be a lack of guidance from the leadership team, abrupt change of corporate directions and priorities. In addition to internal and external competing forces.

Sales Compensation Matters

My experience has shown me that changing compensation plan incentives can, in the short term, change salespeople's behaviors. Salespeople naturally are always looking for ways to maximize their income. Hence, they are always on the lookout for ways to maximize their commissions and bonuses. Conversely, executive managers are always looking for ways to pay the minimum possible for loftier stretch goals, resulting in salespeople's low morale, lack of productivity, and retention issues. Paying higher salaries doesn't guarantee better talent, but it improves the odds of getting better quality candidates and a larger pool of applicants. The best compensation plans pay for high-performance, and high-ethics with no income ceiling, coupled with a competitive base salary that ensures a decent standard of living, which increases employee's loyalty and retention.

A good sales compensation plan should reward salespeople with appropriate incentives for short-term performances and higher incentives for long-term performance. Smart compensation goes beyond paying just for competence and achievements. It should also pay for one's skill and loyalty. Every company has a few employees that are hard to replace, due to a mix of unique knowledge, competency, and creativity. Innovative companies provide financial incentives for economic performances as well as for knowledge sharing. Knowledge sharing is vital to a company growth, and overall improvement of the salesforce.

Peer-To-Peer Knowledge Sharing Policy Upsides

- Eliminate costly missteps that cost money, time, and energy to fix.
- Speed up learning curves that translate to salespeople's quicker financial gains.
- Build confidence and self-autonomy.
- Build an employee-friendly business model.
- Develop colleagues mentoring programs.
- Reinvent peer relationships as needed.
- Find new ways to add value to customers.
- Creates a culture of cohesiveness among employees.
- Improve employee retention and loyalty.
- Discourage knowledge hoarding.
- Improve employee shared practices.

Most companies pay regular salaries for ordinary performances but fail to pay excellent compensation for extraordinary achievements, often putting pay caps, thereby killing sales reps' excitement, and desire to maximize returns. Sales compensation structure reflects the value one adds to an organization. Good salespeople are hard to find and take time to cultivate internally; hence, it's only fair to pay them above market value. Luring talented salespeople from a competitor requires paying above market value to attract ideal salespeople. It's much cheaper to retain the talent you have by paying them above market compensation and bonuses.

Most companies create job descriptions and pay packages comparable to their competitors. Playing even hands attracts average performers, but often fails to attract top producers that are looking for above market norms.

Additionally, pay often reflects past performances, not current or expected performances. The compensation structure should entice the sales rep or manager to stretch further knowing that with every stretch, his compensation structure will grow as well.

Performance and Fair Compensation

I believe that some sales executives are more focused on their compensation plans than their subordinates, resulting in different levels of job satisfaction between the leadership group and its employees. Great performances should generate great payouts and bonus, and poor performances should be reviewed carefully and compensated accordingly.

Now, I stated ‘carefully’ because sometimes circumstances warrant an exception when poor performance is due to external forces beyond the salesperson or manager’s control. For example, a sales manager who was managing the territory of Puerto Rico has ranked for over a decade among the top one percent in the country. In 2017, Hurricane Maria devastated Puerto Rico and crushed the whole business communities.

It was assumed that it would take two to three years before life regained normalcy. Most sales organizations faced with such catastrophe and bleak future would terminate the employment of their salespeople and sales managers and abandon Puerto Rico for good. However, a couple of smart organizations decided to pay their salespeople and managers equal salaries and commissions to their last three years' average.

These companies, hired the best salespeople from their previous competitors who closed their operations in Porto Rico, given them an edge to dominate the whole market and build employee and customer loyalty as they were rebuilding their businesses and communities. The losses incurred will be compensated with many years of market total dominance.

Here is another example. Jack, who worked for a company for 30 years, was diagnosed with brain cancer. He was the sole provider for his family. While he was healthy, he ranked among the top producers in the country, and he routinely made ten times his base salary in commissions. His medical care was devastatingly expensive, and Jack knew that financially, once his saving ran out, he wouldn't be able to meet his mortgage and children's college tuition.

The company senior leadership decided to continue to award him the same compensation, including the average commissions he was producing pre-diagnosis. Jack overcame his cancer, and during an interview that went internally viral, he stated that without the company care he would have probably died. "The company saved not only my life, but also my family from financial ruin, and because of that I'm eternally grateful to the senior management's empathetic humanity and care."

The company gesture and Jack's message spoke volumes. In a confidential interview with several employees, many listed that how the company treated their employees when facing hard times is what drove their loyalty. Jack's story became a beacon of hope in corporate culture.

Salespeople should be compensated fairly, as they drive and fight for the company economic survival and reputation daily.

Your Employees Are Your Future

During the internet boom, Michael Dell demonstrated that sophisticated technology could be sold through a website and without a salesperson's assistance. Many thought the sales profession had reached an end. Today, salespeople are more vital than ever. The complexity of technology that we depend on to run businesses has created a need for skilled salespeople who can generate results through consultative selling.

Technology has interconnected us to new global markets. Today, a local company can sell products/services to markets across the globe. Selling has evolved rapidly, and it has transformed salespeople from being transactional to revenue growth consultants.

Companies depend on revenue for survival, and sales executives rely on middle managers and line managers to drive sales performances. We know that the right activities drive results. Every unit of the business organization should be razor focused on revenue growth metrics.

The key is to do what's right for your employee first. Happy employees will go above and beyond, even sacrifice time, effort, and energy to satisfy your clients, partners, and shareholders. History has demonstrated that companies that purposefully neglected to invest in the well-being of their employees no longer exist.

CHAPTER 10: SUMMARY

- Salespeople's quotas need to be realistic and achievable to allow people to make money while stretching to meet goals that are challenging but doable.
- Sales compensation should be simple, fair, and attractive. A compensation plan that is overly complex, hard to achieve, or

that changes too often is demoralizing to salespeople and destroys productivity. Demotivated salespeople deliberately slow down their productivity to demonstrate their level of dissatisfaction, leave the company, or pretend to work rather than giving it their best every day.

- A smart organization sets clear goals and simple compensation plans that reward effort and pay according to performance.

PART II: COACHING

"You biggest challenge isn't getting your sales reps to believe they are worthy and capable of success.

Your challenge is the voice within that is telling you: you are not good enough, not smart enough, not talented enough to lead your sales reps to achieve what they can't reach themselves.

Your sales rep's performance and success is a mighty force that has the dual power to elevate your sales rep's confidence while suffocating your inner doubts and fear."— Anthony Chaine

"You can motivate by fear, and you can motivate by reward. But both those methods are only temporary. The only lasting thing is self-motivation." — Homer Rice

"I'd say handling people is the most important thing you can do as a coach. I've found every time I've gotten into trouble with a player, it's because I wasn't talking to him enough."— Lou Holtz

CHAPTER ELEVEN: COACHING BENEFITS

Sales managers' primary job is to coach their sales rep to understand the mechanism, behavior, approaches, and best practices to persuade their customers to buy more of their products and services.

Coaching is all about improving your salespeople's efficiency on the job. Coaching is not solving your sales rep's issues, but helping understand how to solve their problems. You may have to provide direction and even assist sometimes when your direct intervention can make a difference. Your sales reps' primarily job is to sell and get educated on how to become more proficient at resolving customers' problems. Good sales managers help their sales reps analyze current circumstances, facts, and challenges, then assist them in discovering alternatives solutions and developing specific courses of action.

Coaching

What do we mean by coaching? One of the best definitions I found is "asking people questions that help them discover the answers that are right for them". Asking questions? The conventional wisdom is the sales leader is an expert, someone who knows the subject well and can provide answers on the subject. Expertise on the domain is the foundation of the leader authority. In contrast, when the leader wears the coach hat, he will need to adopt a different mindset to add value by helping people. Coaches do not tell; instead, they ask well thought-out questions and allow the team member to think and reflect on the subject.

As a sales manager, you set the overall direction but give your sales reps the freedom of initiative and thought to reach their conclusions. Coaching is all about empowering and trusting others to perform their best without supervision. Professional sales reps often know their job requirements intimately, they love their autonomy and independence of thoughts, and welcome coaching opportunities to grow and expand.

The coaching process principles and discipline have multiple layers of merits. However, many sales managers see coaching mainly as a corrective measure to assist and upgrade sales reps' performance. While, senior managers and human resources executives see coaching as an investment to enhance talent performance and effectiveness.

Most sales manager avoid coaching because it's a time-consuming activity and many companies don't have a formal coaching process that has clear expectations and accountability measures. Many sales managers have never been trained on how to coach sales reps. Therefore, they avoid it to minimize the risk of being embarrassed or feeling awkward in front of their reps.

Why Coach?

I recall being promoted to the position of sales director, I inherited a team that was at the bottom of the barrel in term of performance. My new team was way behind most its sales metrics and quota. I thought my past experiences had prepared me for anything, but my team performance level was the biggest challenge I had ever faced in terms of scale and complexity. Turning the team around was a colossal task. I thought I was up for the challenge, so I drafted an aggressive strategy and championed its execution.

During this transformative process, I experimented multiple approaches that led to numerous conflicts with my sales reps. I had to often lean on my boss and mentors to find a better way to resolve conflicts.

I recognized that I was a little frustrated by sales reps who didn't perform as I expected. I found myself trying hard to suppress my emotions analyzing salespeople incompetence without prejudgment or bias. I admit that I had to change my thought process along the way and accept my colleagues' and boss' advice to maintain control, as well as stay cool when confronted with resistance from underperforming sales reps. Some underperforming sales reps were not willing to put the necessary effort to get better, even though they promised otherwise. I couldn't terminate these sales reps. I had to give them the benefit of the doubt, then do my best in terms of coaching, training, and personal development. When all my corrective action fails to make a difference, I accepted the fact that the relationship may not work, and part ways with any underperforming sales rep without remorse or regrets.

Coach the Coach

Numerous studies have proven the positive impact and effect of sales coaching on individual performance. Being coached by my boss helped me understand how I could create a difference as a leader. During this process, I had to go through introspection to change for the better. I couldn't help others if I wasn't able to improve myself, evolve and accept the fact that I was a work-in-progress as well. I had to let go of my ego first. I start delegating more, trusting my salespeople more, while encouraging my sales reps to try new ways, make mistakes and learn. I also started asking reps for frequent, honest feedback and accepting the limitations of my expertise and knowledge. I realize that I didn't have all the answers, and had to learn to ask the right questions. I had to learn to self-analyze myself first before I started self-analyzing others.

Major Benefits of Coaching the Coach

Many sales organizations have adopted leader-mentor type of strategy to develop sales leaders. Many Sales organizations task their vice-president of sales with spending thirty minutes a week coaching their non-direct reports. While this is a good practice, it's certainly not enough to have a meaningful impact, as effective coaching requires time to share knowledge, experience, perspective, and counsel.

Professional coaches can serve as mentors and teachers to help and guide sales managers personal development. Some companies rely on external coaches to support their sales leaders with coaching techniques, methods, and strategies. However, despite the demonstrated value of professional coaching, many companies don't invest enough in external coaching assistance, putting themselves at a disadvantage to develop their sales force and managers.

Value of Coaching

Organizations that have adopted coaching as part of their employees' leadership development and learning initiatives can gain a competitive advantage in the following areas:

1. Improve overall business results.
2. Create a path of learning and development for leaders and sales reps.
3. Create an experimental educational space, where coaches learn new skills and test new innovative approaches.
4. Optimize an organizational culture that promotes positive change, and encourages diversity and risk-taking.
5. Create better communication, sustained dialogue, and honest feedback.

Sales managers often have the most impact on their sales reps' development, as they experience real-life events and challenging situations with customers. Coaching happens in real-life settings; the lessons drawn from specific circumstances can be shared with the whole team, benefiting everyone. These kinds of experiences can expose the organization to situational studies and widen everyone's experiences by adding value to the team's collective knowledge bank.

There is no right way to coach, and every coach has their own ways and methods. It's a trial and error process; what works with a specific individual rep may not work with another. You should be aware that some techniques may only work with people, in some particular situations.

Coaching is challenging, as you may have to reconsider your approach and make the necessary adjustment according to the situation you are in.

What is Directive Coaching?

Directive coaching means telling people what to do or should be doing. This type of coaching may be required to move something along quickly. Non-directive coaching involves allowing people to think on their own and act on their own. You may start thinking, what do I mean? Real coaching requires both directive and non-directive coaching based on the situation and type of work needed.

What is Non-Directive Coaching?

Non-directive coaching focuses on getting the salesperson to take a specific course that will advance her agenda. It primarily focuses on getting the salesperson to identify and resolve their problems. Salespeople tend to deal with multiple issues daily. The sales rep's ability to solve complex issues while advancing the sale is challenging, but success depends on one ability to manage multiple competing demands.

Careful

As a sales manager, it's natural to resist relinquishing control, jump in to save a sale, provide on the spot feedback, or attempt to demonstrate how objections should be managed when your rep is struggling with a tough customer. My advice, step back, and let your sales rep handle the situation even when asked to intervene.

Most sales managers struggle to relax in high-challenge situations. Rather than being uncomfortable and allow the sales rep to learn during these moments, most sales managers jump to the rescue a little too soon. Personal development and true learning happen in times of discomfort, unfamiliarity, and intense pressure. Tenuous situations are golden, and the most-remembered coaching moments are those that occur between the sales manager and their sales rep following tough events.

Be a Role Model

Managers have a huge impact in shaping people's career growth, stimulating their minds, and educating future leaders in the fundamental principles of good leadership and strategy.

People have a job when they work in an environment that confines their personal growth and ambition, where money is the only motivational factor to come to work. People have *careers* when they feel valued and supported by leaders who care about their individual career growth, support learning, promote open communication, life-long education, and promotion that is based on merit.

A CEO who is perceived as a dedicated mentor and teacher will undoubtedly create an organizational culture that advocates positive role modeling that will have a ripple effect on its employees.

Coaching Underperforming Employees

Most of us have at some point given up on an individual because despite our best efforts the person simply didn't put in the necessary effort to change. As a coach, you cannot allow frustration to ruin your ability to influence your reps. People are unique, and they respond to different learning styles and operate at a different pace.

The key is to be patient because low expectations rarely yield to progress and often disguise potential. Experienced managers often fall into the trap of judging people's potential based on prior experiences and gut feelings. It's easy to pass judgment on a sales rep who's behind, fails to meet expectation, or is too slow in comparison to others. However, hold passing a final conclusion until you gather enough facts that support your argument.

Coaching with Compassion

I hired a sales rep to penetrate the Hispanic market in New Jersey, even though he could not speak English fluently. Several managers that interviewed him before me passed on him and advised me to do the same.

My instinct told me to hire him, and I did despite everyone's mockery. His sales performance during the first two months were acceptable, and suddenly his production went bad for the next three months. My peers were telling me we "warned you not to hire him; he cannot survive without being fluent in both Spanish and English in a market like New Jersey."

I couldn't give up on him, so I decided to spend some time with him in the field. We visited several customers, and I was amazed by his sales skills and how he bonded with his customers. So, I asked him, "Jose, what's going on in your life that you are not telling us?" After a long silence, he broke down and told me his mom had been in the hospital for the last three months: she had a terminal cancer and did not have long to live. Moreover, his father was home suffering from

Alzheimer's disease. He was the only son and the sole family they had in the U.S. I was out of words. Most people couldn't operate under these conditions, yet he did.

I promptly made his sales manager aware of the situation, and we gave him all the support he needed. A few months later, Jose broke every record the company had in the last forty years. He became a legend and a perennial President Club goer. His customers loved him, he was always smiling and he had incredible work ethics. I have seen some hard-working sales reps in my career, but Jose was unstoppable. His portfolio had as many English-speaking customers as Spanish speakers, and he turned a language disadvantage into an asset. He was authentic, and people loved his integrity, transparency, and humility.

Having compassion and understanding people's pain and suffering is a critical leadership attribute.

- *Accept your humanity.* It's normal; we all make mistakes and act judgmental. The key is to pause, reflect, and conduct thorough research before you act.
- *Be mindful.* Passing judgment instinctively or too quickly, can be wrong. Slow down, understand the other party's perspective. Put yourself in the other person's position to reframe your thinking and judgment.
- *Never judge a book by its cover.* We naturally harbor biases and prejudgment based on the environment we grew up in, society, school and parental influences. Being open-minded and flexible can allow you to uncover gems in places you may not be familiar with. There are talented people in every corner of the world, and you just need to be open to new perspectives and ideas.
- *Self-educate.* People can create miracles in the right environments. Albert Einstein said, "Everybody is a genius. But

if you judge a fish by its ability to climb a tree, it will live its whole life believing that is stupid." Be open to people potential.

- *Be compassionate.* No one likes to be mean or bad. However, people are complex creatures; give them the benefit of the doubt. People change, help facilitate the transition.
- *Support your people and stand by your beliefs.* Brené Brown quoted the following: "If I feel good about my parenting, I have no interest in judging other people's choices. If I feel good about my body, I don't go around making fun of other people's weight or appearances. We're hard on each other because we're using each other as a launching pad out of our own perceived deficiency."

Before you judge your sales reps, you should conduct a comprehensive introspection of your skills, behaviors, and capabilities. Do you possess sound abilities to help others operate beyond their comfort zone? Do you trust your ability to help your sales reps learn, grow, change and develop? Do you have the right combination of attributes in terms of empathy, compassion, and understanding to affect positive changes?

Using a grounded approach may work with underperforming sales reps who may not be used to or comfortable with coaching sessions. To teach effectively, you must believe strongly in your convictions that underperformance can be overcome with the right level of training. It would help if you also stayed mentally agile to educate and learn from others. Coaching is a dialogue where both parties stimulate one another while evolving at different rates.

Mindset

You cannot coach or educate your sales reps if you believe they are uncoachable. Your mindset defines the outcome you are going to achieve. You are a role model for your salespeople. Hence, everything you do as a manager will reflect your sense of responsibility, experience, personal convictions, and skills. You cannot help develop a person unless you connect and earn their trust. Adopting a growth mindset requires commitment, focus, and effort.

Pause and Reflect

Ted, a sales manager, was reviewing a request-for-proposal (RFP) prepared by one of his sales rep; his first intuition was that he'd done a terrible job and was about to call the account executive to tell him that the RFP needed some serious rework. Then, he realized he never took the time to educate his team on how to create an excellent request-for-proposal document, nor had the company training department ever trained anyone on the subject.

He called the sales rep, thanked him for taking the initiative to draft such a complex document, and proceeded to ask him what he was trying to accomplish. What vital points needed to be incorporated in this document? How many competitors were they up against?

Together, they drafted an excellent RFP. Ted then asked the sales rep if he would be willing to coach his peers on the subject during the next team meeting. The sales rep was thrilled at the opportunity and the confidence bestowed upon him by his manager. He did such a great job that other managers wanted him to educate their teams. The training department took notice, as they needed a training director with experience in sales. With Ted's blessings, he took the job and transformed the training department from its reactive state to a proactive state that created state-of-the-art training material that genuinely worked. Everyone benefited from his promotion, and while he was a great salesperson, he was a better coach and trainer.

Taking time to reflect, before rushing to judgment, requires an open mind and continuous self-inspection, but, it's worthwhile.

Stay Humble and Learn

I believe most sales reps want to add value to the organization they represent. However, it is sometimes hard to do so when one feels way behind in terms of performance achievement and standing.

The larger the gap to meet performance, the higher the desperation level and the lower the morale. A good sales manager takes time to understand the reason for underperformance by listening carefully to the sales rep's reasons and challenges without interruption or dismissal.

You cannot help someone if you don't listen to uncover the root cause of the problem. I've witnessed on multiple occasions where the manager interrupted the sales rep at will, dismissed his explanations and thought processes and acted as though there was nothing he could learn from the situation. The most memorable learning experiences are often not planned. People learn from job experiences more than planned training. People remember these experiences because of the price paid to learn the lesson.

The cost related to the experience can be financial, emotional, or mental. Losing a significant relationship can be financially devastating. Making a significant mistake that tarnishes your reputation in the market can be an emotional catastrophe and losing a considerable partner can be a confidence sinker. Major events like these can be recalled vividly years after they occurred. Business challenges, personal failures, crises, and mistakes tend to become a permanent part of our experience bank.

It's wise to listen to people without passing any judgment. Both the coach and the coachee can learn from mutual experiences. As a sales manager, you should:

- Refrain from excessive interruptions. Instead, ask questions and listen carefully to understand the underlying challenges.
- Refrain from showing impatience or irritation.
- Never suggest solutions and course of action before understanding one's challenge and abilities.

Development Process

- Clarify your understanding of the matter and validate with the sales rep.
- Try to understand the core reasons behind the performance deficiency. Is it a skill issue or a will issue?
- Figure out which role you need to play to help the sales rep meet his goals.
- Leverage all internal and external resources to support the sales rep to overcome challenges.
- Summarize the discussion and agree on an action plan.

By showing respect and humility, your salespeople will open up and their challenges. People can get better, as long as you are supportive and demonstrate patience and leadership.

Self-Inspection is Powerful

As a sales manager you should ask yourself the following questions:

- What strengths do I bring to the job? How can I leverage this ability to help my sales reps?
- What areas should I focus on to develop my team members' skills? What challenges should I expect?

- What aspect of coaching may be the most challenging for me?
- What kind of coaching should I practice to get the best ROI?
- How can I measure and monitor my team coaching progress?
- What's my greatest coaching success? What contributed to it?
- What coaching mistakes have I made year-to-date? What were the lessons extracted from it?
- How can I improve my overall coaching skills?

Your Experiences

It's quite common that a sales managers get in the way to progress. It happens when the sales manager seeks team conformity rather than individuality which met resistance.

People achieve success in different ways, and every individual has unique experiences. People make mistakes, but the lessons learned are priceless. It's the mistakes that educate us on personal resilience, humility, vulnerability, perspective, strengths, and limitations. Work-related hardship is not unique but can give you a wealth of introspective learning.

Your life lessons can be shared with your sales reps to enrich their lives, but you cannot impose your thought process as a path to follow. It would help if you respected people's individuality and free spirit; you can provide guidance but do not force people to follow your directives.

Since, what worked for you in the past may no longer work; you must be prepared to accept new ways and ideas to grow as a manager. Things change fast in the business world. Your role as a sales manager is to provide support, remove obstacles, and create an environment where salespeople can become better.

Coaching is Learning on the Job

Learning from one's experience has its limitations. People don't always recall nor apply self-learned lessons, but they find it easier to remember and apply the lessons learned from people they trust. Most organizations tend to focus on performance goals and rarely on learning goals. We reward people for achieving goals, not for learning. People will naturally gravitate toward achieving financial goals at the expense of continued learning.

Learning new skills and developing new strengths takes time, effort, and practiced refinement. In a fast-paced environment, people rarely take time to pause and reflect on the value of learning new skills, except when one suffers a major defeat or a setback. When learning new skills stems from the consequences of a major failure, we focus on the negative aspect of the learning experience to avoid peril, which erodes one self-confidence and risk-taking initiatives.

Learning from personal failures is challenging, time-consuming, and costly in terms of time, money, and potential. Recognizing personal weakness is hard, but learning from others experiences and leveraging their findings can help one avoid pitfalls.

For example, a senior vice president realized that John, who is a vice president of sales, was creating Power Points presentations that were rudimentary in comparison to what the job demanded. John's overall performance was great and his communication skills were outstanding. However, his major weakness was his computer inadequacies.

The senior vice president knew that John could not keep his job unless he fixed this major weakness. Tom was another successful vice president of sales, and he was towering over his peers in term of performance. He had advanced computer and financial skills. However, he was perceived as an average communicator, because his communication style lacked structure and was long-winded with no pauses.

The senior-vice president encouraged John and Tom to set twice-a-week one-hour sessions to educate one another on their areas of weakness. Within a year, John became an advanced Microsoft Office user and Tom's communication skills improved dramatically.

The above example reflects that leaders' creative thinking is paramount when the time is scarce or organizational support is lacking. Taking the time to evaluate every situation and reflecting on smart solutions can make the difference between solving a problem or rushing to an undesirable course of action.

Promoting Learning on the Job

People naturally want to learn, but when the learning curve is steep, only a few people will have the stamina to complete the task. Most trainings fail because people are not willing to go back to learn and absorb the material provided. Most written training books get shelved permanently post-training, coaching lessons get forgotten unless practiced continuously, personality assessments often get ignored, sales best practice techniques get implemented only after great failures, and development training on-the-job become more of an opportunity to socialize than work.

Peter was a sales director at a major-medical equipment company. Like most managers, he spent most of his time putting fires out, removing obstacles, and helping his team members close deals. Peter realized that while each issue was unique, some similarities and redundancies kept occurring. He started journaling every problem he encountered, how he solved it, and the parties who helped him resolve it. Within one year he realized that his journaling system had reduced the time he spent on issue resolution from 65% to 25%, freeing a lot of his time to learn new things, helping coach his team members, and focus on acquiring more considerable opportunities he wouldn't have dared to touch in the past.

Peter implemented a regular group-think process. He started sending complex issues to his team members and peers to reflect collectively or scheduled short conference calls to discuss and compare thoughts and strategies. This system worked so well that major challenges that once took days to resolve were taking minutes now due to the collective employee mindset and shared experiences. This method proved so successful that senior managers modeled this behavior across the whole organization.

Peter's methods allowed sales reps and managers to learn on the job by using collective reflection techniques such as journaling, problem-solving, and brainstorming. Peter achieved senior management buy-in by creating a learning support tribe within the company, and everyone benefited from this bank of knowledge that was documented and available to all. The price of admission was simple—contribute ideas, insight, and strategies. There were no right or wrong answers; what mattered was thoughtful, genuine solutions.

Peter created a system that promoted collective input and learning to resolve complex issues. Employee confidence went up, and issue resolution became everyone's business. A reward system was set up to encourage people to contribute often and well.

People encounter challenges daily on the job, and these challenges should be part of individual development experiences. Failures and setbacks are natural business events and sharing these collective experiences can be priceless to the whole team as they are powerful development opportunities. People love working for organizations that acknowledge people's wins but recognize the wisdom gained from failures. The latter shouldn't be a subject of shame and incompetence, rather an enriching experience that the whole organization can benefit from.

CHAPTER 11: SUMMARY

- Coaching is the most important job that a sales manager performs to improve his team members' productivity and ability to do their job most effectively and efficiently.
- Coaching your sales manager on how to become better at managing their teams, forging a stable internal relationship with the cross-functional teams, and building relationship with their external partners is vital to the success of the leader.
- You cannot expect a sales manager to coach effectively if they were never coached on the subject. Sales leaders need to continue coaching the coach until the coach become proficient at building future leaders who can coach as effectively as the sales manager does.
- Learning on the job should be a way of life within the organization, along with sharing information and peer-to-peer education. The evolution of the team depends on the level of trust and comfort that team members and leaders share toward the improvement of the group.

CHAPTER TWELVE: COACHING THE COACH TO CREATE LASTING COMPETITIVE ADVANTAGE

You can hire the best salespeople you can afford, but it will be just a matter of time before you start seeing issues related to one's approach, behavior, attitude and overall business management. A good sales manager is always checking their salespeople's vitals to ensure performance while sensing mood changes and frustration and addressing hidden and unspoken issues that may affect productivity.

Sales management is like parenting; parents know when things are not right, even when the child doesn't utter a word. Most parents will approach the child with empathy to gain trust and help. In many ways, good sales managers act the same way; they become intimate with their sales reps to the point where they can sense when their assistance is needed.

It's amazing how even some of the best-managed corporations in the world have little or no official training for managers. Most corporate promotions are made based on taking a leap of faith on someone and hoping that things will turn out well. We accept that the newly-promoted sales manager will project a positive attitude, be responsible, committed, accountable, creative and compassionate. We also expect them to motivate, inspire, reward and serve their team members while meeting company objectives.

The above attributes represent a tiny portion of a long list of capabilities that a sales manager needs to possess to do their job. However, how do you expect the newly promoted manager to master these attributes from day one? This list of attributes requires years of experiences, training, and coaching. Most corporations provide little or no formal training to develop their managers.

Managers Formal Training.

I have witnessed several companies sending their newly promoted sales managers and even senior vice-presidents to the same training created for new sales reps. It may be an excellent way to provide a good understanding of how salespeople are trained, but it's not a managers' specific training.

Most sales managers are not provided with continuous training methodologies that will help them grow as sales leaders who can affect their teams and company positively.

Not all sales managers are effective coaches. I conducted a survey where I interviewed 30 new sales managers in B2B representing different industries.

I asked the following questions:

1. Did your company train you on the tasks that are the most important in getting results? 95 percent of the participants were told that these tasks are left to be learned on the job.
2. Do you believe that your tenured peers master these skills? 80 percent of the participants stated that their tenured peers continue to struggle as they learn through trial and error process.
3. Did your organization provide you with any formal management education related to the development of problem-solving and decision-making skills? 91 percent of the participants stated that they struggle with finding and exploiting available opportunities. Besides, most believed that they are

unprepared to deal with severe problems before they become critical.

Cost of No Training

Across industries, sales managers feel unprepared to spend time in the field with their salespeople because they worry that their gifted sales reps will discover that they are not well equipped to handle tough customers and situations. Some managers experience severe anxiety meeting customers along with their experienced sales reps, knowing that their poor skills and awkwardness may be discernible during these client interactions. To not lose face, most sale managers will bury themselves in administrative tasks to avoid being embarrassed.

You are probably saying that this type of sales manager should not be on the job. Most sales managers spend most their time doing administrative tasks to advance the sale; many go through stretches lasting several weeks and even months without a face-to-face with a client. It's easier to spend time with a sales rep over lunch, discuss business rather than face tough clients where the sales manager along with the sales rep are put to the test. To make things worse, most companies bury their managers in non-revenue driven tasks, giving the non-competent sales manager the perfect alibi to avoid face time with customers.

The best sales managers accept that they will be put to the test often, and despite their best efforts, they will lose sometimes. They accept defeat graciously because they learn from it. They hide nothing from their sales reps and admit that they are learning as well and that they are far from being perfect. Salespeople respect and admire humble sales leaders who are authentic under pressure.

Great sales managers love to spend field time with their sales rep, as it allows them to observe the sales rep's strengths and weaknesses, to coach on the specific deficient areas. Sales managers' impact is vast in most sales organizations. It's a tough job where one is expected to do much with limited resources and authority.

Coaching Impact

A sales manager can only teach what he knows. Sales management is all about coaching. Wait! Coaching? Yes, coaching is the only activity that the sales manager can leverage to drive exceptional performance. As a sales manager, you have a team quota, and you can achieve your quota by driving your team performance up. The way to do it is by ensuring that every individual in your team fulfills their obligations.

How can you ensure that all your sales reps achieve their respective goals? Coaching your sales reps can get you there.

The dictionary definition of coaching is: "*A method of directing, instructing and training a person or group of people, with the aim to achieve some goal or develop specific skills. There are many ways to coach, types of coaching and methods to coaching. A direction may include motivational speaking and training may include seminars, workshops, and supervised practice.*" — Wikipedia, the free encyclopedia.

The purpose of coaching is to improve the performance and skillset of sales reps by providing one-on-one training to develop performances. Coaching:

- Allows the sales manager to observe the sales rep's behaviors and approaches and, when necessary, offer feedback and best practices to enhance one's performance.
- Empowers the sales rep to achieve progress. Personal performance dramatically improves with coaching; behavioral awareness under supervision can eliminate mistakes and enhance one area's strengths.

- Maximizes people's performances on the job. According to several studies, 71% of C-level executives in sales organizations believe that driving sale productivity is a top priority to compete and grow. In addition, 74% of leading sales organizations cite that the most crucial role of a front-line sales manager is to coach and mentor sales reps to achieve their potential.

Sales productivity drives results and revenue.

To drive sales productivity up requires focusing on the following areas:

- Improving sales rep's efficiency
- Improving sales rep's effectiveness
- Efficiency x effectiveness = productivity

Sales Efficiency

Sales efficiency is defined as the smart allocation of company resources to get the job done well. The most important resource is time, how one chooses to spend one's time makes the difference between achieving high sales efficiency or not.

The more productive you are per hour, the more efficient you are. Good sales managers educate their teams to focus on high-value activities while eliminating low-value activities. For example, a sales rep can increase the number of sales calls per hour, increase customer contact frequency, or improve close rate ratio. Greater efficiency coupled with better effectiveness yields higher productivity.

Sales Effectiveness

Sales effectiveness is about how you utilize your sales force's resources to achieve your team goals. If you manage to have your team to place 30 additional calls per hour, you would have improved your team efficiency by a good margin.

If your team members manages to close 50% more of these calls, you would have yielded higher output from the same level of effort and potentially improved your team's close rate and margin. Efficiency is about the willingness to use economic and human resources to get things done better. Effectiveness is about how skillful you are in getting the most out of the opportunity in front of you.

Sales Productivity

To improve your sales productivity, you will need to improve both efficiency and effectiveness. It is much easier to upgrade sales efficiency, as it requires primarily better management of one's time and resources. Improving effectiveness requires planning, reflection, and continual adjustment. It often involves training and coaching to develop one's skill to mastery.

Sales productivity improvement depends on the development of the following areas:

- Sales productivity increases according to the evolution of efficiency and effectiveness.
- Efficiency is easier to achieve as it depends primarily on the allocation of resources and effort.
- Effectiveness requires improving sales reps' skills and capability.

Coaching and Performances

Multiple studies have demonstrated that the sales manager who continuously coaches their sales reps can expect a 20% increase in total performance.

Despite the importance of coaching, the average sales manager only spends 5% of their time developing their sales reps. When asked, most sales managers cite that lack of time is among the most significant obstacle that leads to failure. Sales managers are pulled in many directions throughout the day, and they often have little control over their agenda, allowing multi-directional distraction to sway their focus.

According to Matthew Dixon and Brent Adams, who wrote an article in *Harvard Business Review* in 2011, "even world-class coaching can be wasted on the lowest performers, more likely because they are a bad fit for the role altogether." Star reps often do not benefit much from coaching, so it's best to leave them doing what works best for them. Their research concluded that the greatest beneficiaries from coaching are the core middle group that represents 60% of the team. Focused, targeted coaching can improve that specific group's performance by as much as 20%. This kind of improvement can generate a 6% to 8% performance increase across the board. This kind of improvement means hitting your goals rather than missing it.

We will dive deeper in the following chapters where the sales manager should focus their efforts to generate the highest return-on-effort.

Many large corporations have an established policy about sales force training, but only a few address the importance of coaching. Surprisingly, most managers do not know that coaching is part of their job description, because they never receive any formal training themselves.

Countless sales managers feel that their daily routine interactions with their sales reps constituted coaching sessions. Others have difficulty providing feedback to their sales reps, feeling that their job is to help their sales reps close business to meet their quota, not radically change their way of selling even when it yields poor or no results.

Coaching Yield Results

It takes self-confidence, tactical courage, observational finesse, and psychological diplomacy to coach. These attributes are not necessarily found in abundance in the pool of sales managers

Many managers confuse occasional training, performance review and occasional guidance with coaching. Others deliberately avoid coaching, mostly because they feel inadequately trained on how to do it properly. Coaching is among the most impactful activity that elevates sales reps' selling skills.

Pilots prepare for combat with intensive training and simulation. Intense close observation and coaching goes into the process to ensure the elimination of potential errors, because even the smallest miscalculation in battle field mean destruction and probable death. Civil pilots are trained to deal with engine failures, engine fires, cabin fire, cabin decompression, jammed controls, and unreliable flight instruments. problems can happen, but when they occur, the pilot's flying skills, and sound judgment will be put to the test. Great pilots are all about security, and they work hard to improve their system knowledge, vigilance, deviation tolerance, overall skills, and capability to ensure the safety of their passengers.

Coaching Purpose

Sales is similar in many ways. Using the wrong word, wrong approach, or wrong behavior can potentially mean losing the opportunity. Business decision makers are often experienced buyers. They watch the sales rep's behavior, sales methods, word usage, mannerism, and tone. An amateur salesperson will inadvertently make errors of assumption which leads to losing the customer interest. Professional sales reps understand that sales is a dialogue where the customers do most of the talking and the salespeople do most of the listening, knowing that every chosen word can either advance the sale, stall it, or kill.

The sales manager's coaching session has everything to do with observing the sales reps' interaction closely with their customers. Then, describing the area where the sales rep has done an exceptional job and the areas that require improvement. Providing honest feedback creates awareness, sensitivity, and focus. The idea behind coaching is to minimize errors, grow new capability, enhance existing skills, test and support new approaches, and get feedback from a trained professional. Coaching is all about learning, discovering, and sharing ideas and principles to improve both the salesperson and the sales manager.

Coaching is not telling someone what to do; it's a collaboration, where both parties share their thoughts, insights, ask questions, learn, and apply what works based on field testing. Effective coaching requires mental openness, good listening, and adjustment skills. While the coach and the coachee may possess entrenched ideas, beliefs, and philosophies that are hard to influence, coaching works only when both parties are open to change. The sales manager cannot dictate what needs to be done; instead, they should facilitate and inspire their sales reps to accept gradual changes that will have a long-lasting positive impact on productivity and the sales rep sales career. Coaching is a dialogue that analyzes field behavioral observations with the intent to create progress by eliminating areas of weakness.

Coaching Versus Training

Training is a requirement to develop one skills, knowledge and capability. Training should be an ongoing process to ensure the absorption and stickiness and the application of the newly acquired methods in real life. However, training is not a substitute for coaching. Instead, they complement one another, and not replace one another. They are both vitals and serve complementary purposes.

Many sales managers prefer to train their sales reps rather than coach them, because most managers are more familiar with training than coaching. Coaching tends to happen in live settings, where the stakes are high and mutual scrutiny is heightened.

In a field ride, a manager may have to occasionally assist the sales rep. It's common that the sales rep and manager may have to work in tandem to overcome tough customer's objections to win the deal.

In large organizations, company trainers often facilitates training, while in a small organization, it's usually conducted by the sales manager. Training is all about education, sharing new knowledge, and improving existing sales expertise and capabilities.

A trainer can tell you how to do things from a theoretical standpoint, knowing that your knowledge and skills will be tested during your customer-facing interactions.

Training can educate sales reps on building rapport with prospects, questioning techniques, identifying, prospects, planning, overcoming objections, getting out of comfort zone, setting goals, and enhancing closing skills. The trainer and the sales reps can roleplay different scenarios to learn how to deliver a flawless presentation and how to lead decision makers to accept their business proposal.

Coaching turns training sessions into field practices that enhance the sales rep's overall sales capability. Coaching is the precise art of saying the right thing at the right time to trigger strong emotions or advance the sale. Coaching is all about close observation, discussion, and enhancement of one capability.

When and Where to Coach?

Coaching happens everywhere. The sales manager may observe that a sales rep struggles with some aspect of the sales process, so the manager can dig deep to find out the source of struggle and suggest ideas and best practices to help the sales rep to overcome their inadequacies. Good feedback has more to do with guided self-discovery than telling the sales rep what to do.

The sales managers can ask questions such as:

- At what point did you realize your sales techniques were not working with this customer?
- What could you have done differently to persuade the customer that your customized business solution was superior to your competitor's offer?
- What better questions could you have asked your customer to handle their price objection?

These types of questions will allow the sales rep to reflect on their selling behavior and make the necessary adjustments to improve.

Coaching deal with observable behaviors and communications skills to affect the delivery and impact on the customer. Coaching works best in a one-on-one setting, as it focuses on improving one skill at the time, while training can be delivered in a group setting or individual setting. The training impact has everything to do with the individual's willingness to absorb and apply the information learned.

One-On-One Coaching

The one-on-one weekly meeting that occurs between the sales rep and the sales manager is the most impactful time that leads to transformative changes. During these meeting, critical KPIs get discussed, gaps get uncovered, awareness is heightened, solutions and action plans get drafted, and commitment to execution gets done.

One-on-one weekly or monthly meetings are impactful because they are opportunities to discuss the salesperson's performance and current trends. The sales manager uses these opportunities to listen and coach the salesperson to make tactical and strategic changes that will improve performance.

During these one-on-one meetings, the conversation should focus on the following KPIs:

- Volume achieved and type
- Profitability and margin
- Performance against objectives
- Portfolio management and growth
- Net new acquired business
- Ranking against peers regionally and nationally

These one-on-one meetings provide the following values:

- Keeps salespeople focused on results
- Creates accountability and responsibility
- Promotes sales proactivity and initiative
- Builds on historical data but is future-oriented
- Builds trust and promotes awareness
- Focuses on results by adjusting tactics and sales approaches
- Stimulates growth by affecting mindsets
- Improves honest communication
- Allocates adequate resources to complex issues

Coaching Shared Accountability

Consistent one-on-one sessions with the sales managers drives performance and morale up. The best managers take pride in passionately mentoring and developing their salespeople's skills during these sessions. They provide constructive feedback based on observations derived from customer meetings and discuss things that went well versus what went wrong. These one-on-ones are a great time to give credit, acknowledge the salesperson's efforts and progress while laying out shared goals and responsibility to achieve results.

If a team member fails to achieve results because of lack of effort, then discuss and generate a shared accountability plan to turn the situation around. These meetings are an opportunity to understand your sales reps' struggles and challenges and draft a shared responsibility plan that will get them back on track.

Coaching requires that the coach and the coachee trust one another and believe in the value of these sessions. Both the sales manager and the trainee must be all in to get the information to stick.

I witnessed sales reps on several occasions go through tedious new training while the sales manager was either absent, chatting, disengaged, or busy responding to emails and texts in the back of the room. That kind of management behavior sends a clear message to the sales rep that training is not taken seriously and has little or no value.

Many sales managers speak highly of the importance and impact of training, yet when they are subjected to one, they often show total disinterest. Sales managers' lack of engagement during corporate sales training is rampant, and this reality is usually evident when the sales manager cannot perform basic tasks that most sales reps can easily perform. It is also apparent when the sales manager cannot answer standard questions that have been covered by the training department on multiple occasions.

During these corporate trainings, it is always clear to see people who were fully engaged and committed to learning versus those that were not.

As a sales leader, you cannot expect people to show interest in the training when you are not interested. People follow their leaders' examples. If you are engaged, involved, and hungry to learn, they will do the same. The purpose of training is to develop skilled sales reps who are capable of higher performances to achieve their personal goals along with corporate objectives.

Corporations invest a lot of money and resources in training their sales reps to generate higher profits and productivity. When the sales managers are not engaged in reinforcing the process, the investment gets wasted, the knowledge gets lost, and the sales reps do not benefit.

CSO Insights conducted a study to measure the effectiveness and impact of several companies' training programs. They include a question where the participants got to rate the quality of their company's sales skills training program, and reported 10.7% of participants estimated their company had exceeded expectations, 42.5% met expectations and 43.5% percent needed improvement.

The data showed that companies with sales skills training programs that exceeded expectations averaged spending $2,870 per sales rep, while the company that met expectations invested on average $2,196 per sales rep, and the companies that need improvements invested on average $1,815 per sales rep. This data reflects a direct correlation between the quality of the training and the level of employee satisfaction. The higher the investment on the employee, the higher the level of satisfaction.

The same research has shown that the respondents who ranked their sales training as exceeding expectations scored 54% of forecast deals won, compared to 44% in the needs-improvement group.

Furthermore, participants who rated their sales training as exceeding expectations had 5% fewer losses than the counterpart in the needs-improvement group. Finally, the group that ranked their skills training as exceeding expectations achieved sales 69.4% of the time in comparison with their counterparts 60.5% who ranked as a needed improvement.

This study also revealed that higher investment on better programs yielded better results as the salesperson was better equipped to tell a compelling story that highlighted the company's competitive advantages while aligning business solutions to the customers' needs.

Coaching Reality

Is there a correlation between coaching field reps and performance?

Studies have shown that most sales managers state that time is often the primary barrier to coaching. The clear majority of sales managers who have teams of fewer than twelve sales reps indicate that they spend on average about one hour with each sales rep per week. However, most sales manager find it hard to stick to that schedule as they must deal with other priorities.

Time is always a significant barrier. For example, a manager who was short-handed was interviewing prolifically to find the right candidates, and while she understood the value of coaching, she had no choice but to focus on hiring new candidates. She and her team were stretched way too thin to shift focus from recruiting and training new folks.

Most managers confuse training with coaching and performance planning. When an organization has a loose approach to coaching, then no coaching takes place. Several sales managers stated that most coaching happens during the first three to six months of hiring new candidates. Rather than increasing coaching going forward, it decreases dramatically from that point on as sales managers feel that their time should be best utilized with newer hires.

Some sales managers stated that they are stretched so thin that they provide no coaching at all. Many sales organizations have no coaching programs on place or evaluations measurement to ensure that their sales managers are doing a good job coaching their teams.

Junior sales managers are not comfortable conducting coaching sessions with their sales reps. Many struggles with it, as it takes some level of experience to observe behavior and describe the area where the sales reps can improve their skills. Smart sales managers create coaching cadences to ensure that every sales rep is developed according to their skillset and needs. Some sales reps may require one hour of coaching per week, and others may require several hours to build confidence.

Coaching Whom First?

Many believe that the sales managers need to spend more coaching time with the sales reps that crave it the most. The middle-of-the-road sales reps tend to be the most willing and eager to be coached as they aspire to become A-players, make more money, and get better visibility and recognition. The reality is that every team has their A-players, B-players and C-players. Good sales managers cannot spend an enormous amount of time with one specific tier of sales reps and neglect the rest. A-players, despite their prowess, need coaching as much as C-players. One would argue that C-players would probably benefit the most from coaching, being that they have more latitude and leverage to scale up their game than the A-players.

Some sales managers feel that their middle performers — B-players— are keener to listen and act to improve much faster than the rest, and they represent the largest tier in any team.

Coaching requires the coach to be open to coaching as well. It's an exchange of values that needs the coach and the coachee to be aligned to permeate lessons learned into actionable behaviors.

The question becomes: Where should the sale manager spend most of his time to get the highest ROI?

Coaching Allocation of Time

There are several schools of thoughts on the subject. Some believe that coaching time should be allocated equally among sales reps regardless of their level of performance. Some claim that it makes more sense to coach your bottom and middle performers as they will benefit the most and have plenty of room to grow.

While some studies have shown that proper coaching can elevate low performers' productivity, generally it requires an enormous amount of time and effort to keep these individuals focused on their objectives.

Let's assume the team has 2 A-players and 6 C-players. If your top performers create $250K and you can improve them by 10%, that's $275 x 2 which translates to a $50K incremental gain. Assuming that you bottom producers generate $150K in revenue, a 10% improvement will generate $15K x 6 = $90K gain. You can easily see the overall impact you can have by focusing on your C-players.

Again, the sales manager has the duty to develop their sales reps while helping the company create revenue through their sales reps.

Coaching Your Top Performers

The common theme is that if you don't focus on developing your A-players who generate the most revenue, it will lead to potential team members' disengagement and higher turnover.

A-players, while aware of their impact on the organization, need coaching time to improve their skills as well. Your best producers value coaching sessions because they are always looking for ways to improve their game.

Neglecting to coach your top performers is often a great mistake. Coaching your top players means you care about their careers and progress.

Coaching Your B-Player

Smart sales managers spend time coaching their B-players, knowing they have the skills and potential to become A-players. The highest gain some would argue is found in developing your middle players. In most organizations, this represents 50% to 60% of teams. A sales manager cannot succeed without moving these players upwards.

Some sales managers leverage their A-players to become coaches, to affect and influence their B-player's peers. Many A-players are interested in a future management role, and that activity provides them with a coaching and training opportunity. In addition, sales managers can use rewards and recognition strategies to encourage this kind of behavior. Coaching has a significant impact on results, team morale, and business performance.

Individual Coachability

Being coachable is one of the attributes that sales managers look for when hiring salespeople. While coachability is difficult to measure by even the most astute interviewers, it is a critical attribute to learn and enhance one's skills and ability to perform consistently well.

A sales rep who is coachable can upgrade their capabilities reasonably quickly. A high performer who is not willing to be coached will experience a rapid skill devaluation and difficulty catching up.

Uncoachable high achievers have a short success lifespan, as their skills become outdated without constant upgrades.

We have all seen sales managers who tolerate lone-wolf sales reps as long as they hit their sales targets. Lone-wolf sales reps have a hardened character and often complain about these unnecessary coaching requirements.

As innovative technologies become part of our daily ways of doing business, most of these high-achieving lone-wolves who reject training and coaching will find it harder to catch up —forcing them to start new careers in industries that still do business the old way.

There is a chasm in opinions and techniques on how best to manage salespeople and sales teams. The general opinion is that the sales manager should probably spend most of their time coaching their middle-tier sales reps to get the highest ROI, rather than spend time coaching top and bottom tiers.

I believe that studies, practices, assumptions and results can be highly unreliable. What works well for a specific manager and organization within a specific industry may not work as well for another. Too many variables can affect a study's outcome. The key is to stay open and coach people according to their capabilities, desires, and willingness to put in the right level effort to create worthy results.

CHAPTER 12: SUMMARY

- Some of the best-managed corporations in the world have little or no official training for managers, and that is a grave mistake. A platoon commander should be better equipped, better trained, and better educated than his soldiers; the same should apply to a sales manager and his team. Sales management by osmosis and trial and error is costly, outdated, time-consuming, and often ineffective.

- You cannot bury your sales managers in non-revenue driven operational tasks and expect the manager to spend time in the field driving performance and putting out fires. Coaching requires extreme focus, observation, and orientation via dialogue. Coaching is a time-consuming activity that yields substantial financial gain in the long run.
- A relaxed approach to coaching will create tremendous opportunity lost and poor performances. Coaching hones salespeople and the sales manager's ability to observe and tackle complicated situations when they arise.
- The sales manager would probably generate a higher return-on-effort by coaching their middle and top performers rather than unwilling underperforms.

CHAPTER THIRTEEN: COACHING FOR GROWTH

You cannot expect your sales manager to coach their team if they have never been educated on how to coach effectively. Most senior executive managers, promote managers based on a set of desired capabilities and hope for the best when it comes to coaching. However, that's a terrible strategy and a poor business model!

1. According to *CSO Insights*, in 2016, 60% of salespeople were more likely to leave their job if their manager was a mediocre coach. Companies with dynamic coaching programs achieve 28% higher win rates.
2. Over 47% of sales managers spend less than 30 minutes a week coaching reps on skills and behaviors.
3. According to the *Sales Management Association*, firms that provide an optimal amount of coaching realize 16.7% greater annual revenue than the rest.
4. It's evident that sales coaching proficiency is a requirement for any professional sales manager. For it to work, both parties need to be willing to collaborate and cooperate to create the intended results despite the difference in duties.

Coaching the Unwilling

Even the best coaches in the world cannot bend the will of individuals who are not willing to be coached. How do you coach if someone is not coachable? How can you identify the people who are not willing to be coached?

Types of people you cannot coach:

The unwilling to change: Generally, these are successful individuals with no interest to change. Over the years, they have built a mental rigidity and stubbornness that makes it hard to foster even the slightest changes. Let me give you an example: Mike, a newly promoted sales manager, has been a sales rep for over thirty years.

He spent his first month as a manager educating his team on some of his best practices, and he expected that everyone would adopt his selling methods, being that they worked well for him. He met much resistance as his salespeople preferred to keep their sales individuality. A clash of personalities ensued, performance dropped across the board, and a few salespeople start thinking about resigning.

The VP of sales had to intervene multiple times to stop good producers from leaving the company and keep the team morale at an acceptable level. Despite the VP of sales best efforts to get Mike to change his management style, it became apparent that while he was capable of change, he didn't care to change. There was only one solution left: either reinstate Mike back to his previous role, or terminate his position.

Mike's thought process was fixated; he thought his method was sound, proven, and unquestionably right. When you identify someone as uncoachable, don't waste time, as you will have no impact transforming that unbending individual's behaviors.

The uncommitted: If an individual salesperson lacks initiative and commitment to apply the fundamentals you collectively discussed and agreed upon, you won't accomplish much. The most significant frustration for most coaches is when you invest your time, effort, and energy in getting someone to improve, and realize that person is fundamentally careless or is not willing to even try. Coaching may not work as well when someone is committed but keeps pursuing the wrong strategy. You can always try to steer the salesperson back to the right track, but only if they listen and trust your guidance.

The person in the wrong position: Many professional salespeople take a job hoping it will be a good fit. However, the moment they realized that the job or the company does not meet their expectations, they start sabotaging the process while looking for an exit.

I recall a vice-president of sales who took a job with a competitive company, but he was not thrilled about the job, because he was making half the income he had commanded with his prior employer. He showed his excitement to secure the position, but once on board, he start showing how unhappy he was about his income, team, and company. He did the minimum he could to keep his boss satisfied, but he made every effort to discourage other managers from doing their best. When his lack of commitment to the job became apparent, he became more confrontational, then abruptly left the job.

The Blamer: A manager or a salesperson who continuously points fingers at others as being the source of the problem, when all facts indicate that they are the problem, is a challenge hard to overcome. The key to awareness is openness of mind and acceptance of responsibility.

I have witnessed on several occasions when a salesperson or manager got defensive when coached. Many salespeople view constructive feedback as criticism. Hence, they push back to prove that you are either wrong or your facts are not accurate. It’s tough to help people who believe they don’t have a problem.

Coaching requires cooperation and a dialogue between two willing parties trying to accomplish a better outcome. It's collaboration toward improvement, not a combative or competitive approach.

Coaching Requires Humility

The best sales leaders take the time to identify their coaching strengths and weaknesses. Then they draft a written plan of actionable behaviors that will get them to achieve gradual progress.

Michael Dell is recognized as one of the best CEOs, yet he is more recognized for being someone who is always striving to become better by sharing his challenges with his employees. His humble approach became the unspoken guideline for the company. Being such a great role model made his company extremely desirable to external talent and investors.

People prefer working and doing business with companies that are well-managed. Great CEOs are great bosses, teachers, coaches and sources of inspiration to all. Few CEOs manage to transform and elevate their industries to new heights. In contrast, a bad CEO can destroy employee morale and kill one's commitment to higher performance.

Coaching Requires Stability

Low morale is prevalent in many sales organizations. When you dig deep to find the reason behind it, it often has to do with the CEO club culture. Good CEOs surround themselves with people who are better than they are. Bad CEOs surround themselves with people who are loyal and protective, people who kiss up and kick down. Poor culture often cascades down the chain and erodes performances.

I worked for a Fortune 500 company that changed CEOs every eighteen months on average. A new CEO brought his old crew of executives along with him. He then proceeded to separate the new hired leaders from the existing legacy company leaders. He believed that the new managers represented competence and unique skills, while the old management team members were part of the reason why the company performance was below par. By creating two separate leadership groups, he created animosity, fear, and resistance. The CEO discovered quickly that the people labeled as incompetent were familiar with the history and complexity of the business and industry. Several key executives from the old team resigned. The board of directors suggested that the CEO stop this brain exodus or he may become a vulnerable CEO.

All leaders, regardless of longevity or rank, want to grow and get better. Some people may be smarter than others in some areas, but everyone has a unique capability that can contribute to creating a better company. Every CEO has the obligation and duty to ensure that people work together in harmony to improve their company and themselves.

Behavioral Coaching Approach

The following basic steps work if implemented correctly:

- Determine the desired behavior that needs change. Clarify why the change is needed and how the coachee will benefit from it. Ideally, you want to reach a collective agreement and commitment from both parties to turn this desired behavior into a reality.
- Collect feedback from colleagues and clients to determine if the behaviors that need changes are the right targets. You don't want to spend enormous time and effort before realizing you were pursuing the wrong objectives. Validate that the behavior you believe requires changing is aligned with the coachee.
- Focus only on one or two behaviors at the time to generate real changes. You cannot focus on more than two items at the time, because you will lose the coachee's focus.
- Encourage the coachee to collect feedback from their clients and colleagues; the purpose is to achieve the desired behavior

mastery. As a coach, you cannot dictate what needs to be done. Instead, it would be best if you acted as more of a mental guide to help the coachee improve through self-discovery. Progress occurs only when the coachee realizes they are making progress following a plan they drafted and committed to its execution. Your role as a coach is primarily to encourage development and act as a mental compass to align desired behaviors with the goal.

- Follow-up is critical to avoid relapses. Celebrate upon reaching each milestone, but keep the ball rolling forward by keeping the coachee engaged on reaching new higher levels of desired behaviors. Progress and continuous follow-up creates faithful believers.

- Evaluate results. Have the coachee take a mini-survey asking their colleagues and clients few simple questions pertaining to the areas they were being coached on. If the results are positive, build on that success and start focusing on new desired behaviors for the next 12 months.

Coaching Changes that Sticks

The right coaching can generate permanent changes, but personal commitment and engagement is a must.

- ***Personal long-term commitment to improvement***. Large organizations spend millions of dollars every year on various development programs. While most people benefit from these training sessions and activities in the short-term, many revert to their way of doing business. The reason behind this behavior comes down to lack of commitment to improving, lack of desire to learn and adopt new techniques, lack of belief on the newly discovered methods, or pure laziness. The best coach in the world cannot influence someone who has no desire to change

- ***Application of lessons learned and strategies.*** It's all in the execution; lasting changes happen when education meets practice and the willingness to change. Most trainings can add tremendous value to one's education, but knowing what to do doesn't ignite the desire to do so.

  We all know people who go through life trying millions of diets to lose weight. I had a conversation with a successful heart surgeon who often advised people suffering from a heart issue to go on a specific diet to save their lives. The surgeon was extremely obese, and he knew better than anyone else the negative impact and effect that weight had on his health. He was educated, smart, and successful in many ways. When I asked him why he doesn't apply his own advice, he answered with a sigh, "I love food." Knowing what to do doesn't always translate to the desire to do it, even when it's literally killing you.

- ***Follow-up.*** Coaching effectiveness requires time and practice to stick. You cannot coach for a short period and expect it to work. Coaching success requires time, consistency, and continuous follow-up. Without follow-up, a coachee may feel neglected, she may think that you genuinely don't mean what you preach, and maybe you are doing it because of your job description and to score few positive points. Good coaches follow up often, because they care about their people, want to see progress, and want to evaluate the impact and value of their coaching process. Solid follow-up bonds the coach and coachee, elevates the game, validates what works and what doesn't, and cements the process worth.

- ***Hunger to get better.*** Coaching to create transformative changes takes time; it's a long-term process. Those who view coaching as an occasional event will extract little or no value out of it. A dismissive mindset will quickly forget the significance behind the event. However, a focused mindset will extract value out of the most mundane activities. Personal development is more than an educational program, motivational events, or training excursion. It's an ongoing betterment process that should last a lifetime. The coach's role simply provides tips and orientation on how to maximize the use of the process.

Growth Through Coaching

Smart companies understand that without constant sales growth, they may not survive. Seeking markets and areas of new growth is paramount. Sales executives spend an enormous amount of time gathering and analyzing data to understand market dynamics and allocate the right resources to manage potential growth.

Growth can be achieved by focusing on multiple levels related to process, innovation, economic opportunities, verticals specialization or market expansions targeting specific demographics. Growth can also occur by focusing on performance gaps such as the quality of delivery, sales activity, unique market demands, demographic needs, product appeal, improved sales approaches, analytics, and innovative technologies. Business growth can be dramatically influenced through people training and coaching methods. Good sales practices can be emulated to impact the larger group.

Focus Creates Results.

A sales organization in the payment industry wanted to improve its sales force performance, so it conducted several internal studies to understand the driver behind the higher performance that some salespeople exude.

The first study demonstrated that sales reps among the top ten percent consistently doubled and even tripled their quota in comparison to the sales reps who struggled to meet their goals. To get unbiased results and understand the set of behaviors or attributes that allowed some salespeople to outperform their peers, the company hired outside behavioral consultants to study these top performers. These consultants spent time shadowing and observing how these sales professionals treated and interacted with their prospects and customers.

Observations and Findings

- ***Outcome visualization.*** These top performers could visualize the outcome of their meetings in their mind before it happened. By imagining how their customer was going to benefit from their customized business solution, they were confident that not only could they improve their customer business outcome, but they could also build a strong, lasting relationship that would be mutually beneficial.

  This visualization capability not only self-motivated and energized these individuals, but prepared them mentally to overcome most objections and obstacles. "You cannot fail when you have already visualized a winning outcome. It would help if you saw victory in your mind before the battle begins, as it eliminates fear and doubt," says Bill, who was a top producer.

- ***Right positioning.*** These top gun performers are purpose-driven, not task-driven. They value first impression impact with their customer along with the overall quality of interaction, knowing that every competitor fights to get customer attention and buy-in power. One's ability to leave a positive, memorable impression in the customer's mind is vital to establishing a long-term win-win relationship.

- ***Building an alliance.*** These A-Players understand that winning business is a worthy goal, winning over a customer is terrific, but turning a customer into a believer and a loyal advocate is priceless. Building a tribe of promoters for your cause can transform your career from good to extraordinary. People are skeptical by nature, especially when the price and risk of failure are significant. Customers' purchasing a business solution from a trusted source makes the buying decision more manageable as it minimizes risk, raises confidence and guarantees the desired outcome. These top performers are masters at creating a massive network of trusted followers, business partners, and value-added-promoters. They keep these alliances healthy and robust, through consistent communication and value offers to widen their sphere of influence and trust. These top tier performers offer exceptional, uninterrupted services and access to a tribe of happy customers within diverse industries.

- ***Leading with Questions.*** People buy because of some level of dissatisfaction with the status quo or the desire to achieve some level of improvement. These top performers were great at asking open-ended questions that allowed the customer to feel empowered to be honest concerning areas of current challenges. By asking thought-provoking questions and listening, the salesperson extracted hidden insights and won the respect of the customer.

  Customers trust humble, intelligent salespeople who are genuinely looking to help. You would probably feel way better when a doctor spends time asking you questions about your health before starting a physical examination and giving recommendations. You probably wouldn't be happy with a doctor who rushes to write you a prescription without bothering to ask you any questions about your health

- ***Strong value propositions***. People and businesses buy products because of necessity, the desire for change, product malfunction or deficiencies, slow output or general dissatisfaction of a specific desired area. Business people also buy because of the desire to improve production, increase revenue, speed up the process, compete more efficiently, and innovate current systems to meet market demands. Whether the customer buys out of necessity or desire, there is always a cost of change one must pay.

- ***Cost of Change.*** The cost of not changing means business operations may perform below capacity. For a car assembly line, a breakdown of a robotic system can disrupt the company's production. A convenience store that experiences a malfunction with its POS system may inconvenience its customers and generate a loss of business as well. The degree of difficulty or losses will vary according to the nature of the problem and its impact. The cost of change similarly is defined in terms of gains generated by the time savings, money, and efforts. Additionally, it can be measured by faster production time, higher output, and better customer satisfaction.

- ***Sales outcome.*** Customers buy to acquire a business solution that creates desired benefits and solves a problem, and they move into action when there is a strong financial, mental, or emotional incentive they cannot resist. Tangible or intangible incentives, strong value propositions, and a vivid visualization of the desired outcome can turn unsold customers into new clients.

- ***Communicate to close.*** A-players use authentic dialogues that focus on understanding customer's needs, and purpose which is vital to ensure congruence with the outcome you are collectively trying to create. Precise communication can save time, money, and effort. I have witnessed several instances where the salesperson gets involved in the creation of a solution only to find out at later that they misinterpreted the customer's demands or that corporate needs had shifted, making their business solution irrelevant to the company.

- ***Contracts Value.*** John was working for almost two years on selling a national chain a POS system that would have connected all its two thousand stores. John met several times with the company executive vice-president (EVP) and was verbally promised that if his company could meet several software specific technical criteria, then he got the deal. Excited, he went back and convinced his company executives to start building the internal IT capacity to meet the customer's needs to win the contract. A lot of time, money, and effort went into the process, and several meetings ensued between the executive vice-president and the company management.
- ***Beware of promises.*** Each time they met, newer requests and modifications emerged. Everyone was working in good faith, and a draft contract was in the works between both parties. The customer wouldn't sign any documentation unless they were sure that the company could deliver on its promises and would fulfill satisfactorily all its ongoing contractual maintenance obligations. Eighteen months into the process, the executive vice president left his position suddenly to become the CEO of another organization. Conversations with the new executive vice-president broke down quickly, as he was adamant about bringing on board a POS company he trusted and worked with in the past.
- ***Comprehensive coverage.*** An effective salesperson would have ensured that multiple layers *of management,* including the CEOs, were involved in the decision-making process. Besides,

they should have secured a detailed contract with specific delivery and work stages. It helps asking the following questions during each meeting: "*Has anything that will impact our project changed since we last met?* The answer to this question, will save you a lot of anguish, anxieties, and guessing games.

- ***Personal Accountability.*** Most salespeople view their accountability to the organizations as meeting their quota. Salespeople feel accountable to other people they work with such as customers, partners, and cross-functional teams. However, they rarely feel responsible to the organization as an entity. People commit to give their best to improve their lives first, through positive impact on their customers and partners. Exceptional salespeople view their work as an extension to enhance people's lives along with the organization they represent. This sense of responsibility and duty often gets noticed and opens doors of upward corporate mobility.

One can learn valuable lessons by closely watching these professional sales interactions with their customers. They were strategic in the approaches, building long-lasting, trusted, and profitable relationships with their customers. After analyzing these findings, the company decided to implement and integrate these learned methods into the fiber of its sales training department. It set a new training and coaching program run by top-grade performers, with the support of executive management. Incentives and rewards were given to the "most improved" individuals, teams, and regions.

The results were fascinating; the average salesperson who went through the training improved their performance by an average of 50% within 12 months and 80% within 24 months. These methods were not exceptionally unique; they were more of a philosophy of doing things right in a consistent and methodical fashion. Offers were fair and honest; promises got kept, meetings were value-driven, agreements got honored, and services were rendered as planned.

Additionally, post-sales visits become the norm, follow-ups were maintained and handwritten personal 'thank you' cards were sent regularly. Also, monthly educational materials and valuable industry articles and newsletters were emailed to customers, calls were returned in a timely manner, and concerns and ideas were shared with a group of managers who were responsible for the aggregate retention and growth of the customer base.

CHAPTER 13: SUMMARY

- Coaching is a collaborative agreement between the sales manager and the salesperson. Everyone needs to be on board to achieve the intended outcome.
- People who are not willing to be coached are hard to change. Monitor their performance and let them go if necessary.
- Great coaches use humility, approachability, and inspiration to lead people to achieve higher performances.
- Coaching eliminates wrong behaviors and replaces them with better strategic practices that empower the salesperson and build trust, confidence, and long-lasting relationships with profitable customers.

CHAPTER FOURTEEN: FOCUSED TRANSFORMATIVE COACHING BEHAVIORS

We understand that change is a certainty in life. I believe that people with the right mindset, desire, and willingness to put in the necessary effort can take advantage of what change brings in terms of positive innovation and evolution. This is true even though most major operational and structural change are often feared due to their uncertainty.

People who lead in their respective field tend to see change as a force of good. Change is viewed as a challenge that needs to be accepted and embraced. People in the middle in terms of performance tend to view change as a disruption that may worsen their situation. Hence, they default to wait-and-see approach model. People who operate at the bottom of the pyramid of performance will automatically view any change as a force of disruption of peace and harmony. Hence, the resistance as change is viewed as unwelcome, disruptive, and scary. C-performers already have a hard time dealing with the current company methods, policies and systems; adding any new changes can be a challenge. The B-performers group, along with the C-performers group, will need much convincing in terms of selling the vision to embrace the changes to protect their jobs.

The ladder of productivity becomes the inverse ladder of resistance—the higher the performance, the lower the resistance to change. The lower the performance, the higher the resistance to change.

Is the Transformation Possible?

I genuinely believe in people's ingenuity and capacity to learn, transform, and achieve greatness. I must admit that sometimes I had difficulty turning C-performers into B-performers primarily because of lack of confidence, mental resistance, and lack of willingness to change and improve. I believe that anyone can change with the right amount of effort and time. however, while its possible, no manager or company can afford to spend the necessary time and energy on someone not willing to help themselves. It is much easier to turn a willing B-performer into an A-performer, than to turn a C-performer into a B-performer. (This applies to salespeople and sales managers.)

C-performers

A C-performer is a person who delivers consistently results below specified targets. My experience with C-performers has demonstrated that when coaching and inspection were applied steadily, we experienced a period of incremental progress, often followed by a phase of regress the moment the sales manager shifts focus towards other priorities that require time and energy.

C-performers require a higher level of intensity, coaching, and rigorous follow-up to ensure continuous improvement, which leads me to believe that a C-performer can produce at a higher level, under intense scrutiny and watchfulness. C-performers' root failure can be due to lack of skills, lack of opportunity, personal competencies, or lack of willingness to put in the right level of effort needed to achieve the desired outcome.

With the right training, encouragement, and motivation, C-performers can produce acceptable results. However, continuous supervision, coaching, and support is a must; otherwise, you will start noticing a quick downgrade in performance, followed by lower morale and a relapse to the initial state. Upgrading C-performers is possible, but it's taxing in terms of effort needed by the sales manager to keep these individuals in a productive state. C-performers tend to follow company guidelines but rarely contribute enough value to justify their presence.

Most sales managers admit that conversations with these C-performers who refuse to improve can be tense, emotional, and draining. However, they shouldn't be that way. Here's why.

After years of experience in sales, I concluded that while it's possible to get a C-performer into a B-performer level, it's probably not always worth the time and effort. There are exceptions to this theory, of course, but the overall return on investment is not probable, and the needed level of constant inspection is not possible no matter how you plan for it.

The ten thousand hours of known practice models to attain expertise cannot make champions in every discipline. It has been proven that not everyone can reach the necessary level of performance even with deliberate practice. No amount of training or desire could get you to become the next Michael Jordan unless you have the right mental state, exceptional physical attributes, the right genetic edge, and the unwavering desire to achieve that level of performance regardless of the cost.

While there may be exceptions, I believe that C-performers just do not possess the right ingredients to achieve success within their specific industry. That doesn't mean that they cannot reach stardom in a different field. As a matter of fact, many people enter the sales profession because it has a low barrier of entry and promises great financial rewards subsequent to great performances.

Studies have shown that C-performers represent 10% to 20% of most sales organizations. Many sales organizations hold onto their C-performers for many reasons, including circumvention of emotional conflicts, legal quagmires, prohibiting cost, market perception, brand tarnishing and employee turnover negative rating.

No matter the consequences, it's often a bad idea to hold on to C-performers; as they bring the team morale down and increase tolerance for mediocrity. It's not fair to the rest of the team, and it doesn't do the organization, employee, stakeholders or the customer any good.

Underperformance should not be tolerated to avoid its spread throughout the organization.

You Should Not Be in Sales If…

1. You hate dealing with customers, and you are always bored. It's a dread going to work.
2. You avoid conversations with your manager. You despise team meetings, company social events, and interactions with your peers.
3. You find that company training and your sales manager's coaching sessions to be dry, demotivating, boring and dull. You hate the material, your product, and business solutions.
4. You don't believe in your company's vision and mission.
5. Your work duties don't come naturally. You lack the skills and the willingness to learn.
6. You are frustrated with your company's goals. You believe they are too unrealistic to achieve.
7. You feel you chose the wrong job. You want out but cannot summon the courage to do it, because you like the security of the paycheck.
8. You get the cold shoulder from your sales manager, because you don't listen to their instructions and coaching advice.
9. You get poor feedback from your peers, customers, and manager because of your behavior.

10. Your pipeline is always dry and you don't care. You are looking for another job during working hours.
11. You feel you don't fit in the company's corporate culture, and you are not desperate for a paycheck.
12. You don't feel challenged, and you despise your work-life-balance.
13. You are putting on a fake personality for the job. You feel that you cannot be authentic to keep the job and you don't see yourself staying for long-term.

A-performers

It's much more fun managing a team of A-performers. These top performers have abundant energy, brilliant minds, and unbelievable drive. This group takes daily massive action and is committed to pay the price, serve customers' needs with a level of unparalleled sense of dedication and urgency to create collective mutual success and harmony.

Surprisingly, this group of top performers is very much open to coaching, learning, and growth. They view knowledge as a powerful tool that needs to be updated, enhanced, and challenged continuously. These groups love to be trained on new approaches. A-performers are often eager to demonstrate and share the new exciting news with everyone. Most companies possess a group of top performers who represent 10% to 20% of the sales force but generate 50% to 60% of the company's total revenue. This group is often the pride of the company and their contributions sustain the company growth.

Coaching Focus

A-performers are critical to the organization's survival and prosperity—after all they generate most of the revenue, handle the largest and most complex accounts as well as maintain the relationship between business owners and the company. They are often the face of the company and the ambassadors who promote the company's good will, mission, services, and social responsibility within the community and around the globe. Yet, despite the value this group brings to the company, it is still a small subsection of the entire sales force, and its growth capacity is limited.

Therefore, sales organization must develop a more significant group of its constituents, which is defined by the B-performers group. This group tends to be the largest of most sales organizations. It's often comprised of capable, reliable performers who possess the right skillset that define most A-performers. However, the main difference is B-performers tend to believe they don't have the right competencies to achieve A-performance results or are not willing to put in the effort to accomplish the same status. This mental challenge can be influenced by the right level of training, coaching, and proper psychological fortification.

A-performers are highly coveted to switch jobs. Competitors flood them with lucrative offers to lure them in because most have a solid book of business and have some level of sought-out influence over their customers' decision-making process due to the quality of trust and relationships built over the years.

B-Performers Hold Back for These Reasons.

- Don't know the path to become an A-performer.
- Not sure of the necessary skills, behaviors, and traits required to get there.

- What action plan is needed to become an A-performer?
- What deficiencies does one need to overcome to develop into an A-performer?
- Been there before, not willing to put in the necessary level of commitment.
- Prefer middle road status and better work-life balance.
- Current financial rewards are not worth the effort.
- A-performers risk losing the job if they drop below a certain level, while B-performers tend to have a better safety net being among the B- performers larger group.

The sales manager can play a significant role in assisting with defining the path to achieve A-performer status. Recognizing B-performers' ability and talent can get them to start thinking that their perceived limitations can be overcome with the right level of effort, tenacity, and proper planning.

B-performers represent the backbone of most sales organizations. Neglecting or under-leveraging B-performers' productive capacity can be costly. One-third to half of B-performers can become A-performers.

The transformation will require the sales manager's constant attention, guidance, training, and coaching. Not every B-performer can make it to the "A" category primarily because not every B-performer will be willing to put in the necessary effort to achieve that outcome. Many B-performers value work-life balance and are not mentally ready to go beyond the current level of engagement.

Sales leaders must respect the decision made by some previous A-performers, who decided to perform at a B-performance level, these sales reps made the voluntary transition to scale down their efforts by working less hours to balance their work with family demands. Many

A-performers in the sales profession put in regularly 75 to 85 hours of work per week. While a B-performer may be putting 50 to 65 hours, these individuals are aware they are making less money than they potentially could generate by ascending to the "A" league, but are not willing to make that trade as they value family time and work-life balance more than financial gains.

B-performers' knowledge, depth of expertise, and experience tend to equate often and sometimes even supersede A-performers. In business-to-business there is always a go-to B-performer who everyone goes to for complex situations, tough questions and topics. B-performers tend to be less threatening, more willing to help, and they often possess great temperament. They also tend to be more approachable as they are more relaxed at the job.

Open Yourself to Progress

As a sales leader, you have the amazing opportunity to assist people to develop the necessary skills, behaviors, and attitude essential to achieve significant progress. Most of salespeople are already equipped with the right fundamental characteristics for success; The key is to bring them out of their dormant statues.

Leadership Impact on Coaching and Training

As a sales leader, you will need to evaluate the individual against the job requirements.

Invest time and energy developing your B-performers into A-performers, but if you deem someone not having the right capability for sustainable improvement to become an A-Performer, that's okay, let it be. It would help if you accept the fact that some people are not interested in changing for many personal reasons. Respect their choice, you rather live with a B-performer than allow a C-performer to linger without progress.

As a leader, you should:

- Accept personal responsibility for changing your sales rep's behaviors to improve.
- Implement new best practices, monitor progress and results.
- Notice what's working, what's not, and what needs to be adjusted or eliminated.
- Change course as often as necessary. Stay open minded; true transformative evolution happens when one is willing to accept new realities that yield success and advancement.

CHAPTER 14: SUMMARY

- Focus on your A-players and B-player as they will probably yield the highest results.
- While it's possible to turn around C-performers, the effort, energy, and attention required is often colossal.
- B-players can turn into A-players. Good coaching and skilled attention can speed up the transformation.
- Motivate and inspire your salespeople to reach their potential. However, respect people positions as some people prefer to stay in the middle by choice.

PART III: RECRUITING HIGH PERFORMANCE SALES TALENT

"Sales organizations are in the business of people, and nothing is more important than hiring exceptionally talented people who can soar with minimal assistance. Great people can turn average strategies into great success and average managers into champions."— Anthony Chaine

"Never hire someone who knows less than you do about what he's hired to do."— Malcom Forbes

"Recruiting is hard, it's just finding the needles in the haystack. You can't know enough in a one-hour interview. So, in the end, it's ultimately based on your gut. How do I feel about the person? What are they like when they're challenged? I ask everybody that: "why are you here?" The answers themselves are not what you're looking for. It's the meta-data."— Steve Jobs

CHAPTER FIFTEEN: HIRING AND RETENTION

The Sales Manager's Role in Hiring and Retention

A *Career Builder* survey of 3,697 U. S employees, found that two-third stated they took a job only to realize that it was a bad fit. 46% percent said they left the job due to toxic work culture, 37% realized that the job they had to do didn't match the company job description, and 33% left due to lack of clear expectations about the job. At least half of these new recruits left their position within less than six months.

Millions of people quit their job every year as reported by the Bureau of Labor Statistics. People generally quit their job for better opportunities and to avoid the stress generated from intolerable, toxic workplace environments.

Human resource exit interviews rarely gather the true facts behind employees leaving their jobs, as employees try not to burn bridges or simply don't trust human resource employees.

A sales organization that had a significant new hires retention issue, low morale, and poor sales profits decided to conduct an internal study to understand the main drivers behind these hiring and retention problems and then to craft and implement changes. A quick examination of the current situation revealed that the situation was dire: 70% of new hires left the company within 12 months of employment and 90% left the company within 24 months. The situation was untenable; changes needed to happen fast; otherwise the company risked losing its good reputation to attract talent and harm its market competitiveness. No one wanted to work for an organization that churn and burn its sales force.

A solution was needed fast. The company hired an external consulting company and tasked it with studying its turnover causes.

The consultant created the following list to evaluate salespeople attrition.

1. Known factor and assumptions
2. Unknown factors and assumptions
3. Total attrition of current year versus prior year
4. Voluntary attrition of current year versus prior year
5. Involuntary attrition of current year versus prior year.
6. First-year attrition versus the previous year
7. High-performer attrition of current year versus prior year

Key highlights.

Early trends indicated positive retention of new hires within higher performing teams. Low performing team experienced the highest attrition.

- Senior sales reps with at least three years' tenure and high performance showed great job satisfaction and stability. The top 5% of producers show zero attrition.
- Notable new hires increase of resignations occurred post the first six months in the job.

- Notable increase of resignations happened at a higher rate among the hunters' team category versus non-hunter's category.

In addition, the following questions were covered during employee exit interviews conducted by the human resources department to uncover the main reasons behind these excessive trends of resignation and termination.

- Dissatisfied with or loss of referral source/poor quality of lead flow?
- Dissatisfied with compensation plan?
- Dissatisfied with/lack of support from the manager?
- Dissatisfied with sales culture/direction
- Dissatisfied with the quality of client service and support?
- Better opportunity/ job fit elsewhere?
- Job abandonment?
- Family reasons?
- Better opportunity: leadership role?
- Territory too large/too far away?
- Burned out?
- Retirement?
- Relocation?
- Other?

Below are the top reasons why sales reps left the company.

The number one reason affecting new hires within the first 12 months were as follows:

Key highlights.

- 42% of new hires cited "Dissatisfied with/lack of support from the sales manager".
- 30% of new hires cited "Dissatisfied with the sales culture/direction" and "compensation" as the second-highest reason for leaving.
- 19% cited "Dissatisfied with/or loss of referral source/poor lead flow" as the highest reason for leaving.

<u>Employee Comments Highlights.</u>

Dissatisfied with or Lost Lead Source/Poor Lead Flow.

"I live in a rural area, with poor lead flow. I was promised during my job interview that the company would supplement my self-generated effort with internal leads. Once on board, the promised leads vanished; rather, I was advised to join the Chamber of Commerce at my own expense. Despite my best effort, I failed to meet my goals. The underwriting department rejected most of the self-generated signed accounts for sometimes ridiculous reasons. I was desperate; I pled with my sales manager for help and direction."

My sales manager seemed to be always busy and has never spent a single field day with me, our phone conversations were brief, directionless, and redundant. My manager often stated, "I understand what you are going through, hang tight, it's going to get better, keep doing your best, you will be fine."— Those were my manager's job motivational words. "Find a way." I felt abandoned, and I decided to leave at the first opportunity that came my way. I was willing to work as hard as possible, but I recognized that I needed some assistance and occasional coaching. Alas, no one seems to care about whether I make it or not genuinely. So, I decided to leave to work for a smaller competitor that seems to care.

Dissatisfied with Sales Culture and Direction.

Another veteran salesperson felt that he was being "forced out" by his sales manager because he tended to be more vocal simply because he was concerned.

I felt that my manager and the company do not care much about me, my career, or anyone for that matter. We were COGs, robotic units of productions, used to the maximum, but the moment we need some assistance, we become needy, aggressive non-compliant. The sales manager and the company treat sales reps as disposable machines. "I felt as the company has moved away from recruiting top talent to hiring warm bodies to fill in the gap, and I no longer feel valuable; I no longer feel wanted." The sales reps added his morale was remarkably low because of management dictatorship approaches.

You are forced to produce results at an ever-growing untenable pace, and if you fail, you get terminated. You feel hopeless serving a company that pretends to care, and a sales manager who pretends to help. New hires get lost in a corporate maze, with no training and no assistance. You get torn between trying to build a relationship with your customer in an unforgiven, complex service environment or focus on getting the required transactional deals to meet the company goals to keep your job and your manager at bay regardless of whether you meet your customer needs or not. No one seems to recognize that leadership is amending our goals regularly without explanation. You are pulled in every direction, making it harder to deliver on all your revenue buckets.

Dissatisfied with Sales Compensation

A sales rep cited the following: "Within three years with the company I saw nine amendments to the compensation plan, most made it hard to make money — recently, I lost 50% of my residual income compensation with the last modification. I went overnight from being among the top 5% of performers in the entire company to the bottom 50%. I felt that I could not get ahead within a chaotic system. I was miserable for a while; my conversations with senior management were ignored. I had no choice but to join a competitor.

The irony of the matter is when I presented them with my two weeks' resignation notice, my previously ignored requests were suddenly accepted. My senior vice president (a man I never met or spoke with since I joined the company) was begging me to stay in order not to disrupt the relationship I had with several large national accounts that I had acquired. Unfortunately, the company had me all along, heart, soul, and mind, but no one ever cared before. I had no value while I'm serving the company; it's customers and shareholders with faith and integrity.

My value became apparent and increased dramatically only when I had a competitor offer at hand. Without a job offer in hand, I had no value, I was worthless, couldn't get a raise, or even secure a conversation with my vice-president of sales. I was presumed to go nowhere until I did."

Why does a company have to be reactive when it should be proactive; why take salespeople's efforts and loyalty for granted when you can retain them? Why do you have to lose something or someone to realize their value?

Exit Interviews Tell Half the Story

Exit interviews are great, but they don't always portray the whole picture or the main reason for leaving the job. Here are a few examples that depict the exit interview shortfalls.

- ***Hiding the truth.*** Most employees don't want to burn bridges on their way out. Some employees may provide unauthentic feedback, misleading experiences and falsehood to keep a good face, avoid potential retaliations and burning bridges.

- ***Identify real reasons.*** Not all employees are a good fit for the position. Every organization has its share of employees who met their corporate goals, by using questionable approaches and methods leaving a trail of unhappy customers behind. I have witnessed situations where an underperforming sales rep forged his client's signatures to only be discovered post his employment resignation or termination, others guaranteed unauthorized transactions knowing that they will be quitting the job soon. Some unethical employees maybe too toxic for a healthy sales organization culture. Competence is one thing, good corporate fit is another. Human resource employees must identify the exact reason behind the employee departure to learn from it and take preventive measures to avoid reocurance.

- ***Not all employee turnover can be prevented.*** Employees leave for financial reasons, upper mobility opportunities, and dissatisfaction with the organization sales management team. Additionally, the employee may not always be sincere, and they may pin the blame of resentment on their sales manager behaviors. Taking the time to understand the source of displeasure is essential to mitigate future risks.

- ***Fix the root of the problem.*** When faced with several sudden resignations, have an honest conversation with the employees who are sticking around. Exiting employees will be more open with a peer than with a human resource employee during the exit interview.

- ***Knowing is not doing.*** Most sales organizations invest incredible resources in understanding the reason behind turnover. Then, they either implement poor strategies to remedy the issue or file these findings and facts into a forgotten folder. It's vital to understand the problem and implement a policy that promotes radical changes to stop current losses while making progressive improvements consistently to turn the company from a talent repellent to a talent magnet.

How to Attract and Retain Top Talent

Build a company that truly embodies its mission and vision. Words matter, but more importantly, your deeds must be congruent with your company's purpose.

- Hire fans or turn your employees into fans. Empower them to do what you collectively believe is right for the company and customers.
- Hold on tight to your existing talent, not with ridiculous "non-compete" contracts, but by winning their minds and hearts. Make people feel at home, and be loyal to them rather than ask for their loyalty.
- Make your working environment so inspirational and stimulating that no one will desire to leave. Make the workplace feel like a home where creativity meets curiosity and friendship.
- Be as flexible as possible; don't judge people by their working hours, but rather by their contributions. Measure your people by their value-add, not political savvy. Reward and promote people based on merit, not internal affinity or personal partiality.
- Encourage hiring remote employees, and allow for flexible working hours and flexible vacation time. Don't promote what's convenient for you; support what's right for your salespeople.

- Offer challenging projects, listen to people's ideas, input and insight and implement and reward creativity, while recognizing and celebrating people's genius and contributions.
- Allow your employees to promote and speak about the company on social media, accept suggestions for improvement from both employees and customers without retaliation and with sincere gratitude. People want to help employers who care for their employees, the community they serve, and society.
- Hire with diversity in mind. Nature is diverse for a reason — creating balance. Nature has crevasses and mountains, valleys and dunes, oceans and deserts, mammals and amphibians, predators and preys. Business should emulate nature's characteristics to generate harmony and balance. You need to hire people who look different, sound different, and act differently than what you are used to. Your salespeople should be as diverse as your customers. Diversity is a mental force that spurs creativity and growth.
- Pay above average and be generous with your benefits. It pays ultimately multiple folds in the long run. By paying your salespeople above market price, you win your employees' loyalty, creativity, minds, and hearts. A happy employee will promote your brand for free and attract great external talent. Additionally, happy employees are more productive, and your company will save money through employee and customer retention.

The CXO Disconnect

Faced with survey comments "dissatisfied with lack of support from the sales manager" most heads of sales will go on condemning their first-line managers almost immediately. I was part of a meeting in a large Fortune 500 company. The senior-vice-president (SVP) of human resources shared her survey findings, observations, and conclusions with the executive sales team.

The chief-sales-officer (CSO) recapped the area that surprised him the most and almost immediately started blaming his SVPs of sales for allowing their sales managers to experience this massive failure. “Salespeople are leaving us because you are not spending enough time in the field with them, they are unhappy because you are not training, coaching and educating them on how to sell. You are not doing your job, you are neglecting your duties towards you people, you are a disgrace, and truthfully I’m ashamed to be your leader, this has to change starting immediately.” These were the CSO’s paraphrased words.

I was floored. The CSO didn’t ask any questions of his team, and he didn’t attempt to understand the underlying complexity behind these results. He didn’t ask anyone for input, feedback, or thoughts and he didn’t ask how he could assist or what kind of resources or expertise was needed to remedy the issue. He immediately jumped the gun, pointing fingers and started to blame everyone but himself. This type of poor leadership is often the reason that creates the problem in the first place. You cannot resolve a complex issue of this magnitude with fuzzy directives and intimidating gestures.

The employee exit interview was the first step toward issues resolution. However, more work was needed to conclude the matter. That survey revealed the symptoms of the problem, but not the nature of the disease, but the CSO had no clue that he was part of the problem and part of the dysfunctional culture that contributed to salespeople resignations.

Corporate Norms

In most organizations, when the boss speaks, everyone listens. It's natural to value your boss’ directives and shared wisdom. However, it’s common to listen in silence to a boss who bullies everyone. It takes courage to respond, knowing that your words may be misinterpreted, wrongly assessed, or simply challenged.

Senior managers are diplomatic and know how to avoid the appearance of a verbal confrontation; no one wants to be on the wrong side of the boss. Being vocal requires courage of mind and spirit, you may fear retaliation, passive-aggressive fallout, loss of upward mobility consideration, demotions or even terminations. As the saying goes, you are "damned if you do, damned if you don't."

Most heads of sales do not know what's happening in the field; most hardly spend any field time with their sales reps or customers. However, they expect their subordinates to do so consistently. In large organizations, the chief sales officer (CSO) may spend ten to twenty-four working hours a year in the field with his top salespeople to check a box.

A senior vice president may spend half a day to a whole day a month or less with a top gun to observe the interaction with a large a client and to check the field visit box and respond favorably in case he is asked about field time by his boss. The regional vice president of sales will spend on average one to three days a week observing salespeople's behaviors, gathering strategic market data from the conversation with customers and sales reps, and share this intel with his boss to demonstrate initiative and proactivity. A sales director or sales manager is often expected to spend three to five days in the field helping his salespeople to close deals, along with coaching and training in the trenches.

Most sales organizations' CEOs and CXOs will tell you that the most crucial part of their business is customer satisfaction and improvement of brand loyalty. According to Harvard business school professor Michael Porter, most CEOs spend less than 3% on average in customer-facing time with their customers.

While these CEOs felt that these customer interactions provide valuable independent information about the company's progress, industry trends and competitors innovative advents, many CEOs stated that the scope of the organization managerial responsibilities encompassing functional duties, business agendas, multiple department demands, and myriad internal and external issues is time-consuming and prevents them from spending additional time with their customers.

It's easy to understand why the head of a sales organization can easily place the blame on his subordinates. He hired them and trusted them with managing the business and their employees in a manner that produces results. Most failures can commonly be traced back to failures in the leadership of the organization.

The blame is usually put on the parties who can defend themselves the least. The sales manager stands at the bottom of the management hierarchy, despite the fact that they control revenue production and people's performance. When the sales manager does a great job, the bosses share the credit, but when they fail the sales manager will take the fall alone.

Being a line manager is a tough job, but the position gets harder when you report to a leader who is not empathetic to people challenges and pain.

CHAPTER 15: SUMMARY

- Low performing teams often experience the highest level of employee attrition.
- Salespeople leave their sales organization because they are dissatisfied with:
    - ✓ Quality of leads received from the company or the difficulty to self-source business via cold-calling or canvassing.

    - ✓ A compensation plan that is perceived as too complicated, hard to achieve or tilts the balance toward the company rather than the employee.
    - ✓ Lack of support from the manager
    - ✓ Dissatisfied with the company culture or direction

- Attracting new candidates is essential, but retaining the talent you have is crucial to the survival of the organization.
- Senior executives should never rush into judgment by blaming their sales managers for poor leadership. Strategic organizational missteps often trigger systematic retention issues.
- Senior executives should encourage their employees to share their concerns and dissatisfaction while at the job, rather than express it during their human resource exit interviews. The truth may hurt, but it's better than allowing hypocrisy and intimidation to contaminate the whole organization.

CHAPTER SIXTEEN: TALENT MANAGEMENT

A team is a group of individuals who create synergy to achieve success. Great sales managers understand that the success of the team begins with the right selection of talent. People selection errors can be financially damaging and erode morale. An employee termination may require a lengthy process of performance management to document and justify the dismissal. Additionally, terminations are a painful process that a manager must go through, even when justified. Some terminations generate anger, resentment, and include potential legal challenges. Then a new selection cycle starts again to find and develop the right candidate for the job.

As a sales manager, your greatness is defined by your ability to create a team that operates at a high level of performance continuously and in a predictable fashion. Your success can only be realized through others. Hence, selecting the right salespeople is vital. Salespeople want to be part of a great team, to learn, grow, and produce. The team worth and the sales manager appeal and competence can act as a magnet that either attract talent or repels it.

Hiring from Within Policy

Many sales organizations promote within, which is a great way to create upward mobility and improve salespeople's morale, especially for people who are more interested in leadership roles. Hiring from within promotes employee stability and loyalty. It's undoubtedly an excellent motivator for competent, talented people who would otherwise seek employment outside when the company hires primarily outside talent. Great employees crave appreciation and relevance, so promoting people from within is a great way to build dependable employees and retain your top talent.

However, there should be some level of flexibility to hire competent external candidates as well. I have observed several sales organizations that had a strict policy of promoting only from within.

The Advantage of Hiring from Within.

- Predictable outcome
- Familiarity with the product, systems, and client database
- Faster transition ramps period
- Knowledge of company culture, vision, and mission
- Proven skills required for the job

The disadvantage of Hiring from Within.

- Lack of fresh perspective
- May be biased toward some ideas or concepts
- Replacement issues
- Limited creativity and contrarianism

Sometimes the best salesperson makes the worst manager. A star performer does not always translate to a teacher-coach. Great coaches create an environment for excellence. Coaches develop strategies that help the team to win, and then they step back and watch the magic happen. Great coaches will continue to provide guidance to advance toward the achievement of goals.

Advantage of Hiring from Without.

- New ideas and perspectives
- Access to a new talent pool
- Access to new experiences
- Ability to be selective

Disadvantage of Hiring from Without.

- Requires time to become part of the company culture
- Choke effect in comparison with the previous job
- You don't know what to expect
- Hard to adapt to company culture
- Longer transition time

Ideally, you want to consider both options when you fill a vacant position. Look within at the pool of candidates that are available first, but consider external candidates as well. What matters is to hire the best person for the job.

Hiring Right

Easier said than done; every sales organization hopes to recruit the right candidates once and never have to replace them again. The reality, every time you hire a new candidate, you are taking a chance, every new candidate comes with capabilities and deficiencies. Some turn out to be outstanding assets, others huge liabilities. Some add value, other decrease value, some enhance the team capability, others poison morale and affect performance.

Historical success could be a good sign that the candidate may have the propensity to repeat the same progress. However, performances in the job do not necessarily reflect the salesperson's character, work ethic, internal motives, and mental state.

Did I say mental state? I have hired what seemed like great candidates, only to discover that they were impossible to work with because the salesperson's mental state was questionable at best.

Every organization wants to hire A-players. This group of top performers represents 10% to 20% of the total sales force yet they drive 80% of the company's total revenue. This group of people tends to be consistent, dependable, trustworthy, hardworking and talented in many ways.

These top producers love to work in environments that promote and reward exceptional performance, while allowing the freedom of action and thoughts. This group of people believes that they can do things better than most people.

They live in a stretch zone because they think they can handle stress and intensity with a calmness of mind and confidence of spirit. This group wins most contests and special incentive programs, they are perennial president club goers, and they are the most vocal during roundtables meetings. They possess the right level of knowledge, experience, and creativity to take the most challenging issues and find a plausible solution.

A-players Need Your Attention

One of the biggest misconceptions is that many sales managers believe that your top A-players do not need help; nothing could be further from reality. A-players deal with complex deals, difficult decisions, bidding against stronger opponents, and often working in unchartered territories. Their clients are demanding, unforgiving, pressed for time, and seeking unconventional solutions for unique challenges.

A-players don't have all the answers, but their customers expect them to find the right solution to their business problems. Things can get rough sometimes, and the sharpest minds weaken under pressure, the most robust spirit allows doubt to creep under hardship.

The sales managers can help at this moment by taking some of the pressure and sharing the burden of the responsibility. Hardships become the cement that binds the A-player to his manager. When the managers act as a mental support shield, it empowers the A-player to learn how to handle the pressure better while serving the best interest of his customers and the company.

Keep the Job Description Real

I have read multiple job descriptions. While I understand that recruiters want to cover every aspect of the job's requirements, it often seems that the required package is not entirely realistic. Everyone has strengths and weaknesses, and no one is good at everything.

Critical attributes to do the job should be a requirement, as lesser attributes can be learned on the job. Sales are all about results, and depending on the size of your company and industry, you'd rather have more sales specialists than generalists.

Sales can range from commodity products and services to overwhelmingly complex large enterprise solutions. Selling in a business-to-business environment to government or states requires not only unique knowledge of your products and services but also an in-depth understanding of how the government operates.

Selling complex products like airplanes, yachts, and helicopters requires a specialist with in-depth knowledge of his products and customers. Selling within a small-to-medium business involves some level of expertise as well, but the learning curve is shorter and less steep. Hence, a sales generalist will do just fine.

The more complex the product, the higher the price tag; and the larger the pool of decision makers, the higher the requirement for a certain level of polished communication and sophistication to advance through this lengthy sales cycle. Hiring the right candidate for multiple long sales cycles is vital to achieving the teams goal.

Conversely, you cannot hire a salesperson who is ideal for this type of complex sales-cycle and expect him to thrive in a small-to-medium business environment. Someone who loves the complexity and long sales cycles will get frustrated quickly in a fast-paced environment that lacks mental challenges.

Hire a salesperson who is suitable for the position, hire someone who is going to be excited, passionate, willing to learn and progress within the role. Building a good team means developing people you have and retain them for as long as possible. Stability is essential for the morale and cohesiveness of the team.

So, hire the right people according to the competency needed for the job, but you have to be flexible on what important attributes are needed for the job and what characteristics are desirable and learnable.

Talent Retention

Great sales managers strive to do a great job wrapping their arms around their top producers. They take every opportunity to recognize and thank them for a job well done and for going above and beyond the line of duty.

According to a DePaul University study, the average turnover cost per sales rep is $97,690, which includes recruiting costs, training costs, and lost sales. Losing just ten salespeople a year will cost your organization one million dollars. However, I have seen large sales organizations that churn half of their sales force every year costing them millions. Additionally, it takes 3 to 5 months of intensive research to replace a vacant salesperson position with a new hire.

Another Glassdoor survey found that 19% of sales reps have no immediate plan to leave their companies, while 86% plan to look for another job within the next year and 45% are planning to look for another position within the next three months.

Recognize People's Intrinsic Motivators

I saw several excellent sales managers who constantly promoted their top producer's unique accomplishments to their senior management team; they were proud to recognize the value and contributions of their team members. These sales managers worked closely to understand their top producer's motives, fundamental needs, and then they work to affect these triggers.

Consider the following facts:

- 60% of salespeople left because of a poor relationship with their managers.
- 73% of salespeople who left for pay reasons were in the bottom half of performance ranking.
- 70% of people who left citing lack of promotion opportunities were in the top half of performance rankings.

Top producers may be motivated by financial gain, individual recognition from the head of sales or their CEO, winning family trips, bonuses, promotion opportunities, or a chance to coach the team and new rookies.

Many top caliber salespeople love the opportunity and platform to voice their thoughts and concerns on how to improve specific areas of the business. Many top producers see themselves as equals to senior management in terms of brain power and ability, and they feel empowered when their input is considered and valued.

These top producers genuinely care about their careers, the company, and its direction. They want to help, and they want to be recognized as strategy contributors, and thought leaders. After all, they are the revenue generators that the company depends on.

Employee Retention Starts from the Heart

It's a mistake to omit to recognize top producer's unique effort in one-on-one settings.

Do not believe that earned financial rewards is enough. It's not. Salespeople have multiple triggers that often have little to do with money. Knowing your salespeople's domestic situation can allow the sales manager to affect the direction of the conversation and the outcome you are trying to create.

Tactics to Retain Your Talent.

True challenges. Ask your top salespeople what they would love to do, and try to fulfill it. For example. Allow a senior salesperson to lead your weekly call, act as a manager for a day, lead training sessions, conference calls or champion a product and be a management advisor in a specific topic. These simple initiatives promote employees retention and loyalty.

- ***Emotional engagement.*** Salespeople who are genuinely engaged on different projects, individual advisory boards, or educational programs are four times more likely to stay in the job rather than leave. The higher the salesperson's engagement in company activities, the higher the retention.

- ***Smart Financial incentives.*** Be creative, offer short- and long-term incentives that appeal to people's needs and curiosity.
  - Offer bonuses that can pay someone's three to six months' mortgage or rent
  - Offer short-term bonuses that cover one to two weeks of groceries from their favorite place.
  - Offer bonus that pays part of the sales rep's student loan.
  - Offer one-year car leases to your top sales reps.
  - Offer extra all paid vacations for a family trip to your top-producing sales reps twice a year.
  - Offer all-expense-paid online professional education every a year.
- ***Coach to develop.*** Allocate time where you are dedicated to developing your people to elevate their capabilities to the next level. Keep development sessions separated from KPI discussions. Development is about them. Quota, pipeline and KPI discussions should be conducted on separate times.
- ***Your team is a tribe.*** Salespeople stay longer in a friendly environment that encourages camaraderie and friendship. According to OfficeVibe, 70 of employees say that having friends at work is the most crucial element to a happy working life. Getting your people together as often as possible where you collectively do fun things is a great way to bond and decrease churn.
- ***Stay in celebration mode.*** Recognizing your people's successes motivates everyone. People love to see their efforts paying off, but more importantly, being publicly acknowledged and

encouraged. People crave earned recognition and appreciate the leader that promotes it.

- ***Promote based on Merit.*** Recognize salespeople who exude signs that they are ready for promotions and assist them during the transition. If someone is qualified, don't stay in their way to benefit from their production. Have a backup plan, but encourage them to move forward. Salespeople love to see their peers being promoted as it energizes them.

People are different and their motivational triggers are different. Find what each of them values and use that specific value to motivate them. Invest in your A-players and B-players as much as possible.

As a vice president of sales, I recognized that some of my sales directors craved to grow personally, so every three months, I sent them a business book related to their aspirations and areas where they needed growth.

I allocated fifteen minutes per week to discuss a specific chapter. We had to read the chapter the prior week, discuss it, share our thoughts and findings and swap notes. This creative idea was so well-received that we added a group discussion once a month, we took turns on who led the call. This idea became so popular that the company decided to adopt it nationwide.

A friend of mine who was the head of sales traveled the whole country to meet salespeople and conduct business. Each night, he invited five A-players-and B-players to join him. During these dinner sessions, he merely listened to his salespeople's concerns and proposed solutions. He took notes and acted on many of their interests.

He sent the dinner pics to the whole region, and he recognized people who suggested solutions to their current challenges. This practice became so popular that people came prepared with several solutions along with their problems. The company benefited from people's honesty and initiatives to find solutions to some daunting issues that the company faced.

Small gestures can go a long way. Retaining your top talent is vital; finding ways to make people happy at work is paramount. Invest in people's development, growth, and emotional connectedness. Listen, think, and challenge the status-quo. Do not underestimate your people's mental potential.

You are not hiring people for their hands only; the essential element in your employee package is the brain. People do not leave companies like Google and Apple easily, and the reason is not the money. Instead, it's the environment and the culture that allows employees to think and express their thoughts without being ridiculed or dismissed. People stay in jobs where they feel worthy of making a positive difference.

Hunters Are Predators. Farmers Are Protectors.

I attended a company all-hands call arranged by the head of sales. He sounded worried—sales growth was going the opposite direction, a sales force of 800 salespersons was not creating the needed revenue, margins were down, conversion rates and win rates were at all-time low, sales volume had plummeted, and account sizes decreased. The head of sales was under intense pressure from his executive management team. His days were numbered; he knew that unless he turned these numbers around quickly, he was history.

He spent thirty minutes describing how dire the situation was, then he appealed to everyone to double productivity within the next thirty days and hung up. Thirty minutes later, I joined a mandatory call for regional vice presidents only. During that call, the same head of sales asked all regional vice presidents to conduct daily blitzes to spur productivity. All salespeople and sales managers needed to canvass daily for new business. Sales managers set up mandated regular calls to inspect activity and results.

Every salesperson had to be on these calls at 8 am and 6 pm to report their success. A week went by and productivity continued to decline and call attendance start to dropping as well. Salespeople start complaining that this level of inspection started to weigh on them, as they had other obligations to attend to. Managers didn't let up, and rather, they increased the level of pressure to ensure compliance.

Within two weeks, it was apparent this initiative wasn't working. These salespeople had relied on leads being provided by their marketing department and referral partners. They were accustomed to getting hot leads. The company had hired these salespeople and guaranteed that they would be given 20 to 30 leads per months. The average close ratio hovered around 30% per account executive.

A quick conversation with several sales managers revealed that most of the sales force had joined the company because they were assured that they would be provided good leads and their job was to close them with a sense of urgency and professionalism. The company referral partners found it harder to generate qualified leads, which affected salespeople's closing ratio and performance.

Farmers

The whole sales force was never trained on self-generation of business, and most salespeople had poor hunting capabilities and despised cold-calling and canvassing. Asking these farmers to become hunters overnight was an impossible task. The head of sales believed that with some level of pressure, these salespeople could turn dormant skills up quickly. What he failed to understand is that these skills were not inactive; they were non-existent. They needed to be developed through intensive training, mental conditioning, and field modeling.

Sales farmers have honed skills like nurturing existing customer relationships, people management, and relationship building. They are great at building long-term relationships, they are exceptional nurturers, and they can build a fantastic relationship with clients who have a lasting impact on the company revenue.

These sales farmers cannot become sales hunters overnight. Sales hunter are trained to be aggressive, tactical, and result-focused.

Hunters

Hunters are almost a different breed; they are wired differently, and they think and act differently. They work with a sense of urgency and thrive under pressure. They love challenges, resistance, and ambiguity. However, with few exceptions, they are not wired well to service customers, and they don't manage post-sales issues well. They are wired to kill, not repair wounds. They are predators, tough and resilient. Like it or not, that's their tendency, and that's what makes them good at what they do.

Hunters are money makers, and the key is to recognize their talent early in the game and connect them with peer hunters. While they are mostly lone wolves, they also draw energy from one another. They love to hear other team members' successes, as it motivates them to be more and do more. They are great at business acquisition but do poorly servicing accounts, handling escalations, and building a long-term relationship. They thrive building new relationships, but tend to fail to maintain long-term relationships.

Requiring hunters to become account managers and vice versa is insanity and a sure recipe for disaster. Account managers thrive at account maintenance, retention, expansion, as well as cross-sell and up-sell. Hunters excel at chasing new wins.

Asking a sales farmer to do a sales hunter job is just like asking a drone pilot to fly without training a Boeing F-22 Raptor fighter. Piloting an advanced aircraft is not the same as piloting a high-tech drone. They are both stressful and unique piloting systems that require exceptional skills. These skills can be learned, but they take time, effort, and resources.

The head of sales didn't know what type of sales force he had; he managed people through data and reporting, not knowing that he had, all along, been leading order-takers and farmers. Only when he became desperate, he thought that maybe he could transform the nature of his salespeople quickly from farmers to hunters. However, it doesn't work that way in real life.

CHAPTER 16: SUMMARY

- Employee termination is always hard to perform, even when necessary. Employee termination should be dealt with care, sensitivity, and humility.
- Promote from within whenever possible, but don't hesitate to hire from outside when it's the better option. Hire the best candidate for the job based on merits.
- Understand your people's intrinsic and extrinsic motivational factors to retain your best talent.
- Be generous, pay above market compensation to retain your best talent and attract your competitors' best people.

CHAPTER SEVENTEEN: SMART HIRING

Salespeople are the lifeblood of most sales organizations. Hiring a new salesperson is always like playing Russian roulette— you hold your breath, hope for the best, but cannot help but think that it may not turn out as expected. Over the years, I hired hundreds of sales reps, I worked for several Fortune 500 companies that were experiencing high turnover due to multiple reasons and I probably interviewed thousands of salespeople. I followed company hiring processes when it was a mandated, and deviated when it didn't work for me, I had my own set of questions, and I certainly strived to get to know the real candidate potential even when they were poor interviewees. I hired several rock stars, many average producers, and some bad candidates. Over the years, I became good at reading people; when I followed my instinct, I did well. When I ignored it and followed the company human resources directives and processes, it was a 50-50 probability of success, which is no better than flipping a coin — heads, you are hired; tails, you are not.

Most candidates had to go through five interviews with different managers to get the job. You would think that if five intelligent people interview the same candidate, the probability of hiring the right candidate would increase dramatically. Nothing could be further from the truth, as these interviewers tend to influence or reinforce the decision maker's thought process indirectly.

Each new hire is like a new child. The sales manager hopes that they made the right choice. No sales interview or technique will guarantee the success of any individual. You always take a chance. I hired candidates who everyone told me to pass on, as they didn't look great on paper or their interview skills were not great. Some of these candidates turned out to be the best hires I ever brought on board. I have also hired promising, talented candidates whom we collectively thought were going to outdo, outsmart, and outwork everyone else in the company.

Several times, I witnessed brilliant candidates go straight to the bottom despite sales managers' coaching and training efforts. I sometimes wonder how perceptions and collective judgment could go so wrong. Despite your best effort to hire the best talent, there is always a question mark that follows the new hire until they manifest their inner genius. I would agree that careful planning is vital to hiring quality salespeople who fit well within and make positive contributions to the organization. My experience made me realize that some salespeople are hard to replace in terms of unique knowledge and competency—their losses are often devastating to the organization, at least in the short-term.

The key is to retain your best salespeople and continually hire the best talent you can afford, or at a minimum, create a pool of tested candidates that can replace lost talent in a short notice. You want to hire talented salespeople who are willing to be with you through great times and bad times. Sales is hard, and it requires strong-minded individuals who are eager to support the organization's success when things get tough.

Create a Pool of Potential Hires

Hire with Strategy in Mind. Business growth is great, however, do not hire additional salespeople unless it's necessary. I witnessed several sales organizations changing their hiring strategy due to a sudden growth and saw new executive leadership directives to fail miserably because of lack of planning and poor market demand study.

Hiring many sales reps without any consideration of the company's sustainability model, available opportunities, or financial impact on the existing sales force can be counterproductive and potentially destructive. Hiring too many salespeople over a short period will decrease efficiency and productivity, affect morale and may force loyal salespeople to consider moving out — furthermore, massive hiring increase hiring errors. Hiring should only occur for fully developed roles, and specialization should be the goal to create a sales force's competitive advantage. To win specific channels and new markets, you will need sales specialists with an industry focus.

Hire Synergistically.

Great teams reflect people's diverse backgrounds, cultures, and experiences. Groups' gender, belief, and thought process differences keep creativity up and curiosity at the forefront of performance and innovation. As a sales manager, you should hire salespeople who understand the company's vision and believe in its corporate and social mission. You should hire salespeople who are willing to challenge the status quo, existing paradigms, and processes to improve the company by contributing ideas and new ways that will benefit everyone.

Hire salespeople who are willing to share their knowledge freely and exchange information to overcome tough challenges and elevate performance. New hires can add new perspective and value to the team; be open to learning from new hires' past experiences, challenges and solutions. Some best practices that worked on specific markets and industries could apply to your industry; stay open-minded, you have everything to gain from other experiences. Great new hires fuel internal competitiveness, increase awareness, speed the team learning curve, and add value through new skills. They also bring in new energy and excitement that keeps team productivity and morale up.

Refuse to Accept Underperformance

Continuous underperformance should never be tolerated under any circumstance. I worked for a large organization that had a high employee turnover and struggled with retention to the point where sales managers were praised and rewarded for salespeople retention regardless of performance.

Yes, sales leadership became tolerant of mediocrity, because the company wanted to go public and was afraid of analysts' judgment and market perception. For the first time in my career, I witnessed a sales organization where sales performances didn't matter. There were salespeople midyear standing at 30% to quota attainment, while their sales managers and the leadership team totally ignored it. Many sales managers were instructed by human resources not to put their underperforming sales reps in performances plan as it triggered the following timeline that led to termination within ninety days for continuous failure to achieve company set quota. Incredible, you may think! I would totally agree, but it's very true.

Even today, many large corporations still suffer from underperformance syndrome, yet they do not know how to address it. Many look at it as just too big of a challenge to resolve; it requires shifting priorities, time, and resources they don't have. Others believe that the psychology of sales is a matter too complicated to deal with while some organizations fear that too many terminations may trigger people to question their people's leadership capability, so complacency becomes the option of choice and the route of least resistance.

Underperformance should not be accepted for any reason as it erodes top sales performers morale, making them question why they should be working so hard for an organization that allows below par performances to become the norm. Great performers want to be part of an A-team and an A-company that requires everyone to stretch their abilities to attain tough goals. Having to work along with "B" producers can be tolerated but the A-players, but C-players acceptance cannot be tolerated or normalized. The sales leadership role is to help them up or out because, holding on to too many underperformers weakens the organization's productivity and contributes to its economic demise.

Hire Slowly and Terminate Swiftly

It's easier to hire than to terminate an employee. Urgent hiring needs do not need to translate into a desperation hiring. Take your time to avoid regrets, ask the right questions, validate references, ensure uniformity with the hiring process, and involve several managers and sales reps in the evaluation of the new candidate before making a hiring decision. Have team leaders interview all new candidates. Have new candidates shadow a veteran sales rep for a couple of days and evaluate their ride-along feedback carefully. This ride-along has been precious to my hiring decisions, as I often learned valuable insights I would never have expected from my current sales reps. I had a candidate once who stated during a ride along with a friendly sales veteran that his whole interest to joining the company was because it was a work-from-home position; therefore, he would be able to manage his personal online business who was his main priority, while drawing the corporate job salary and benefits. Another instance revealed a candidate who already had a job with a competitor that he never disclosed, which created a direct conflict of interest and was against company policy. The list goes on, but you get the message.

Hire right, train and coach continuously, and terminate quickly.

Reasonable quota attainment should be the norm, and no one should be left behind. However, if despite your best efforts, the sales rep is not willing to improve, then terminations should be swift. However, all job terminations should be human, fair, documented, and with no surprises. You should prepare your sales reps about what will come if they continue to fall behind without an effort to remedy the situation.

Hire Sales Leaders

Hire high-caliber sales leaders who are committed and capable of doing a great job. The quality of your new hires will define your team and organization success. If you can land intellectually curious individuals who are smart and able to self-manage their careers with little help from you, the outcome could be outstanding.

Talented salespeople act as magnets to attract similar successful individuals. Happy, successful new hires attract competent individuals who are employed by other organizations. Employee happiness is a measure that draws talented individuals from the competition faster than any lucrative compensation package. People want to work somewhere they are valued and respected.

There was a time when my organization needed to hire people quickly because of partnership obligations, stress on the current sales force, and opportunity cost loss. I learned that despite the pressure, it's always better to wait to hire the right person than suffer the consequences of offering the job to the wrong candidate.

For example, years ago, I was a regional-vice-president of sales managing a sales force of more than 200. A new hire recently assigned to work a banking partnership relationship accidently sent a shocking picture to a female banker partner. The image made it to the senior vice president who was not happy with the organization. The SVP was looking for a way out of his contractual obligation, and that incident was his perfect opportunity to claim breach of contract.

The situation became so tense that the company CEO had to get involved in salvaging the relationship. The sales rep was terminated and the organization suffered financial losses and humiliations. One wrong hire can cause the company irreparable damage and loss of repute. Take your time, dig deep, and hire ethical salespeople.

In another case, I heard from a colleague of mine that three promising new hires got extremely intoxicated while drinking during their out-of-state first week on-the-job training. They got into a local bar fight with some local guys over disrespecting their female friends, and got arrested for assault. Can you imagine the audacity, weak character, and lack of professionalism of these new hires?

Hire salespeople who exude leadership flair and traits, people who can motivate and inspire their peers to go the extra mile. Hiring high-caliber individuals improves morale, creates competitiveness, broadens creative intelligence and increases productivity and efficiency.

Create a Hiring Profile of an Ideal Candidate

Many sales organizations rely on a human resource question templates to create hiring uniformity across the organization. However, this mechanical process created by human resources is flawed and lax. The salespeople hiring process should be as rigorous as hiring, at a minimum, a sales manager. You certainly wouldn't hire a sales manager or a sales-vice-president who won't last with the company for more than six months.

It would be best if you resisted hiring sales reps who you may have to terminate within few months. It's better to pay way above industry norms and attract high-quality individuals that will create real value and grow with the company than pay average or low compensation package and be forced to hire from a pool of mediocre candidates.

Attributes to Seek

Intellectual curiosity. Hire sales individuals who are part-book smart, part-street smart, and possess problem-solving skills that rely on raw intelligence, logic, and intuition. Curious salespeople are always asking questions that no one thought of before; their antennas are always up sensing changes in the air. They are sensitive to prospects' mood changes, meaning behind unspoken words, body behaviors, and thought process shifts.

Intellectual curiosity requires the individual to continually self-educate, learn new trends, and learn about the competitions product services and strategies to overcome prospects' objections and offer better alternatives. These individuals can understand the company's holistic business solutions but only offer the right business solution to the customer.

Smarts. Smart people come from different backgrounds, have a diverse level of education and may come from various industries and cultures. Try to evaluate people's smarts without biases or pre-judgments. Intelligence comes in different shapes and packages. Look for personal initiatives, past personal and professional accomplishments as well as the courage and confidence to take major projects even if they led to failure. Smart individuals take chances based on their self-belief and confidence.

Resourcefulness. These individuals are resilient to find a solution when confronted with a challenge. They find a way to the obstacles, where most salespeople give up. Resourceful salespeople will keep working the problem from different angles until they find the ideal solution. They love the challenges because it motivates them to stretch beyond their comfort zone. They are often the salespeople who come up with unusual solutions that no one thought of before.

Competitiveness. Salespeople are driven by competitiveness to win. Operating on a high level requires focus, stamina, grit, thinking, planning, research, proactivity, and a good dose of old-fashioned hard work. Competitiveness is a mental and emotional state that forces the individual to keep going against tough odds, keep crawling inch by inch until they achieves the goal.

Coachability. Hire salespeople who are open to coaching. Everyone needs to learn new skills to grow, evolve and improve. The sales manager primary job is to coach his salespeople to get better. Hire people who love to coach and be coached.

Leadership. Hire salespeople who have the potential to lead others, who love to help and educate their peers and customers. Salespeople who possess leadership qualities take chances, love challenges, crave additional responsibilities, speak their mind, possess mental courage and emotional fortitude, and are often confident in any setting.

Detail-oriented. Success in sales requires attention to detail and being visionary. Details matter in drafting contracts, following up with customers, organizing one's pipeline, structuring daily activities, and winning deals. As the adage says, "The devil is in the details." Being detail-oriented is the essence of a job well done.

For example, a few years ago, I dealt with a situation. A new hire omitted to get the customer to initial three areas of the contract that stipulate "The customer must initial here, failure to initial this box may result on the customer not being charged for this purchase."

The sales administrator caught the error. The sales rep felt that he had built a good rapport with the customer, the latter was aware of this cost, and it shouldn't have been a big deal as it was an innocent mistake.

To his surprise, the customer refused to initialize the contract and demanded that the company hold onto their end of the bargain to avoid a lawsuit.

This error cost the company over $10,000. Lesson learned, details matters, and contract purpose to secure that both parties hold on to their end of the bargain.

Persistence. Sales is a tough job; winners require a high level of endurance. Constant rejections, pushbacks, and setbacks can erode confidence and excitement. Additionally, hearing hundreds of NOs can wear you out. Winning requires persistence and toughness of mind. For example, marathon runners build feet blisters that make every step painfully excruciating, yet without strong mental tenacity, they would never reach the finish line.

Teamwork. Lone wolves can manage to do well. However, the sales landscapes has changed so much that collaboration becomes essential to individual success. Working with others can make the difference between struggling alone or tapping into collective wisdom, feedback, and experiences.

The above characteristics provide you with a solid foundation to hire a salesperson who will probably succeed on your team. However, you will need to be careful when hiring people with some level of professional experience. Your job description needs to be accurate, and you must highlight the non-negotiable areas and the areas that are desirable but not a must.

Industry Specification. Focus on the job requirement that is critical to having a good start. Some companies don't have the luxury of time to wait and train an individual to reach the level of proficiency and sophistication required to succeed.

For example, if you are looking to hire a salesperson with experience selling to the C-level suite, you may be tempted to hire someone from a different industry. However, banking and manufacturing CEOs thought processes and buying behaviors are different. Your salesperson may find the transition difficult although she is accustomed to working with C-level suite.

Additionally, a salesperson who specialized in retail may find it difficult to work in a B2B environment.

Job Nature. A new hire who worked as a relationship manager handling long-cycle national accounts, while occasionally cross-selling and up-selling his customers, may transition poorly into a high-pressure, fast-paced, short sales cycle, revenue-driven sales hunter position. You must be careful in reviewing one's capability versus job demand and the efforts necessary to transform willing individuals.

Sales Cycle Requirement. Hiring someone who is used to multi-level long sales cycles that take months and even years, and where teams work synergistically to customize business solutions that meet customer's needs, may not be capable of one-call close-selling to small and medium businesses.

Industry Legends. Historical President Club members may not be your ideal candidates. Some of these legendary producers may have operated for years under privileged conditions that you cannot provide nor be aware of. The risk of losing these individuals is extremely high. These sales reps will start looking for an exit the moment they realize they no longer have the same privileges they are accustomed to with prior employers. Hire people who meet your current needs and who will grow as your company grows.

CHAPTER 17: SUMMARY

- Follow company hiring questioning processes when it's a mandate, but deviate from it whenever it doesn't meet your needs. After all, generic templates create by human resources folks often miss the target. In addition, no one knows more about what you want in a candidate more than you.

- Adopt a constant hiring mode, create a pool of candidates that you can tap into in case of emergency.

- Hire smart candidates who can add value to the whole organization by taking leadership roles.

- Create a profile for your ideal candidates. Work to identify the right match and reach out to introduce yourself and build rapport.

CHAPTER EIGHTEEN: PROMOTING & STIMULATING HEALTHY SALES CULTURE

People are always self-employed. In a nation like the United States, most employees operate under "at will" job contracts; one can walk away from a job for any reason and at any time.

People stay in the position for a variety of reasons; some are intrinsic and others are extrinsic, such as: job satisfaction, the opportunity for upward mobility, financial rewards, company culture, company values, quality of leadership, professional development, comfort on the job, peer friendships, community relations, and company brand reputation among others.

Employee job satisfaction includes job responsibility, level of achievement, recognition, and opportunity for growth, as well as other matters related to the quality of leadership and peer bond.

Staying in the Job for the Right Reasons

In sales, you want people to stay in the job for the right reasons; these are attributes that are beneficial to the company and the employee. Management's role is to understand and reinforce the drivers that increase employee satisfaction, loyalty, and retention.

Several studies have revealed that employees cited that personal bond with their peers and sometimes their sales manager as the main reasons for staying on the job.

Ask any U.S Marine why they are doing what they protecting us. Besides the love for God and their country, the answer will always be the same: "I'm doing it for my brothers and sisters in the corp." Organizations like the military are all about the bond created among people, friends, and colleagues.

Pay close attention to the principles:

1. Know yourself and seek self-improvement
2. Be technically and tactically proficient
3. Develop a shared sense of responsibility among your subordinates
4. Make sound and timeless decisions
5. Set an example
6. Know your people and look for their well-being
7. Keep your people informed
8. Seek responsibility and embrace responsibility for your actions
9. Ensure assigned tasks are understood, supervised, and accomplished
10. Train your people to work as a force of one

These principles above could belong to any Fortune 500 company, yet they are part of timeless military principles and leadership lists. These sound principles are operational pillars of a well-managed organization and people.

Compassion Matters

Working for a leader who cares and shows appreciation and gratitude can be a strong reason to stay on the job. A sales manager who genuinely cares about his people's career growth and knows how to stimulate his people's minds and hearts wins their trust and confidence easily.

Business, like war, is a constant battle that requires constant adaptation to internal challenges and external events. A good sales leader serves as a strategic moral guide when you don't know if you should be on offensive or defensive mode, attack or hide, spend time, energy or save resources, move forward or backward, speed up or slow down, take initiative, or wait.

A good manager serves as a guiding compass. You can make your own decisions, but an occasional glimpse at your compass will tell you if you are still on the right course or you deviated from it. It's the little adjustments that keep you on track; small deviations can lead off your destination. Your sales manager acts as your inner voice that guides you back toward safety.

Wrong Reasons to Stay on the Job.

There will come a time when it makes sense to change jobs or career. Inertia can be a force to reckon with. However, if your mind, heart, and passion are gone, move on. You cannot delude yourself into staying in a job you no longer love or appreciate, or keep working in an environment that become toxic. If you are not happy, take a chance toward a better future somewhere else. It may be tough to leave the security of a paycheck towards the unknown, but it often worth the leap.

<u>*Don't stay on a job you loathe because of*</u>

- Financial security
- Good relationships with your co-workers
- Familiarity with the job operations and complexity

- Fear of the unknown moving to a new position
- Age-related concerns or social fit
- Fear of not securing a job within the same industry
- Fear of retaliation from your manager

Poor Performance Needs to be Addressed

Most sales reps fail to achieve their goals because of inadequate training, lack of motivation, poor work ethics, attitudinal issues or lack of confidence. As a sales manager, you ought to know your employees intimately to ignite their spirit and trigger the desire to achieve the necessary change required for betterment. Many sales reps get into sales for the wrong reasons. When faced with the complexity and the difficulty of the job, many give up mentally, procrastination becomes the norm, meeting customers become a dread, doing nonproductive work becomes an escape to avoid facing clients or prospecting for new business. As a good sales manager, you should pay attention to these behavioral cues and address them with the sales rep before they reach an irreversible stage.

The salesperson who chronically underperforms might be simply in the wrong job. Assist to your best ability that salesperson with the transition to a more suitable position either within the company or outside. Your role is to instill confidence in your salespeople to improve morale and performance. By creating an environment of trust and accountability, you can help your sales reps meet their sales objectives.

Communication Breeds Confidence

You can easily tell if the sales rep is not excited about their job; lack of enthusiasm, excitement, and passion will be apparent. It's hard to sell yourself and the product you represent if you don't believe in yourself and the value you bring to your customer. This behavior can stem from an attitude problem, lack of confidence, or poor work ethic.

People who are unhappy about their job complain incessantly, lack energy, desire, exude grumpiness and dissatisfaction. They come late to work, leave early, hesitate to attend conference calls, and rarely speak, add value, or provide feedback. These sales reps are often competent but demotivated.

Having a one-on-one conversation with these sales reps can bring to the surface the reasons behind their behavior and lack of performance.

Multiple studies have shown that a good number of sales managers neglect to have an honest conversation with a challenged sales rep to avoid being entangled in personal stories. Finding out the reason behind an employee's lack of motivation is part of the sales manager's job. After all, you are responsible for your team's performance, work ethics, and morale. The simple act of starting a conversation with the purpose of helping your sales rep overcome their challenges can make a huge difference in building personal trust, boosting confidence, and overcoming obstacles.

It would help if you encouraged everyone to be open and share private information; we all have private lives that can get messy sometimes. Having a team of friendly colleagues and managers you respect and trust to be open can give you a morale boost and renewed confidence that things will get better.

Your people should feel that you have their back, during both good times and bad. Supporting your people is the right thing to do, and it's the essence of good management. By taking the initiative and protecting peoples' personal secrets, you create an environment where salespeople strive for openness and excellence. Good sales leadership is a set of behaviors and decisions enrobed in empathy and care. You earn loyal employees by showing genuine concern when people are vulnerable.

Connect to Serve

People who feel connected perform better. A team is a group of people who care for one another while serving the company and its customers to attain its objectives. The relationship and trust that people forge among them become the glue that unites them to stay on the job and sacrifice as necessary to help their peers, boss, and company. People can become loyal to a fault when they believe that their work creates value, support their community and company to achieve a worthy goal.

People love to work for a leader and with peers who appreciate their work and contributions. Salespeople stop performing their best and lose morale when they reach out to the sales manager for assistance and get ignored. Multiple surveys have shown that the fastest way for a manager to lose respect is to ignore a sales rep in distress for an extended period.

Some sales managers tend to dismiss their sales reps too quickly, ignore their plea, avoid their calls under the pretense they were busy, and hope that the issue will vanish or the sales rep will resolve the issue on their own.

Salespeople regularly deal with unpredictable situations and urgencies. Few know how to navigate the internal company systems to resolve pending issues, but most salespeople get stuck in the process of figuring out what to do and who to go to for assistance. Nothing is more infuriating to a salesperson than having a sales manager ignores their call for help, especially when the issue is critical.

As a leader, nothing can damage your reputation faster than ignoring people who depend on your guidance in moments of distress.

You don't have to have all the answers, as you can figure it out later, but what's important is to respond to distress calls and be there when it matters the most.

Faith in Your Product

Selling is hard, especially during the days where you are overwhelmed with customers' problems. Issue resolution can be harder than selling itself because it's mentally exhausting. It's hard to deal with a customer's wrath when your sales operation comes to a halt because of product failure that you sold.

The inability to rapidly resolve critical customer issues will damage your professional repute. Nothing does more damage to a sales rep's morale than the failure to solve pressing customer issue quickly and efficiently. When the company support systems are inadequate, a sales rep starts questioning if they're working for the right company.

Unsupported salespeople lose faith in the organization's ability to stand behind its products and fulfill its duties of providing excellent service to its customers. Lack of internal support is among the biggest reasons why salespeople quit their job. You cannot ask your salespeople to sell dysfunctional products that keep failing and require constant repair or replacement.

Salespeople sell the idea of better outcomes, functionality, and performance. They want to sell a product that lives up to their promises. A product below standards or poor customer service is perceived as a personal threat to the sales rep's reputation and integrity.

The customer can exert tremendous mental pressure on the salesperson if the product doesn't produce what it claims. Your salespeople should feel good about the product they are offering rather than having to defend its merits at the risk of alienating the customer.

Some customers can be brutal, calling sales reps liars and cheats when the product fails to produce the level of performance sold and expected.

Selling is Believing

Salespeople are not actors, contrary to what we hear; they are honest, hard-working people who are in the people's business. While it's possible for some people to sell a product they don't believe in, most professional salespeople cannot do the same, because they know they will sound phony, dishonest and will lose respect for themselves and the profession of selling. That is why it's vital to believe in your products, services, company, and the value you add to people's lives and society. To sell is to believe in your products, services, and company. Your enthusiasm and excitement are sourced from your belief systems. It's is more comfortable to sell a product, idea or concept you genuinely believe in.

How to Build Excitement for Your Product/Services?

Encourage creativity. Educate your salespeople on your product and services features, advantages, benefits and value. You can assist initially your sales reps with sales pitches that will help build their confidence during role-plays. However, you should encourage your sales reps to customize and improve their sales scripts, approach and methodologies to influence their customers.

Share product flaws. Educate your salespeople on the pros and cons of your products before going to the market. Your salespeople will need to understand how to position your products' worth without hiding its shortcomings, while comparing it to competitors' products. Honesty is the best policy. Your salespeople should sell your products confidently, but your products quality and durability should withstand the test of time and expectancy. Customers often don't use all product functionality, and your business solution may be just right for them.

Customizable solutions. Promote the fact that your product is not a solution that fits all. Instead, it's a solution that meets specific customers' and business's needs. Customers buy products that meet their requirements and budgets. A salesperson `who believes in their products' capabilities and flaws sells with passion, conviction, and integrity.

Team Bonding

Products and systems will occasionally break; how you choose to handle the issue matters. A cardinal rule for a sales leader is to never fail to assist your salespeople in times of need. Sales management is all about building bridges and trust, and the latter is built in moments of need. The issue will pass, but if you fail to support your salespeople in critical moments, your repute will suffer, and the damage will linger for a long time.

It takes continuous effort to bond with team members. The trust that took years to build brick by brick can come tumbling down quickly in a matter of minutes. Never hesitate to aid in the resolution of an issue that is beyond the scope, power, knowledge, and capability of your sales reps. If the problem cannot be resolved based on the available resources, be honest and ensure that you will continue to research for alternative solutions. The challenge will pass, but how you make your sales rep feel will be remembered for a long time.

Human beings feel safer, empowered, and perform better when connected with others. Great sales managers build trust by serving their people.

How Can You Help?

Connect with your employees at a deeper level. Get to know them intimately, assist and coach to elevate your salespeople's ability to resolve issues.

Encourage your sales rep to be authentic with you. There should be no pretense in the process, keep it simple and real. People love authentic leaders who care and are willing to share the blame when things go wrong. As a sales leader, you should be prepared to defend your salespeople and take the heat when necessary to earn the team trust and loyalty.

Promote conversation as much as possible. Use all types of communication methods preferred by your salespeople; you should be accessible and aware. Getting back to your people within a reasonable time should be the norm and not the exception.

When the emotions are high, stay calm and try to have a face-to-face with the salesperson.

People become more pragmatic and reasonable when they realize you are doing everything possible to resolve the issue to their satisfaction.

Educate your sales reps on how to approach the problem from a different angle to come up with alternative solutions. Train them on how to diffuse difficult escalations and how to minimize these occurrences.

Take your sales reps to social events, share a drink, have dinner together, and try to build personal relationship beyond just work. Create a work-family environment that promotes openness and healthy collaboration.

Make the work place enjoyable, make people feel home. Most of the day is spent at work anyhow, so make it pleasant.

Peak Performance and Fun

Only a few managers recognize the importance of having fun at work. Peak performance is attained when employees are happy. People enjoy their work environment when they perform well while enjoying working with their peers in a culture that promotes meaningful work and a healthy work-life balance. Having fun means creative problem-solving and working as a force of one toward a worthy goal that benefits employees, shareholders, community and company.

Companies that promote hard work and work-play-time tend to achieve greater employee performance and job satisfaction. Here is how to move your team from standard output to extraordinary accomplishments.

Rather than provide answers, educate your sales reps on how to ask meaningful questions that challenges one's thinking, broadens personal perspective and allows for deep reflection and imagination to discover new solutions. Here are few examples:

- What didn't work and how can you avoid its reoccurrence?
- What did you learn from it? What part surprised you the most?
- What changes are necessary to meet these challenges?
- How can we get better? What are your thoughts on the subject?
- What can we do differently next time? Why do you think may be a better alternative?
- What are we missing? Where are we losing the game?
- What are we doing right? What are we doing wrong? What can we improve or eliminate?

Encourage people to disagree, debate, and add value continuously. There are no wrong ideas or concepts. Listening to everyone's ideas and insights can create a culture that promotes individual creativity and limitlessness of thoughts and action.

Peak performance requires an environment where leaders promotes individuality, respect, uniqueness, connectedness, fun, and creativity to be your best.

Be a good leader, show gratitude, praise people for a job well done, recognize and praise exceptional work and performances, glorify selfless acts and salespeople who support others in times of need. It's the little things that matter to people the most, it's the little things that bond people and create desirable work cultures.

CHAPTER 18: SUMMARY

- Treat your salespeople with the ultimate respect. Companies that poorly treat their sales force close doors.
- As a leader, show appreciation and gratitude to your people. You will gain their commitment, understanding and loyalty.
- Connect and communicate with your employees regularly. Leaders who show their humanity, vulnerability, and candor command respect and allegiance from their employees.
- Be willing to serve others, but don't forget to have fun while working hard. Work is joy when people's minds and spirits are aligned behind the same purpose.

PART IV: CRITICAL CORPORATE SUCCESS FACTOR

"People are the ultimate competitive advantage in any organization. Healthy organization culture has the transformative power and synergy to turn poor strategies into success. Employers have a moral obligation to invest in their people's social, financial, personal and professional development to create a harmonious environment where employees look forward to coming to work and contribute every day. Healthy organization culture has the transformative power and synergy to turn poor strategies into success. " – Anthony Chaine

"Customers will never love a company until the employees love it first." — Simon Sinek

"I think a large part of that is the fact that I'm a large believer in hiring the right people and giving them unbelievable amounts of power and autonomy." — Blake Mycoskie

CHAPTER NINETEEN: SALES CULTURE AND HIGH PERFORMANCE

Many sales leaders are still discussing how to get the highest level of performance from their teams. Sales culture efficiency and effectiveness stands at the heart of the matter. Great sales leaders strive to create a positive sales culture that promotes learning, growth, development, sustained high performance, and execution as well as internal harmony.

What Is Sales Culture?

Sales culture has been a buzzword in the corporate space for decades. Many define it as a mix of values, beliefs, and behaviors developed internally over a period; some describe it as the personality of the organization or its core DNA.

Sales culture reflects how teams are built and developed and how business gets accomplished; it's the set of behaviors that drive daily operations. It comprises, but is not limited to, how people interact with one another, how decisions and expectations get communicated, what gets rewarded, and how rewards are disseminated.

Sales Culture Drives Organizational Behaviors and Results.

Ultimately, it's the system that connects people and resources to create sustained value. People are wired differently and they get motivated differently. Money motivates some people, others are driven by recognition and opportunities. Sales leaders' understanding of what motivates their salespeople is vital to performance, as unmotivated sales reps often generate dreadful performances.

According to The Gallup organization's research, the salesperson's direct sales manager influences 80% of salespeople's perception of a company. The sales VP or even the CEO has little impact on the sales culture because salespeople view their impact only through the prism of their direct sales managers. When a salesperson joins a sales organization, they will report to a single manager.

Gallup found that 70% of the top producers who left their company did so because of a breakdown in their relationship with their direct sales manager. Conversely, behind every single sales star, you find a great sales manager in the shadows.

A Columbia University study demonstrated that organizations with healthy sales culture experienced a mere 13.9% job turnover, while job turnover in companies with poor sales culture averaged 48.4%.

Another study conducted by The Department of Economics at the University of Warwick found that happy employees were 12% more productive than average workers, and unhappy workers were 10% less productive, costing the American businesses more than $300 billion each year.

A statistic from New Century Financial Corporation reflects that non-engaged, unhappy account executives at a banking company produced 28% less than those who were engaged. Conversely, happy employees outperformed the competition by 20%, earned 2.1% above industry benchmarks and managed to solve difficult problems much faster.

Sales Culture and Organizational Strategy Disconnect

A favorable sales culture enhances the sales organization opportunity cost, improves sales reps' effectiveness (doing the right things) and efficiency (doing things right) as clarified by Peter Drucker.

Sales efficiency initiatives, like CRM, training, and KPI dashboards empower salespeople to do their job better. While sales effectiveness optimizes decisions, such as customer selection, high-value customers targeting and alignment of sales tasks with organizational strategy, it's a trajectory or roadmap to progress.

Executive management can develop the foundation upon which the sales culture can flourish. According to a survey of 1,800 executives, 53% of the respondents said their employees don't understand their company's strategy. The reality is that corporate strategic goals are the aggregate results of multiple individual business units' goals. Most work independently and hope the results will fit within the organization's go-to-market strategy.

Furthermore, corporate strategic planning is often disconnected from frontline decision-making, as well as customer buying processes, which creates constant friction and frustration at all levels. Executive management feel they are not understood, while frontline management feel alienated from the decision process.

Fundamentally, all opportunities are not equal, and smart sales organizations target specific verticals within specific market niches. The organization evaluate each opportunities by taking into consideration the cost to serve, order volume, profit margin, delivery logistics, and other critical driving KPIs.

Sales Culture and Profit

Companies who do not specialize force their sales reps to suppress margin to compete and win over slim to unprofitable deals. It's naïve to expect salespeople to follow company strategy without a deliberate effort from the executive management team to align sales objectives with the company's overall strategic goals.

Positive sales culture can make the difference between having a holistic, successful business or an operationally segregated struggling multi-unit divisions. Vibrant work sales culture allow talented individuals to work synergistically to elevate the company performance.

Negative sales culture creates toxic environments that lack structure, discipline, and operational flexibility. Some of the signs of negative sales culture include low employee morale, high turnover, lack of trust and resentment towards sales leadership, lack of synergy and excitement and a total absence of interest in camaraderie between employees and leadership.

How to Build a Positive Corporate Sales Culture.

Hire right the first time. Despite high turnover, it is wise to take the time to hire the best talent you can afford. Great talent attracts similar likeminded individuals. Do not settle for average performers; think long-term. You can contribute to the betterment of your sales culture, or you can undermine your intent.

All new hires need to have the required characteristics that will allow them to succeed within the company. Nothing is more destructive than hiring under-performers that do not fit the job description or requirements.

Proper sales culture maintenance requires hiring only top talent individuals consistently. Great performers love to work with peers who are just as good to stretch and push performance boundaries. A-players like to work and compete alongside similar competent peers.

Celebrate Successes and Learn from Failures. Healthy sales culture requires celebrating wins and acknowledging defeats to learn.

When a team works hard and achieve specific goals, you should recognize the collective team efforts and celebrate their victory. Success attainment propels salespeople to strive to recreate the same emotions by winning frequently.

Never shy away from celebrating joint victories. Never berate the team when they miss their goals. Look at it objectively as it happens to the best of the best. Missing the goal can be a learning moment, so extract a lesson from it, discuss it, and move on.

You will experience new challenges, and you need a team that is cohesive, supportive, interdependent and shares positive feedback and encouragement. You will also, need to keep your salespeople enthusiastically focused on their goal attainment. By helping one another, removing obstacles and simplifying the process. Life and work are meant to be celebrated with the people you lead and care for every day.

Manage Activity and Results. Managing both action and results is imperative. Activity drives results, the latter creates momentum, revenue, and employee satisfaction.

We all know that sales is a numbers game. The outcome of the game changes according to the exerted intensity and the deliberate effort that goes into finding qualified prospects and turning them from unsold prospects to sold customers.

Focus and intensity create results. No amount of activity or hard work can predict an exact outcome. However, there is a definite correlation between effort equity and results. The proper sales process can create predictable wins.

Enhance Morale and Self-Esteem. The sales profession is hard; the number of rejections that a salesperson receives daily will erode the confidence of the most resilient sales reps. The sales manager can create a counterbalance by uplifting morale and motivating the team with words, actions and incentives.

Your salespeople should understand that they are creators of revenue, the pioneers of all relationships, and the plasma that connects the organization and its customers. Hence, salespeople work, and contributions should be glorified and appreciated. The organization derives significant value from its salespeople. As a matter of fact, it owns its existence to them—no sales, means no revenue, hence no company. Therefore, top sales producers should be put on a higher pedestal to entice others to emulate their behaviors to achieve similar success.

Recognition is Everything. People work for money, recognition, and being part of something greater than themselves. Most sales organizations reward their salespeople with bonuses and prizes for attaining lofty objectives. Conversely, many fail to create smaller and attainable incentives that promote morale in pursuit of more significant awards and bonuses.

Based on progress, most salespeople can mentally calculate their probability quota attainment. Many give up the quest when the likelihood of goal realization is low. Celebrating the attainment of smaller, benchmarks along the way will keep everyone excited and focused to on the achievement of loftier goals.

Educational Empowerment

Empowering your salespeople with the right level of training and coaching can prepare them to win sales battles. Healthy sales cultures have processes and systems that promote on-the-job employee development. These growth platforms build employee loyalty and create a culture of ongoing education.

Training can take shape online, in a class setting, or in a one-on-one environment. However, the best training courses are when you get your sales team to collaborate and share ideas and proven best practices with one another. Education in the workplace matters and an ongoing employee development process is vital to meet innovation acceleration and increasingly complex customer demand.

Fostering an environment that endorses continued learning will improve business growth, reduce turnover, promote employee job satisfaction, and will ultimately cascade down to enhance customer satisfaction.

Healthy Corporate Cultures Benefits

Positive sales culture is like an invisible magnetic field that attracts everyone towards it. It's almost like a hidden glue that bonds people marching in the same direction. At its core, it's the DNA of the organization where people are engaged in fulfilling the company vision, mission and core values through a system that encourages performance, transparency and accountability. And where upward mobility is based on character, capabilities and merit.

Healthy Sales Culture Promotes Learning

In a healthy sales culture, mistakes are accepted as part of the learning process. Excellent company culture encourages creativity and innovations by supporting employees ideas and concepts, even when they seem far-fetched. When employees feel valued and respected, their productivity, and imagination skyrockets and the company benefit from having a healthy, vibrant environment that promotes growth.

CHAPTER 19: SUMMARY

- Positive sales culture promotes growth and sustained high-performance.
- Sales culture is the DNA of your organization. It reflects who you are, what you believe in, and what you stand for to accomplish your purpose.
- Companies with healthy sales cultures experience higher employee satisfaction rates and higher retention rates than their peers in the industry.
- Sales organizations with healthy sales culture, enjoy better employee engagement, higher loyalty, attract better talent, retain customers longer and are more profitable. Happy employees tend to sell more complete business solutions that benefit their customers and their company.

CHAPTER TWENTY: HEALTHY SALES ORGANIZATION DNA

Organizational culture is the personality and the DNA of any organization; it's the aggregate sum of the organization's values, norms, expectations, and history. Healthy sales culture promotes company growth, innovation, creativity, and employee happiness.

In the B2B sales space, you depend on your sales rep's job satisfaction and ability to create revenue, promote your company mission, brand, products, and services — however, only a few companies put in sincere effort measuring employee satisfaction and happiness. Revenue can be easily tracked and measured, but it's harder to evaluate a salesperson's belief in the company values and mission or their excitement level towards their work, and their willingness to promote the company vision and social responsibilities investments.

Healthy corporate culture has employees who are happy about their work because they feel they are part of an organization that supports its employees' growth by promoting team-work, learning on the job, friendship, and fun.

Employees love to work in an environment where they consider their coworkers and management team as a second family. Healthy corporate culture requires transparency, uniformity, and a clear mission statement and value that are congruent across the board. The company should provide the same level of care to its customers, shareholders, and employees.

A good example is Southwest Airlines and the Walt Disney Company. Chevron promotes 'the Chevron way', which consists of practicing safety first, being supportive, and always looking out for your team members.

Japanese companies invest tremendous resources in training staff to care exceptionally well for their customers and assure quality service every time. Good corporate culture is not accidental; it requires planning, training, and constant improvement. In the airlines industry, ANA Airlines ranks consistently among the world's top rated airlines. Japanese and business travelers prefer to pay more and fly ANA than opt for cheaper competitors.

Japanese employees go above and beyond across industries to provide excellent service. They take enormous pride doing their job to the best of their ability, knowing that they help their company to serve the community and grow and prosper. Additionally, Japanese companies invest in training their employees while ensuring safety and career stability. It's common in the Japanese corporate culture that employees consider their co-workers like a real family and share a strong sense of bonding and team spirit. Many employees see the company and their co-workers as a central force and balance in their life.

Fanatic Brand Ambassadors

Salespeople who believe in their company's mission often create more loyal customers than what the marketing department could ever achieve. A believer is a passionate, tenacious person who radiates confidence and comes off as credible and trustworthy. Your B2B salespeople have a considerable influence over the businesses they interact with. A salesperson who profoundly believes in the company's mission is a powerful promotional tool that promotes the company values, vision, and mission along with its business solutions that improve these business' lives. Positive growth-driven sales cultures turn every employee into a walking, talking marketing billboard that promotes the company to the community and society.

Employees Creativity

Happy, empowered employees who work for a company that fosters a healthy sales cultures take it on them to find solutions to challenges.

In a survey released in July 2010, IBM asked more than 1,500 global CEOs the following question: What are the essential skills for success in today's world? 60% stated that creativity was a necessary quality over the next five years.

Creativity is the power source behind new ideas and innovation. Creative minds create new products and improve on existing products, services, and ideas. Creativity is a valuable and desired characteristic of employees.

Yet in B2B, creativity is often suppressed by executive leaders who spend years working within a structured traditional system that focuses on rewarding salespeople for reaching specific objectives.

Creativity is often left to the R&D or marketing folks. Salespeople are not perceived as creative people in general. But they are incredibly creative, finding gaps and ways to take advantages of these gaps. For example, I witnessed salespeople taking advantages of gaps in the company compensation plan, pricing structures, business solution bundles, and competitors' errors.

Salespeople can be extremely smart and creative to overcome obstacles. But most companies pay them for their work and not so much for their creativity, which can be had for free.

Encouraging open creativity while providing some incentive to the sales force can promote new ideas, initiatives, and innovations that will yield creative efforts and better results.

Employees Happiness

According to a *Harvard Business Review* study, happy employees outperform their competitors more than 20%. Additionally, their job performance exceeded industry standards by 2.1%. Happy employees increase company value and profit by retaining existing clients and acquiring new ones at a much faster rate than the employees who are just doing it for the money.

Happy Employees Are More:

1. Productive and responsible
2. Healthy and active
3. Profitable and work more extended hours with no absenteeism
4. Creative and innovative

How to Increase Your Employee's Happiness Factor?

- Celebrate individuals and team wins often
- Establish activities that increase team cohesiveness
- Promote people based on merit and often
- Demonstrate the value and impact of their work.

Happiness takes a collective effort to improve job satisfaction and mental satisfaction. Positive corporate or organizational culture has a direct impact on revenue, employee satisfaction, and retention.

CHAPTER 20: SUMMARY

- It's harder to evaluate a salesperson's belief in the company values and mission.
- Measuring your employee job satisfaction is difficult. It's the aura in the air that tells you how people feel, work, and interact. Survey data and interviews may not always reflect the truth.
- Good corporate culture is not accidental; it requires planning, training, and constant improvement.
- Happy employees outperform their competitors, increase company value and profit, and generate loyal repeat buying customers.

CHAPTER TWENTY-ONE: SALES CULTURE AND REVENUE CORRELATION

A direct correlation exists between sales culture and revenue generation. Sales output require the right tool-set and resources. When senior executives value sales, sales culture flourish, employee morale goes up, and their synergy propels revenue creation. Sales culture is built from the top-down, not the bottom-up. Leaders who are pro-sales drive the whole organization towards revenue generation and profit single-mindedness.

Sales culture requires that the company's leaders sell their vision consistently and empower all managers to drive its fundamentals across the organization. Allocation of resources is necessary to ensure adoption and conformity across the branches of the organization. Leaders should celebrate progress, study setbacks, and coach the short-term and long-term benefits behind the company strategy and vision. Winning paths need to be identified; obstacles need to be cleared, and issues need to be addressed.

Everyone Should Understand the Why Behind the Vision.

No one should be allowed to sabotage the sales culture. Everyone should understand that the survival of the organization depends on revenue creation, brand perception, and client relationships. The goal of the organization should be to improve its employees, clients and shareholders lives. Finally, a sales culture should be built on rewarding the right behaviors and achievements. They both matter equally we often reward performance while ignoring behaviors, yet behaviors matter as much as achievements because of the essence of a healthy sales culture.

The success and longevity of healthy sales culture depends on the leader's teaching style, level of engagement, belief, and mental influence. Top leaders must work hard to transfer their belief to become the organization common belief. It takes enormous effort to turn the company purpose and vision into core principles that all employee believe in.

Faithful leaders will spread their cultural belief throughout the organization ranks. Over time, it will change the mental wiring of the organization and how employees communicate with one another. Just like in the military, the core belief are set at the very top, and there is an unwavering understanding that these fundamental are the accepted norms, and there is no deviation to its tenet. That rigidity becomes the culture. One beliefs, cannot change the core belief of the military regardless of rank.

Sales Culture Require Empathy and Strength of Mind

Sales culture change and evolution generally start at the very top, often at the CEO level. The CEO has the power to align people and bring them together around a joint mission and standard set of values. The larger the organization, the more critical the alignment of everyone behind the company sales culture. The CEO must ensure that the sales culture conformity and uniformity span across the whole organization. Allowing deviations will erode the sales culture and will start allowing exceptions to be made, which in the long run will dilute the sales culture fundamentals. Strong work cultures create revenue, improve innovation, and serve the company, its employees, and shareholders well.

Sales culture is like a good reputation; it takes time to build but is easy to destroy. CEOs must work hard to protect their organization work culture, as it is just like currency, it can appreciate and depreciate as well.

I saw a CEO of a Fortune 500 company, who spent his entire life in banking, coming onstage and start lecturing many lifelong sales professionals on how to sell. He explained that he believes that selling is easy and that he cannot understand why professional salespeople cannot sell better, faster, and at higher margins. He honestly thought he knew it all. Sales reps were listening and thinking how ignorant he must have been, and how full of ego he was. Being an executive financial banker doesn't mean that you are a great salesperson. A little research revealed that the same CEO suffered in his previous job from high turnover, low employee morale, low conversion rates, massive customer dissatisfaction, and high leadership attrition.

The CEO must wear many hats to maintain the organization's growth. Sales culture is a total experience that defines the organization purpose and ensures its long-term health.

CHAPTER 21: SUMMARY

- Leaders drive vision and behavior changes. Sales culture is fundamentally built from the top-down, not the bottom-up.
- A sales culture that is not perceived by every employee as a way of life and a core evolutionary proces will fizzle and die.
- Deliberate effort is required by senior leaderships to ensure adherence to the company sales culture. No deviation or short cuts should be tolerated.
- Strong sales culture brings people together to accomplish a worthy purpose that all employees believes in.

CHAPTER TWENTY-TWO: SALES CULTURE UNWRITTEN GUIDELINES

Every sales force, every sales organization, and every sales team has a unique personality, a distinctive fingerprint, approach, and method. This personality is what defines a sales culture. Sales culture is the undefined, unwritten sales guidelines that form salespeople and sales management behaviors based on a set of beliefs often prescribed by senior executives.

Great sales cultures are a set of unwritten behavioral guidelines that govern everyone. They are often unrecorded and undefined because they encompass ethics, emotions, behaviors, decisions making, preconceived assumptions and belief. Great work cultures tolerate, mistakes and errors of judgment, failed well intentioned initiatives do not get reprimanded and penalized.

Great cultures have top performers voluntarily teaching their peers on best practices to allow them to win, make money, and stay on the job. Happy employees do not leave their leaders or their companies; they are delighted to show up, work hard, and make a difference. Great cultures promote mostly from within giving anyone a chance for upward mobility and leadership access. They pay well for exceptional performance and above fair market value to keep their employees happy. Great cultures are all about corporate harmony, employee retention and satisfaction, and exponential growth to invest in their employee innovation and long-term growth.

Sales culture must be defined and reinforced from the top of the organization. Every employee should be trusted and empowered to make the right decision to advance the company goals. While culture is a set of unwritten guidelines, it helps to articulate a framework of fundamental behaviors that should drive these expected actions.

Sales leaders should evaluate the company sales culture by asking the following questions.

1. What is the overall organizational sentiment toward salespeople and the sales department?
2. What is the predominant shared mental state of salespeople and sales managers?
3. What is the predominant shared customer feedback toward our salespeople?
4. Can your salespeople collectively articulate your culture shared values?
5. What is the level of variance in terms of shared value among different sales teams?
6. What's the level of tolerance allowing individual initiative to drive sales culture fundamentals?
7. What's the general attitude towards the flexibility of the sales culture?

Sales Cultures That Yield Joy

Many years ago, I worked for Jerome Tacobi, a fast-moving sales organization. Jerome understood the fundamentals of sales, and he was a masterful empowering chief executive officer (CEO). He watched closely salespeople's performances, got involved to learn, approved things quickly, got personally involved in aiding and advancing major deals. He was humble and loved to lead from the front. He also knew when not to get involved, when to play the helper instead of the chief. He coached and trained, but he was just as good a student, absorbing new methods and putting them immediately into practices. He was not afraid to make mistakes and encouraged everyone to make mistakes to learn. He encouraged creativity and wild thinking; nothing was impossible for him and his employees. His employees loved him, goofed around with him, and enjoyed coming to work, because for many, work was joy.

The sales culture was healthy, vibrant, and joyful, but focused on revenue generation. Salespeople and sales managers came early to work and often left late by choice; every employee was proactively looking for opportunities to make more money for the company and support their peers. Jerome created a sales culture that encouraged creativity, shared responsibility and success. Jerome had everyone's back, and every salesperson felt they were making a difference, they were valued and appreciated. He knew how to push everyone to the limit, and he loved to stretch people to do what was accepted as impossible.

People went above and beyond and delivered incredible results, knowing they would be celebrated for a while, until someone else dethroned them. Commissions were based on gross margins, forcing people to do what was right for the company. Not just giving away the margin to ensure a quick sale, salespeople were leveraging selling value to justify the price. Everyone was focused on selling value with a sense of urgency and vigor. It was an intense, competitive environment, but it was also a friendly, loving, and caring place. The extra efforts created incredible growth, huge brand recognition, and happy customers, as these happy employees made every customer feel golden.

Additionally, Jerome was a chief surprise officer; he loved to surprise his employees by being involved in their lives, like the time he helped a financially-struggling employee pay for his kid's bar-mitzvah or the time he paid one year's rent to help a sick employee, or the all-expenses-paid family vacation for four to Italy to thank an employee for going above and beyond to help other employees. He was listening and doing things that most CEOs would not care to do. Like the time when he paid out of his pocket for the surgery an employee needed but couldn't afford, or the time when he bought a car for an employee that has his car stolen and couldn't afford another one.

The Leader Sets the Tone

Alternatively, I worked for a similar business within the same industry. The products and services were almost the same; the location was only a few blocks away, same demographics, same buying power. The only difference was the CEO. Steve, was reserved, controlling, disengaged, stubborn, disrespectful and often spoiled the sale. There was no sales culture, as everything was subject to his mood. His salespeople felt undervalued, underappreciated, and were often subjected to ridicule. His sales managers, while unhappy, were mirroring his behaviors by belittling their salespeople and making fun of their performance. There was a wall between management and salespeople.

The only reason salespeople stuck around was that the company paid above average to keep them onboard. There were no top performers, and no one could make any decisions at all. Even the smallest decisions required Steve's approval; failure to do so would expose everyone to his wrath. This was a well-financed company with incredible potential. However, having blind, clueless CEO with poor perspective and careless attitude created a common sales culture where the best salespeople and sales managers fled, and customers had to deal with regularly with new faces.

The above true stories reflect how leadership can create a sales culture where employee thrives or cannot wait to run away.

As a sales professional, consultant, and sales leader, I saw multiple organizations that promoted sales professionals the right way, by creating thriving work cultures where employees are well-compensated, encouraged to pursue higher education, and get involved in exciting projects. I also witnessed poor leadership, antagonistic sales cultures within Fortune 200 companies where sales professionals were blamed for everything. Despite corporate investments on innovative products, services, and partnerships, the results continued to reflect paltry gains, because dissatisfied and underappreciated employees produce the minimum to keep the job, but not enough to improve the company financial standing.

The CEO with a background in finance and banking surrounded himself with prior colleagues that thought alike, and viewed sales reps as a bunch of disposable organisms that should execute the strategy as told. The same CEO was a huge advocate to lower the commission structure of salespeople every year. Finance people found creative ways to tweak salespeople's compensation making it hard to understand or even explain. I witnessed not long ago five regional vice presidents trying to explain the new comp plan that was dropped into their lap on a late Friday.

They had to read a fifty-pages puzzle, understand it, and discuss it among themselves on Sunday as they had to present it on Monday (The compensation plan for the given year was provided end of February, effective retroactively January first). The VP's job requires to put a positive twist on everything to ensure that they wouldn't lose top performers. The plan was horrible, and it was worse than the year before, these VPs were struggling to explain it because they didn't understand it as well. On several instances, their logic differed from the analyst logic, it was total chaos, no one understood the compensation plan, but everyone was urged just to adopt it.

The head of sales who was part of this plan discussion all along didn't say a word, deferring to his VPs and expecting them to convince

800 salespersons that this plan was the best they ever had. The CEO and his top executives were getting a larger bonus every year, but they were pushing their sales force towards the poor house every year. Most of these sales executives felt that they should put a cap on salespeople's commissions. Yet, they were asking all employees to do much more, with fewer resources. These executives had no real of salespeople challenges, yet they acted like they knew how to run a sales organization to profitability without lifting a finger.

Signs of Great Culture

I recall my first interview day with a mid-sized B2B company. Nat Mosery was the CEO of the organization, and his brother Steve was the president. After a one-hour conversation, I felt that Nat was welcoming, friendly more knowledgeable and overall more professional. Steve was quite the opposite in every way, unsure, mean, demeaning, fiery, and harsh in his observations.

Nat managed the day-to-day operations as well as sales. The sales culture that Nat had created was positively infectious, there was an air of freedom, creativity, acceptance, tolerance, and casualness among salespeople and sales managers. Everyone worked hard; everyone was razor-focused on advancing the company agenda, closing deals, and stretching above and beyond while providing excellent customer experience. Nat was funny, he told jokes, encouraged productivity, and pushed people because he genuinely believed they could make miracles happen. He provided the necessary resources and moral support.

He was brutally honest, composed, and knew how to affect positively salespeople's minds and hearts. He understood that the job was a home from home, so he ensured that people were comfortable and happy while at work.

Nat had an open communication system, and he was a good listener; he understood and empathized with his people. He was willing to listen to everyone about everything and was always there to help. His salespeople and sales managers would have done anything for him. He was an outstanding leader, not because of his title, but because of who he was. Performance reviews were honest, direct, and helpful. Sales managers provided feedback with steps on how to improve. Great performers were glorified; they often spoke during conference calls and in front of their peers and management team sharing their best practices, unique experiences, and the know-how that generated radical repeated result improvement.

Nat celebrated monthly top performers on multiple critical categories; he celebrated great performance, every month and every quarter and he loved to celebrate the twice a year president club achievers event. People loved the culture he created, and everyone wants to be recognized as a winner. Nat sent the high winner's family on an all-expenses-paid vacation every quarter. This action alone created a frenzy, as these competitive salespeople wanted to win to have a chance to show to their families how great the company they worked for.

Nat was willing to pay great rewards for high production, and he was happy to hand-deliver the check. He often gave his employees hugs and thanked them along with the check. The sales managers reflected Nat's behaviors. He cared, and he understood that high production was directly related to people's states of mind. Nat was always encouraging people's creativity, flexibility, and spontaneity. He was customer-focused, goal-oriented, and result-focused.

Nat was a great at touching people's hearts and minds, and people delivered every day; the company prospered. The clients were thrilled with the service and attention given by everyone. People knew their salespeople by name and knew their managers as well. The level of transparency was incredible, testimonials flooded the company website, and people trusted the sales culture to the point where sales became easier. The company's brand was supported by an extensive web of employees empowered and willing to do what was right for its customers every time.

Unfortunately, Nat lost his life in an avalanche in the Alpes, and his brother Steve took over sales and operations. Within less than two years, this growing, ascending, and flourishing company went bankrupt. Nat built the company and took it from a startup to great statues, and Steve took it from great to oblivion. Steve's views of sales culture were that you are paid to do a job: get it done, and you will get paid. He eliminated recognitions days, family quarterly reward trips, and president club events. He lowered compensation to meet market targets, and he didn't permit the smooth flow of communication. Work became mechanical, controlled, inflexible, and followed specific orders. Steve avoided meetings and canceled yearly company events.

Sales morale collapsed quickly, and sales managers had to embrace the new sales cultures to keep their jobs. Customers deserted in droves as their salespeople were no longer supported to make any decisions. Revenue vanished, debts increased. Steve blamed people's incompetence, the economy, the bank and even customers. At no time did he ever point his finger inwards, he was incapable of recognizing that he was an incompetent leader.

The top leadership often defines organizational sales cultures. If a company does not have an established sales culture, it will allow everyone to fill in the void. Sales managers and salespeople will determine their own. Absence of sales culture creates havoc within an organization as it deprives it of a cohesive, unifying business model and vision. Salespeople, faced with a tough decision, will refer to what's best for them instead of what's best for the client and company.

The sales manager's feedback is often tied to the sales culture he operate within. Appropriate choices are made based on the sales culture the company wants to portray and encourage. Strong sales culture provides clear guidance based on preset norms and values. All sales cultures are based on standards and values. Norm describes how a salesperson should behave when faced with a choice, while values should explain how a salesperson would want to act when faced with a decision. The value should be supported by management's actions to ensure conformity.

The sales force decisions, if supported by sales management, can affect results. Cultures may encourage teamwork or individualism, and it can be emphatic or cutthroat.

CHAPTER 22: SUMMARY

- Sales culture is the undefined, unwritten sales guidelines that guide employees to live by a set of beliefs embraced by senior executives.
- Healthy sales culture encourages employee decision-making and accepts mistakes as a way of learning and growth.
- Employees are empowered to do what's right, and errors of judgment are never penalized nor frowned upon.
- Good sales culture encourages creativity, innovation, and spontaneity in decision-making to create an ideal outcome.
- Good leadership is a requirement to create and maintain a healthy sales culture. Poor leadership can quickly destroy a great sales culture that took years to build.

CHAPTER TWENTY-THREE: BUSINESS ETHICS AND CORPORATE REPUTATION

The Sarbanes-Oxley Act's purpose was to restore public trust by promoting ethical business practices, internal communication, and corporate financial transparency.

Salespeople must meet customers' expectations along with the employer's expectations. In the process, even the most experienced salesperson struggles when facing complex ethical dilemmas where a decision needs to be made quickly with little or no guidance from knowledgeable sources.

Salespeople often feel like warriors in a battle that has an uncertain outcome. The competitive nature of the profession, coupled with the pressure to meet sales objectives, can lead some salespeople or managers to engage in unethical behaviors that can damage the company's brand, expose the company to legal challenges, and lead to loss of customer loyalty.

In the same industries, unethical practices are almost expected. A customer buying a used car from a local dealer that has a questionable reputation online would probably be suspicious of the salesperson assisting him with the purchase. The customer may be guarded to protect himself against any attempt by the salesperson to inflate the price or be sold a lemon. The salesperson may be honest; however, the unethical dealer reputation will overshadow the ethical sales reps best attempts.

Unethical behaviors and shady sales practices should not be allowed. As a sales manager, you should reinforce the fact that you will not tolerate any deviation from ethical behavior even when temptations are high and risks are low. No deal is worth losing your job over or putting at risk the company's reputation. Ethical team's performances are paramount in the pursuit of one's sales objectives.

Following the organization's code of ethics is critical to win business, cement the company's good reputation, and improve customers trust and retention. Several studies have shown that committed salespeople are less likely to commit unethical sales practices.

Sales Ethics is Good Business

Marketing, advertising, and sales professionals tend to rank at the bottom of the ethical ladder. Most large organizations offer a once-a-year mandatory online ethical course and many have some form of a written code of conduct that the salesperson is required to sign-in to validate that the company did its part. However, organizations rarely promote or speak about good ethical behaviors throughout the year. Understanding the purpose and value of good work ethics is a foundation for a successful career free of wrongdoing and full of accomplishment.

Code of Ethic Example.

1. Maintain the highest standards of integrity in all business affairs.
2. Provide your customers with a great buying experience by doing the right thing every time.
3. Use company best practices and make the right decisions that benefit your customers and the company.

4. Follow the organization code of ethics along with the laws that govern your business.

The above Sales Code of Conduct is a sample example. However, unless senior managers and line managers live by its principles, people under pressure will deviate from it for personal gain.

Being ethical in any profession means that you do what you believe is right while serving your company code of conduct, following company policy, and your moral belief. In the absence of organization guidance, follow your mental and heart guidance. When your decision has a major impact on the organization or the customer's business, don't rush your decisions making despite temptations. Tell the concerned party that you will do your research and find the best course of action based on the company policy and code of ethics and you will get back to them as soon as possible.

Several years ago, I was driving on my way to a meeting held in Greenwich, Connecticut. Suddenly, my car started making rattling noises, concerned I took the first exit and went to the first small mechanic garage I could find. The mechanic opened the hood of the car and looked at the car for about five minutes. "Mercedes parts are expensive, and your car seems to have a major engine problem. Repairs will take about three hours, parts and labor will cost you $2,500. By the way, my credit card system is down, but you can get cash from a bank four blocks up the street

I was flabbergasted by the amount he asked for based on his shallow observations. My car was only two years old, so I told him that I would think about it, and I needed to go to my preferred bank to avoid paying any additional fees.

"Leave your car here, It won't run for another mile, and if we have to tow it back to the garage, that will be another $500. My apprentice can take you to your bank to withdraw the money," he added.

I became alarmed, and felt somewhat pressured by a mechanic that sounded more like a crook. So, I took my chances, knowing that my two-year-old car could stop any minute (I know very little about car mechanics). Using my GPS, I drove to the Mercedes-Benz of Greenwich dealership service center. The mechanic checked the car thoroughly and stated that it was a negligible issue. I was out of the dealer repair center within less than 10 minutes, and my total cost was zero dollars.

The point of the story is that ethics matters. Years have passed, and I've never stopped talking about this unethical mechanic's behavior. If his business was listed online, I would have written my story on social media and given him a bad review, which would have affected his business reputation negatively for many years. This encounter with an unethical mechanic made me extra cautious dealing with any mechanic garage. "one bad apple spoil the whole bunch." is an old adage, but very true, one person lack of ethic can affect many honest, hardworking professionals.

Customer Needs Come First

Quota achievement is vital for all organizations, teams, and individuals, but how it's achieved is even more critical than the attainment of the goal. Your salespeople should put the customer's interest ahead of their gains. Customers hate being ripped off or overcharged. Using social media, a customer who is subjected to unethical behavior can affect the vendor reputation in the market with a message that may be read online by thousands of potential future buyers. Negative online reviews can damage the company reputation, cost major loses in term of opportunity cost and speed up the loss of loyal customer lifetime value.

Account managers do not necessarily understand the complexity of ethics and governance as much as they know the sales process. Large corporate accounts, government, state, and municipalities are often assigned compliance and legal folks to assist with ethical matters. An organization known to successfully handle ethical complexity tends to have a competitive advantage over their competitors. Higher ethical standards and professionalism leads to great performance, promote brand recognition and repute.

Impact of Good Ethics

Corporations and businesses that enjoy a favorable reputation attract the best talent and shareholders and have higher customer loyalty. Companies with an excellent reputation such as Microsoft, Google and Apple find it easier to attract the world's best talent, devoted customers and investors. A good reputation takes years to build, but it takes very little to destroy it. Ethic is the cloak that protect reputation, the thicker it is the better.

Throughout my sales career, I witnessed several ethical dilemmas that cost company's money, loss of trustworthiness, and destroyed good relationships with customers and partners which triggered new policies to prevent reoccurrence.

Disgruntled, unethical, desperate or merely unaware salespeople can create issues that could be massively damaging to the organization. A good sales manager should watch for these signs to prevent harmful consequences. For example, soon after the termination of an underperforming employee, the company discovered that the salesperson submitted several contracts where he forged clients' signatures. Luckily, the company had a robust system that validated each submitted contract before it billed its customers. This kind of unethical behavior can have severe and lasting damages to a company.

I experienced a situation where a sizeable B2B company went through a draconian company restructuring, where most of its legal and compliance folks were forced to take compensation packages or get terminated.

Overnight, salespeople and sales managers found themselves having to deal with sensitive, complex documents and contracts primarily handled by legal folks. Tons of aberrations and wrong estimations occurred, causing employees' frustrations and anxieties, and forcing the company to seek external help to manage this complex area. The inaccuracy that occurred during this period may have appeared unethical, but they were honest errors committed by untrained employees.

As sales managers, you can have an impact in forging your salespeople's character by discouraging deviant behavior and wrongdoing. You can also raise your salespeople's awareness to embrace organizational standards that encourage honesty, integrity, professionalism, corporate responsibility, and good citizenship

Addressing Challenging Behavior

We have witnessed recent corporate unethical behavioral events affecting large companies such as the Volkswagen diesel scandal, Wells-Fargo having to pay $185 million in fines, and Mylan's Epi-pen life-saving drug prices soaring to unrealistic levels. These scandals affected CEO's and low ranking employees.

Strengthening corporate culture ensures that employees are committed to their job and careers. Good corporate culture prevent unethical employees from taking advantage of system gaps to enrich themselves by cheating the company, its customers, and investors. Good organizational cultures require placing the right processes and guidelines that define and encourage accountability and good governance.

Having an equitable compensation system can spur productivity and motivate people. For example, a B2B manufacture had a compensation plan that rewarded its sales force for achieving their monthly goals but didn't incentivize salespeople who exceeded their quota month after month, which led to top producers stopping from putting extra efforts due to lack of incentives.

Another sales organization paid its sales force for their submitted car mileage without question. Many underperforming salespeople were grossly inflating their monthly mileage log. Once the company implemented a GPS system that tracked individual salespeople's driving itineraries, underperforming salespeople mileage expenses dropped by almost half, while performing salespeople stayed virtually the same.

Corporates' obsessive focus on short-term goals can lead to dangerous behaviors. Most sales managers will not question dubious extraordinary performance if they benefit from them to achieve their bonus and presidential club status. There is no motivation to challenge someone's ambiguous performances especially when the rest of the team is struggling.

Unethical behaviors are often driven by fear and desire to achieve status or financial objectives. Some industries have a high propensity to embrace low integrity comportments in a highly transactional and competitive environments. Multinational salespeople often operate in environments and countries where questionable and unethical behaviors tend to be rampant.

Variable Compensation

Industries operating in a high-risk environment should compensate their salespeople for cultivating ethical relationships with ethical companies, a process that takes years sometimes to establish. Hence, the compensation plan variable should be relationship-based rather than performance-based. Conversely, performance-based compensation plans work best in markets and countries that operate similarly to the American standards.

Fair Compensation and Integrity

In the payment industry, Merchant Services have huge employee turnover, primarily due to false expectations and incorrect promises. Many of these companies hire 100% commission-only salespeople, promising them a lifetime residual commission income on their signed accounts or the ability to sell their whole portfolio for a specific multiplier and get a lump sum once vested.

Many employees are lured by this idea of securing an income for life. However, most of these companies resort to deceitful behaviors once these employee acquired a substantial residual income, many lawsuits had revealed that these companies terminated these sales reps based on questionable reasons or simply stopped paying them once they voluntarily left the company. Scores of hard-working salespeople have been cheated and discarded after years of hard loyal service.

I'm not against a 100% commission structure, as long as any hard-working salesperson can make an acceptable living, but I'm against companies and managers that make false promises to lure in talent, but fail to live up to their promises. Providing a base salary to cover someone's living necessities is a good retention approach, and variable compensation should be adequate to motivate people to perform with integrity and vigor. "Eat what you kill" compensation methods encourage unethical behaviors, especial in tough economies and when the product or service perceived value and utility is substandard.

Selling with integrity requires salespeople to build trusted rapport and relationships with their customers. Winners sell with integrity and never cheat even in difficult times. Connecting with customers at a deeper level takes time, effort, and energy, but it builds satisfied profitable relationships and loyal customers. The practice of "Eat what you kill" encourages bad behaviors even in the most bountiful markets.

You should adopt a compensation plan that rewards people based on their performances, but you should take into consideration the collective success of the organization. All contributors should be rewarded according to their output, impact, and value-added.

Smart Compensation Prevents Bad Behaviors.

I witnessed a large corporation lose almost half of its sales force every year, primarily due to its irresponsible compensation plan and careless executive team. The compensation plan was so complicated that the management team couldn't explain it to their team. Not only was it over-complicated, but it was also purposefully delayed and released in the second quarter of the year to prevent smart salespeople from leaving the company early into the year. Furthermore, to make things worse, the company introduced several retroactive modifications throughout the year that benefited the company at the expense of the sales force.

Salespeople witnessed their commissions dwindle year after year, although they were performing at higher levels than the prior years. It didn't help that this was a public company and the sales executives' salaries were public knowledge, reflecting the exorbitant executive bonus payouts.

Companies that operate in such fashion trigger employees distrust, fear and low morale, which prompts destructive, careless unethical behaviors.

I experienced a situation where the head of sales bluntly stated to his regional vice presidents of sales the following: "Listen, if we don't double our sales performance within the next quarter, I won't be here. Please sign the following pledge that you will deliver on it. Failure to do so may mean that you and I will not have a job." Talk about poor leadership and extreme pressure! What would you expect these sales leaders to do? Naturally, his commands become the law of the land.

These vice-presidents passed verbatim their boss's directive on to their sales managers; now everyone was under pressure. Salespeople felt tremendous daily pressure from their superiors.

Tactical calls were conducted three times a day to ramp up production and accountability. This was a small- to medium-business credit card payment environment. While it was possible to increase output marginally, everyone knew that it was impossible to double it. During the next quarter, despite the intense daily pressure, performances decreased dramatically, while employee resignations increased frighteningly to unsafe levels.

Sales managers and their vice-presidents were perplexed, confused, and concerned. The head of sales blamed his salespeople for sabotaging the company's vision and his sales managers for being ineffective at channeling their salespeople to meet their goals. The reality was apparent, demanding unrealistic performance from your salespeople without checking the market demand, and the economic reality was a recipe for disaster. Merchant Services was a mature industry, operating in a saturated market, using an overstretched sales force that operated at maximum capacity during tough times. Doubling production in the best times is stretch a goal, but during these times it was a delusion. The head of sales should have known better. And his subordinates should have pushed back by sharing market facts, data, and statistics demonstrating that his requests were not realizable.

Ethical Violation

Sales managers need to act as role models promoting ethical behaviors by always coaching, training, and education their employees on best practices. Reinforcing ethical awareness should be the norm; anyone who deliberately violates these guidelines should not be employed with the organization, regardless of performances.

My years of experience working with several large sales organizations has shown me that strict reinforcement by sales managers affects low performers more so than over-achievers. Under-performers are often terminated for minor infractions, while management gets more lenient with high performers. These unusual behaviors should not be acceptable, as they create double standards of improper management. Sales managers worry that if they chastise these big players, they risk losing them to welcoming devious competitors, knowing that they are highly marketable. Great sales managers thrive on being perceived as fair players.

Performance is one thing; violation of ethics is an issue that needs to be dealt with swiftly to eliminate recurrences.

Good ethical corporate culture and improved work harmony creates disciplined employees and increased productivity and employee retention.

CHAPTER 23: SUMMARY

- Ethical behaviors can salvage the company's reputation, prevent legal challenges, and improve customer loyalty.
- Ethical behaviors should be core to the sales organization, continuous education on the subject is a must, and adherence to its principles should be a mandate.
- Organizations that expertly manage ethical complexity tend to have a competitive advantage over their competitors.
- Sales executives should act as a role model by embracing the right ethical approaches despite market pressure and potential

opportunity lost. The risk of reputational and morale loss will always far outweigh any financial gains.

PART V: BUSINESS STRATEGY

"Strategy execution requires people to faithfully believe in its purpose, merits, and value to drive forward and persist by turning failed tactics into possibilities and possibilities into successful choices."— Anthony Chaine

"What we need to do is always lean into the future; when the world changes around you and when it changes against you – what used to be a tail wind is now a head wind – you have to lean into that and figure out what to do because complaining isn't a strategy." —Jeff Bezos

"Strategy without tactics is the slowest route to victory. Tactics without strategy is the noise before defeat." — Sun Tzu

CHAPTER TWENTY-FOUR: STRATEGIC THINKING

Have you worked in a chaotic corporate environment where leadership adopts a project they believe is a game changer, only to turn out to be a complete failure?

I lived through such a situation more times than I can count. Senior management came up with a new strategy and decided to implement it immediately, forcing sales reps to execute on it or risk losing their job for lack of compliance. Naturally, a group of sales reps will follow the new instructions, while another group will resist the implemented changes until its workability factor is proven.

When the adoption and usage is below par, sales managers often reinforce the company directive to ensure compliance despite the fact that the supposed game-changer is proven to be a failure.

Executive managers facing a significant investment credibility loss will naturally blame their line managers and sales reps for resisting change, lack of adoption and inadequate training.

I witnessed multiple major projects launched as game-changers, where millions of dollars were invested with the purpose to drive incremental profits, increase revenue and reduce cost only to vanish or die within a short period post-launch. The reason behind the lack of adoption is that the solution did not live up to its proclaimed transformative capabilities or the solution benefits was never thoroughly explained to the sales rep who would be using it.

Recently, I observed a company that adopted a new software that was supposed to provide its salespeople with additional access to local leads. The concept was simple: While meeting a customer within a specific geographic area, the software would allow the salesperson to view several similar businesses within the same territory allowing the sales rep to call, drop by for a quick introduction, and potentially schedule a meeting. Except that the system provided information was not always up to date; the name of decision makers was not always correct making the first call or interaction somewhat awkward. Sales managers pushed hard their sales reps to adopt the usage of this promising cold calling tool that had the potential to increase salespeople's lead flow and reach.

Due to these inaccuracies, salespeople adoption of this new tool was anemic at best; under executive pressure, these sales managers got on the phone with their sales reps to understand why the tool isn't creating the anticipated results. Sales reps massively responded that the integrity of the data provided was somewhat below par. Upon doing some digging, another factor resurfaced, salespeople were neither trained nor coached on cold calling or cold prospecting. They were used to a culture that handed them enough warm leads to keep them from quitting, but not enough to flourish. These salespeople were unequipped to handle cold calling and they didn't stand a chance to overcome the level of rejections that tend to be part of cold calling businesses.

The project went from being the hottest item of the year to another failed project that needed to be abandoned. Executive managers may have the best intentions in the world to add value and empower their salespeople, however, good intentions do not mean good business decisions. An internal study should have preceded the implementation of this project. Employee awareness and feedback can prevent investment losses, the market changes fast, and ideas that seem great today may not be what the market needs tomorrow. Sales reps will easily adopt a product that will enhance their ability to grow their pipeline and will be more engaged and willing to learn and integrate the product benefits in their daily sales endeavors.

Sound Strategy Drive Revenue

Sound sales management strategy can increase revenue and profitability. A business sales strategy is a plan that defines how your products and services will be sold to increase profits. Sales strategies are often generated by the company administration, with the assistance of multiple cross-functional departments. Good sales management focuses on getting salespeople to achieve their goals in the most effective way possible. The clearer the sales strategy the better the results.

How to Build a Good Sale Management Strategy

1. Establish well-defined goals and objectives for your sales team. Ensure that your goals are challenging, timely, practical, and attainable based on your specific, verticals, markets and industry.

2. Your products must add value to your customers. Salespeople need to be educated on the value and benefits of your business solution to be able to recommend it to their customers.

3. Hire great talent. Salespeople's job is to position the company's products and services in a way that appeals to the customer. The company revenue creation has a direct correlation with the quality of its salespeople.

4. Know your competitive advantage. You and your sales team should know your products and services' competitive advantages and distinctions against your competitors. Your

ability to recognize your strength, weakness, opportunities, and threats can define your success and failure.

a. A competitor can introduce a substitute product to the market that has the potential to steer away a segment of your customer base. A supplier you depend on may increase his prices excessively forcing you to suppress your margin. A competitor may establish an alliance with other partners to gain considerable buying scale power forcing you to compete on prices. New entrants to the market may come up with innovative products that render your business model obsolete. All these scenarios are possible, and your business survival will depend on how you navigate these challenges. You can achieve performance advantages by differentiating your products, lowering costs or being an innovative powerhouse.

5. Salespeople's preparation is key. Great interaction with customers requires intensive training. The sales manager can train and coach their salespeople to handle tough questions and challenging situations.

6. Manage salespeople's performances. Trust but verify your salespeople's daily activities and accomplishments to ensure everyone is on pace and trends are aligned with the established plan.

Good Sales Strategies Require Strategic Thinking

According to business and management expert Henry Mintzberg, "Many practitioners and theorists have wrongly assumed that strategic planning, strategic thinking, and strategy making are all synonyms, at least in best practice." Many studies used the following definition to define strategic thinking: "*To discover novel, imaginative strategies which can rewrite the rules of the competitive game; and to envision potential futures significantly different from the present.*"

Strategic thinking is a distinctive management activity often conceived as an idea in the mind of a sales leader and honed by a group of people before its execution.

Several studies argue the concept of leadership strategic thinking capability: is it nature or nurture? While there is no definitive answer yet, many thought leaders believe that the answer is somewhere in the middle. Natural capabilities can enhance one's strategic thinking capability, but life-learned experiences and reflection are vital to hone this skill.

Strategic thinking is the aggregate culmination of one's life experiences along with the influence of internal and external controls one has been subjected to. These controls range from one's upbringing, education, work experiences, exposure to a high level of responsibilities, and acquired knowledge while dealing with challenging projects and external threats.

These experiences and interactions broaden one business perspectives, stretches one's mental capability to turn around the organization, and exposes one to challenging situations. Challenging events and difficult times can force one to think strategically as it takes time to become adept at being comfortable dealing with a high level of complexity and ambiguity.

Strategic Thinking Mapping Process.

- *Alternative perspectives.* Every problem has a solution. The key is to expand your thinking capability by viewing the problem from all angles, the solution lies on your positioning.

- *Clear Planning.* This mapping approach requires three steps: where you stand, where you want to be in a specific period, and the method you are going to use to get there.
- *Progressive growth.* This is a gradual responsibility increase derived from your upward mobility or exposure to multiple industries that broaden your overall thinking process. More significant roles often face greater challenging demands and risks.
- *Exposure.* Using the above strategic mapping mix can improve your ability to think strategically, along with leveraging other people's experiences and expertise.

Strategic thinking mastery require a lifetime of progressive improvement. Your logical thinking and experiences are foundational stepping stone to better decision-making.

A venture capital organization acquired a company and placed a new CEO in charge. It was quite apparent that the new CEO had much to learn in the job. The parent company charged the vice chairman, an experienced past CEO, with the role of mentoring the new apprentice CEO for a period of three years to develop his strategic thinking skills. Strategic thinking capabilities is not a capability you develop by occupying the corner office, rather it's developed through experience, education and mentorship. Gradual improvement takes time, energy, and effort; however, by exposing oneself to great mentors, experienced colleagues, and strategy experts, one can shorten the learning curve.

Strategic Thinking Importance

Strategic thinking is critical to influence subordinates' development, promote a vision and unite people behind it. As per the example above, the parent company understood that without honed strategic thinking skills the CEO would waste considerable time and valuable resources originating and executing on strategies that may fail.

Leader Role

Many sales leaders love to use words like "think strategically, focus on the big picture, be a visionary" when addressing people and crowds that aspire to grow beyond their current role. People get passed over for promotions because of these undefined requirements that no executive takes the time to define with clarity and precision, leaving people wondering what they should do to improve.

A leader's role is to ensure that his people are empowered with crucial information to make the right decisions and improve their strategic thinking skills. Vital thinking skills take practice and a lifelong process of mentoring and self-education. Smart leaders understand that all employees, regardless of hierarchy, can benefit from the application of strategic thinking to solve big problems facing the company, its customers, and shareholders.

How to Improve Your Strategic Thinking Skills

- Think two levels up. Despite your workload, focus on your job strategic purpose. A good understanding of your boss's boss needs is critical to resolving major obstacles that are not part of your day-to-day job. Strategic thinking requires proactive knowledge of all internal and external forces that have the potential to disrupt and impact your industry trajectory.

- Communicate with precision. Strategic thinking is a thought and communication process. Your ideas and communication needs to be structured in such a manner that it is succinct, thought-provoking, and compelling to drive congruence and action.

- Think big, reflect, and adjust. Allocate time to think on large issues and challenges that your industry is facing and anticipate major future problems. Additionally, learn to make good decisions despite limited access to data.
- Be fluid. Challenges and conflicts will test your beliefs and assumptions. Fluid thinking forces you to think creatively and to open your mind to all possibilities, even when the solutions seem farfetched or difficult to realize. Strategic thinking involves a significant amount of risk-taking while making decisions that are based on facts, hypotheses, and predictive theories. The risk is always yours, and so is the result.

Sales Strategy Start at the Top

Strategic thinking starts at the top and is often championed by an executive who has a vision that they believes in and wants to implement to improve the organization and people's lives. Strategic thinking is critical to a company's performance.

A good sales strategy success requires focus and action. A strategy is a battle plan and a set of tactics a business should implement to achieve specific results. Not all business strategies can be successful. As a matter of fact, the majority fail because of poor communication, poor execution or misaligned belief. Additionally, many good strategic plan due to: partial commitment, involving unqualified people, lack of execution, unwillingness to evolve, wrong leadership, ignoring economic signs, absence of follow up, and lack of resources.

Good competitive sales strategies require creativity, innovation, and a distinctive edge to attract customers. Being different requires choosing a path of action that delivers a mix of values.

Uber, took the market by surprise and transformed the public transportation industry by providing a unique way of serving its customers. Uber's cutting edge business model has several components that made it successful.

- It delivered a unique value proposition to its customers.
- It made strategic trade-offs. Uber did not acquire its fleet; rather it leveraged local drivers who were willing to use their own cars to make extra income.
- It continued its strategic direction to create value for its customer while expanding its business model by leveraging customers' needs.

Sales management's role is to explain the vision behind the strategy, anticipate challenges, the impact on customers and the actionable go-to-market strategy to achieve the company goals.

Working Harder is Not a Strategy

A few years ago, I attended a Fortune 500 sales kickoff in New York. There was much excitement on the air. The company had just hired a new head of sales who had spent most his career working for IBM. This event was the perfect setting to present his vision for this struggling fintech company that needed some significant changes to get back to profitability.

High hopes were lodged on this new executive to turn the company back to profit and stability. The new executive went on for two hours talking about his experiences and accomplishments with IBM. He showed several PowerPoint presentations that had more to do with everything but sells. His presentation seemed somewhat misguided, longwinded, and infuriating; his presentation was all about himself rather than his employees. He couldn't articulate with clarity and simplicity his new strategy, his approach was "transform instantly, or you will be terminated." After his presentation, people were livid, confused, and worried. People were disappointed, and want to go home. Many thought that was the end of an organization that promoted for decades empowering its sales people and managers to do what's right for the customer

Sales kickoffs in the past were all about energizing and motivating the sales reps. This events had historically been about getting the sales force under one roof to celebrate past successes, share current and future innovative products and services, meet internal and external partners, conduct training, and educate people on the company vision, mission, and direction.

Following the meeting, these pumped salespeople went on their way empowered and feeling great that they were part of a great sales organization that helped its customers, enabled its employees and improved society by adding value to its communities. That's was the concept, anyhow.

Unfortunately, this ego-driven new sales leader managed to destroy his salespeople and managers' morale in their first meeting with him. This new head of sales was knowledgeable of information technology, he was analytical, methodical, and brilliant in many ways. However, he was impatient, self-serving, and apathetic to his people's needs.

I was told by several vice-presidents that the CEO introduced him during their kick-off event. Then, all the managers head towards the open bar to mingle, network, and have fun. The new head of sales was sitting in the bar with his laptop open. Upon shaking someone's hand, he looked at that person's current numbers and reprimanded the person in public without any understanding of the personal circumstances or market conditions. Many sales managers were surprised and stunned by his harsh, misplaced and insensitive approach. Several managers simply avoided shaking his hand to circumvent being publicly embarrassed.

This sales leader used his background in IT to improve sales managers' ability to view different reports using company CRMs. He believed that he could enhance team performances by providing them with better visuals and excel measurement tools to evaluate specific KPIs such as MTD leads, close rates, approved accounts, productivity ratio, etc.

His management style was focused on providing better CRM reports to manage the sales force metrics, thinking that will change the sales dynamics and create more sales. He was wrong, and no one dare to tell him! He believed that by adding this tracking capability, he was empowering his sales manager to hold their salespeople more accountable to drive their team productivity up. But, adding an additional KPI column in an excel file doesn't change mindset or inspire people.

The essence of his sales strategy was: "We've got to sell more, so you've got to push your people to work harder. If you are not hitting your goals, it's because of lack of leadership."

He asked questions during team meetings and answered them, and he often interrupted people's responses in a disrespectful manner. In desperation, to show better sales numbers, he mandated that the entire sales leadership reporting to him to become a quota carrying sales executives. Several senior vice-presidents and regional vice-president's find it impossible to sell while managing their insane work load.

Please understand that this was a B2B environment of a complex structure. Some senior vice-presidents had not been directly selling for a long time. Asking them to hit the ground selling in addition to their job responsibilities was counterproductive and hard to achieve. Forced to build a pipeline and start selling, several senior vice-presidents and regional vice-presidents began looking for jobs outside the company.

Many felt that their boss was not only clueless about sales management, but he was a desperate tyrant that needed to go. This head of sales' job tenure lasted less than a year, but the damage he generated was extensive in terms of talent exodus and morale destruction.

As a sales leader, you may have an aggressive agenda, lofty goals, and challenging vision. However, you will need to articulate clearly your vision in a manner that generates a consensus from people who are responsible for driving its execution. Strategic plans drive tactical performance plans, and the latter is an outcome of the aggregate efforts of your sales force.

CHAPTER 24: SUMMARY

- A good sales strategy should not force salespeople to comply. Instead, it should allow people to willingly embrace its fundamentals as a path of growth and evolution.
- Sales executive often invest time, effort, and resources in tools they believe will increase revenue and productivity. However, they commonly fail to sell their vision and share their passion with their end users constituents.
- Strategic thinking requires creativity, imagination, and innovation to resolve complex challenges. Visionary, inspiring leaders drive higher performance and command people respect.
- Strategic change requires training, education and paradigm shift in people's thought process.

CHAPTER TWENTY-FIVE: GROWTH STRATEGY

History has proven that the prepared win. Well, almost. Do you remember AskJeeves.com? It was ahead of its time for a short period, and then it faltered because the technology wasn't good enough. AskJeeves had multiple innovative technologies that were ahead of their time and most of these advanced technologies became part of Google's platform. Innovations like semantic search and ranking web pages were among the competitive advantages that belonged to AskJeeves. These technological features contributed to the success of Google. However, they weren't good enough to sustain the AskJeeves' business model when the global supporting technologies weren't advanced enough.

Idea Ahead of Their Time

You may remember WebTV; the founding vision was to bring the internet to TV. Microsoft bought the company because it had a good financial outcome. However, the market wasn't ready for such an innovative, bold move, so this promising Internet TV concept died. Was the idea too early for its time? Probably.

The above examples demonstrate that great business ideas and concepts may not always turn into success. Every great idea requires a robust underlying system to support its growth. For example, you can build a state-of-the-art school, but without good teachers, the school will be nothing more than beautiful architectural edifices.

The market may not always respond favorably. Current supporting technologies may not be advanced enough to support the company vision or strategy, and governing policies may not allow the realization of the project.

Imagine Apple launching the iPhone as we know it today, thirty years ago! What level of success would it have achieved? Without the current internet download speed capability, and today's wireless infrastructure capability, the iPhone would have failed miserably.

Toys R Us squandered the opportunity to develop a great toy e-commerce platform. The company continued to focus on its physical stores, while the market moved toward buying toys online. Toys R Us signed a 10-year toy exclusivity agreement with Amazon in 2000, but Amazon allowed other toy competitors to sell toys on its platform. Toys R Us sued Amazon for breach of the agreement and the contract ended in 2004. Consequently, Toys R Us missed the opportunity to build a substantial online presence.

Many startups with great innovative ideas, great people, and sound financial backing went out of business. Market trends can be anticipated; innovative technologies can be tested and improved upon. However, none of these elements can guarantee success.

Anticipate the Future

Successful organizations study major market shift and trends, knowing that the first successful market entrant secures top-line growth and market domination. Opportunistic organizations gains trend surfers and first-movers advantage. Market domination is much harder to establish at a later stage in the game. Reading the market and anticipating potential new demands is critical to own the future.

Alibaba scored the biggest Internet IPO since Google's by raising \$1.5 billion. Jack Ma, the founder, realized back in 1999 that China had

42 million small and medium businesses, and many of these businesses were eager to become part of the global market. Alibaba has created a point-and-click e-commerce system for suppliers to connect with distributors and consumers online. Today, Alibaba reaches millions of users all over the world. Amazon today stands as a global e-commerce leader. It expanded its reach by allowing consumers to purchase directly from Amazon or its affiliates. You practically can buy anything from Amazon today; products range from e-books, videos, music to health food. Their menu of options and its global consumers base keep expanding as well. Not long ago, people thought Walmart would never have a challenging worthy competitor, especially one that operates as a pure e-commerce business.

Disruption Is Innovation

Square Inc. was founded in 2009 by Jack Dorsey its CEO. Since then, it has evolved into a significant payment platform. Its ideas were ahead of their time. It focused initially in the micro-merchant arena by having a unique value proposition along with a simple, transparent pricing model. The company has been averaging a 50% to 75% increase year-over-year, which is impressive based on the competitive nature of the industry today.

Square was initially viewed as a disruptor and a fad that would not survive for more than a couple of years. Most payment industry CEOs thought that Square Inc. business model was not sustainable and would soon go out of business. Against the doubter and the skeptics, Jack Dorsey pressed on with innovative ideas that transformed the very nature of the payment industry. Square introduced the first innovative mobile card reader payment hardware. Industry legacy leaders took notice and struggled to emulate Square's innovative technologies and later its business model. With the implementation of Europay-Master-Visa (EMV) chip-embedded card, Square designed the quickest EMV transaction reader in the industry, giving major competitors another challenge. Recently, the company launched Square Capital to help small entrepreneurs with business loans that are payable gradually as a percentage of their transactions. While this is not a novel idea, Square secured the backing and loyalty of many small entrepreneurs and startups that are denied access to loans based on risk factors associated with business longevity.

Organizations that are forward-looking in terms of business ideas, innovation, and creativity can become a dominant industry force within a short period. Alibaba, Apple, and Square would never have succeeded without the advent of technological and infrastructure systems that made it possible. Every technological innovation is another stepping stone that made it likely to succeed. These technological advances, ranging from the internet to information technology, communication tools, transportation capabilities and financial services, made it possible for these companies to take an idea or business model and turn it into a global company.

Take Risk Invest Early

Great ideas cannot succeed without the right level of exposure and resources. History has shown that many great startups sank just before they could make it big. Too many startups went out of business without ever knowing they could have been great success stories, if only they had a little more time, more resources, or better guidance.

Scrub Daddy brought in about $80 million in revenue, according to Lori Greiner, CEO. Aaron Krause went to *Shark Tank* asking for $200,000 in exchange for 20% equity. Eight months of prior sales generated a total of $100,000. The company was struggling to stay afloat. Greiner realized Scrub Daddy's signature product potential. She jumped on the opportunity to help Krause to cement and expand his product line; she used her business connections and know-how to generate and secure additional shelf-space for Scrub Daddy with few major national stores such as Bed Bath and Beyond as well as QVC where the product became an instant TV major best sellers.

Greiner knew there was risk investing in such company, but her honed business skills allowed her to see the opportunity and product potential. More importantly, she had a tremendous mental business flair that was honed through experience and a sense of risk-taking. Forward-looking leaders make wise decisions, based on product potential and risk tolerance.

Significant wins are often preceded by risky investments. As the adage states, "no pain, no gain". It was right then, and it's still true today. Risk-taking is the foundation of most breakthroughs. That ability to commit in advance to an improbable future is the factor that differentiates exceptional winners from the rest. Significant wins are often preceded by long periods of insecurities, hard times, and crippling challenges. The ability to keep pushing forward in uncharted territories is what separates the audacious winners from losers.

Think Ahead

Jack Welch in his book *Winning* stated that he loved to hire leaders who have an edge. An edge for Jack was the leader's ability to see around the corners and identify opportunities that could only materialize in the future. These leaders can visualize a mental concept and transform it into a vivid reality in their mind. The rationale of these leaders is based on innate ideas built on imagination, intuition, experience, market study, business modeling and predictive data analysis.

Jeff Bezos' vision is that e-commerce will become the future of global commerce. Bezos' vision would have been unrealistic a few decades ago without the internet. Technological innovation and the internet were the backbone that allowed Amazon to become a super multinational organization. In addition, a reliable transportation delivery systems along with sophisticated storage logistic systems and progress in robotics capabilities contributed enormously to Amazon success.

Leading sales organization focus on the future; they use today's consumer shopping trends data along with market studies of client desires, struggles, and future possibilities to create tomorrow's winning concepts. Steve Jobs was obsessed with customer experience; he analyzed reports related to customer behavior and created future solutions that disrupted several legacy industries ranging from telecommunication to entertainment.

Great leaders pay incredible attention to details, knowing that customer loyalty is won by delivering exceptional products that focus on quality, transparency, speed of delivery, and simplicity. The chess game is all about predicting future adversarial moves before it happens, and leading organizations act the same way. They anticipate customer demand by looking forward into the industry future both at a macro-level as well as at micro-level.

Authority Is Not Influence

Many heads of sales and CEOs have been promoted over the years because of unique talent, intellect, business savvy, operational ability, analytical capability, and special managerial and leadership aptitude. However, few know how to influence a buyer.

Yet many feel they ought to be great just because they manage salespeople. I witnessed on multiple occasions corporate leaders (CEOs level) destroy deals that were certain to close. Often, these authoritative corporate leaders feel the same way talking to potential customers as they speak to their reports. When the CEO speaks, people listen, they don't interrupt because of perceived authority, wisdom and experience, but out of respect and proper business etiquette. CEOs get accustomed to speaking in a monologue fashion rather than a dialogue. Many of these CEOs brag about their success, power, accomplishment, or how they transformed or built their company (no one cares how great your company is—they can do their online research—what matters is what you can do for them to improve their lives; it's all about them, because they support the business).

I cringed on many occasions, listening to these monologues, while I believed that few corporate leaders could add value and credibility to the sales demonstration when done well. However, CEOs that think they're master salesmen often talk themselves out of the deal due to personal egoistic behaviors.

The salesperson and the CEO entourage tends to yield more speak time to the CEO, rather than intercept when necessary. These calls often produce the opposite results because they don't address the customer's needs. Leveraging the CEO's presence can be great if it's controlled, client-focused, and purpose-driven.

Sales is all about positively influencing and getting customers to align their thoughts with yours to advance the deal. Sales is earning the right to recommend a business solution that adds value to the client business.

Learn from Your Customers.

The CEO should be the head teacher within an organization. Teaching allows learning; therefore a healthy organization should encourage self-education and transmit the acquired knowledge to others via instruction. Managers should create a setting that enables learning and promotes thinking. Managers' victories should be celebrated as everyone's victory. The role of head teachers is to challenge current perspectives by broadening the conversation and even offering contradictory views to improve the organizational thought dynamics.

Customer's meetings should be all about them. That is the time where the teacher-in-chief should wear the hat of the learner in-chief. Customer meetings are all about understanding the customer's issue without rushing to offer a business solution that is cure to all challenges. Great managers know they need to suppress their desire to pitch and immerse themselves on understanding the challenge the customer is trying to address.

In the pursuit of revenue, one should never forget the purpose of the company, which is to provide value to its customers. The companies that ignore this reality eventually will be at risk of going out of business. So it's critical that the company and its employees create value for their customers to survive and flourish.

Growth is All About Solving People's Problems.

Sales has always been about solving a problem and bettering people's lives by adding value. So if sales is all about value, then the majority of sales organizations failures happen because they fail to demonstrate a compelling value worthy of investment. Opportunities surround us; the key is to create a difference in people's lives. Many companies want to generate revenue and profit but focus on the wrong priorities to create the desired outcome. When the business solution value becomes apparent and necessary, the allocation of the budget becomes justifiable.

How to Bond with Your Customers

Even in today's competitive sales environment, great sales managers understand that their customers expect more and deserve more. Customers today have more options to choose from than ever before. Therefore, they expect to work with a salesperson and a sales company that understands their values and tries to customize a business solution that spurs growth and long term relationships. Customers want a customer-centric relationship that is based on transparency, trust, credibility, and competency.

Great sales managers understand these requirements, and they encourage a sales culture that serves its customers. Companies with a stellar brand can charge more for their products and services, yet they will continue to increase their customer base. Customers are always willing to pay more for a product and service where there is alignment, innovation, and collaboration.

Where there is understanding, there is an opportunity. Understanding your customer's organization, culture, industry, objectives, drivers, challenges, values, buying process and history will allow you to build a value proposition that is based on thorough knowledge.

CHAPTER 25: SUMMARY

- Advanced technological features may not provide a competitive edge unless local and global supporting technologies are also advanced enough to support growth and expansion.
- Every great idea requires a robust underlying system to support its growth.
- Successful organizations study major market shift and trends. Opportunistic organizations gains early trend surfers and first-movers advantage.
- Significant wins are often preceded by risky investment. Take calculated risks; you cannot win without strategic audacity and smart tactics. Opportunity and growth lies where problems can be found and solved.

PART VI: STRATEGIC SALES TOOLS

"I do believe that the smart sales professional has to be able to leverage their organization's technology and processes proficiently to qualify existing opportunities and deliver memorable customer experiences. Used well, sales tools can be an advantage; used poorly, they can become a hindrance."— Anthony Chaine

"Left to their own devices, the one thing your customers want to avoid is change."— Brent Adamson

"The first rule of any technology used in a business is that automation applied to an efficient operation will magnify the efficiency. The second is that automation applied to an inefficient operation will magnify the inefficiency."— Bill Gates

CHAPTER TWENTY-SIX: YOUR CRM IS A TOOL, NOT A TOY

You probably have witnessed, at some point in your career, your company spending an enormous amount of money on tools like productivity software, tracking systems, and CRMs that promise better, faster production and performance improvement. But after the implementation, training, and execution phase, nothing works as intended. The project fails to deliver on its widely-anticipated results. A period of confusion follows where senior management conducts surveys, interviews managers, human resource personnel, and other cross-functional teams to figure out what happened, and what adjustments need to occur to deliver on the expected promised results.

The account executive who sold the company its business solution will initially justify it as a natural event that occurs during the learning and adoption phase. However, as the pressure mounts from senior management who need to explain the ROI of the business solution to the board of directors, the seller will shift strategy to blaming the company training process, lower employee usage adoption, employees' resistance to change, and inadequate management support.

As the intensity rises, the executive team starts pressuring the sales management team to push their salespeople to leverage this new technology to generate incremental revenue as many other companies did successfully. The training folks are summoned to double their efforts training their sales force in order to turn this massive investment into a revenue-cranking machine.

When all these initiatives fail, the executive team gives strict instructions to terminate anyone who is not complying with the company directives to embrace the new technology to spur performance.

CRM Is Just a Tool, Not a Success Path

What these sales executives fail to understand is that technology is a tool that can facilitate, coordinate, and manage efforts that drive sales. However, technology by itself cannot move the sales needle upward. It's a tool, just like a hammer in the hand of an experienced carpenter. No matter how sophisticated the ram, it needs an expert hand that will guide it to get the job done. A hammer is a potent tool in the palm of an expert, just as Salesforce.com is a fantastic CRM software and a stable enterprise cloud ecosystem in the hands of expert salespeople. It has the potential to facilitate business growth by streamlining sales and marketing. However, it's nothing more than a process improvement tool that organizes customers contacts, sales processes, market trends, and data. It's evident that no matter how sophisticated your CRM, it cannot make a sales call, negotiate a contract, or close a deal.

Many sales managers and executive managers have spent an enormous amount of time studying their corporate CRMs. Hundreds of hours went into the process of learning, dissecting, and customizing different reports, trying to figure out a way to spur sales. Data analysis is vital for identifying your best customers and satisfying their needs. However, a transaction occurs only when the salesperson proactively engages his customers with the purpose of understanding their needs and customizing a business solution that works.

CRM Is Not a Sales Strategy

I had a conversation with the chief revenue officer (CRO) of a large corporation recently. He was fuming because his division sales were down and he was not satisfied with the reasons given by his sales managers.

CRO: We invested tons of money in a new CRM, product development software, training, sales tools, and mobile technology to ensure that our salespeople are equipped to dominate the market. The CEO gave us all the resources needed, expecting a spike in sales. Surprisingly, we experienced a decrease in sales figures beyond anything we had seen in the past. Despite our brand recognition, partner loyalty, and resources, we are losing ground to smaller competitors. I cannot understand it, and if this trend continues, I may not be here next year!

Me: How much time did you spent in the field with your salespeople last month to understand the reason behind their performances?

CRO: I honestly didn't spend any time at all with any of them. We have a quarterly roundtable that is managed by regional managers that occur around the country. I try to attend some events to understand the sales reps' challenges, so we can address them by allocating the right resources to the problem.

Me: How long do these meetings last? Also, do you feel you are getting honest feedback from your sales reps?

CRO: The meetings last about two hours. The feedback is not great, and only a few salespeople venture to talk during these sessions. I often get a sense that our sales reps don't have a total grasp of all the solutions we offer our customers. I started to believe that we have launched way too many products into the market, without taking the time to educate adequately our salespeople creating a knowledge gap.

Me: How often do you spend time with your regional sales vice-presidents and their sales managers to try to understand the main reasons behind this lack of sales?

CRO: You saw my calendar. I try to allocate 30 minutes on a one-on-one conference call with each regional vice-president to discuss challenges, action plan, and progress. Unfortunately, my schedule is always overextended, not permitting me to allocate any time to meaningful conversation with my first-line sales managers.

Me: How often do you review sales reports in Salesforce? Also, where do you focus your attention most?

CRO: I review Salesforce reports at a minimum of eight times per day. I primarily focus on critical reports such as lead flow, conversion rate, close rate velocity, equipment installs rate, loyalty programs, dynamic pricing, and deals in the pipeline.

Me: In terms of salesforce usage, how many hours do your field salespeople and your sales manager spend daily at it?

CRO: Since implementing our CRM, we initially experienced much resistance from our salespeople. Many resisted preferring on a note book. Some salespeople felt they would be losing control over their client database by allowing management to access it at will. I had to implement some severe policies to get some of them to comply, but we are totally compliant now.

I assume that the average sales rep spends a couple of hours a day managing their customer portfolio. My sales managers probably spend two to three hours daily reviewing the team progress and managing sales gaps. Most of my sales managers devote half of the day or two-thirds of the day in the field assisting, training, and coaching their team members. Then, spend the rest of the day doing administrative work and returning calls.

Myopic Strategy

It was apparent I was looking at a scenario of myopic executive strategy. This chief revenue officer was spending much time managing a CRM screen that couldn't generate additional sales or fix the current sales gaps. Sales needs to operate as a matrix with a singular focus—revenue generation, but sales tool are not the solution. Revenue generation requires creating a winning strategy and drive its impeccable execution.

This leader was extremely busy, but he was managing his people by monitoring salesforce reports and watching daily screen progress trends. Sales requires a deep dive to understand market dynamics, buyer behavior, salespeople morale, product desirability, value delivery systems, company brand perception, market gaps, and area of opportunities.

The head of sales must spend time with their salespeople and line managers to capture valuable insight and understand their market challenges and constraints to develop smart strategies that meet market demands and future trends. Senior managers cannot manage salespeople effectively behind a desk screening different reports and shooting directives.

Encourage Transparency

Accurate field intelligence is rarely shared with executive management. People are naturally afraid to tell the truth, especially when the management team is dismissive of people's feedback, observations, insights, and ideas. Managers who ignore people's input often end up living shielded from reality in a self-created bubble until their career derails. Managers who are perceived as such usually end up getting sugar-coated false truths or no feedback at all.

Several studies have demonstrated that people refrain from sharing critical negative information for fear of retaliation or even job termination. The head of sales must incentivize people to tell the truth by empowering them through authentic engagement and reward systems. Honesty should always be encouraged no matter how difficult it may be to digest.

The reality in most corporate organizations the higher you go, the less truth you get. Truth-telling is found at the bottom of the corporate pyramid. As you climb up, people become better at bending the truth, disguising it, and changing its initial state to a newer state that protects one's interest. False truth generates financial loss, bureaucracy, redundancies, and it erodes people's confidence in the company's future and its management integrity.

Employees perform according to their belief and confidence level, and rise and fall according to their fears and anxieties. If the employee worries about their safety or job security, they will hide the truth to self-protect against retaliation, biased investigation, and potential unfair targeting.

What should senior management do to encourage truth-telling across the organization?

1. Everyone is accountable to tell nothing but the truth. No retaliation ironclad policy.

2. Discuss all field intelligence and assess its validity without judgment or retaliations.

3. Use dialogue and collaboration to resolve conflicts and significant problems.

4. Senior management needs to be vulnerable, transparent at all levels. Improving people's lives should be the organization central goal.

5. Listen with the intent to understand the speaker's warnings without hasty judgments.

6. Encourage vulnerability and forbid backlash.

Field Feedback

Senior managers often neglect field or market intelligence until it's too late. The irony is salespeople are trained to be in constant contact with their customers and their continual customer engagement exposes them to developing in-depth market knowledge on customer's specific needs and future desires. In addition their customer interactions expose them to competitors' strategic offerings and value bundles. Smart sales organizations study continuously competitors' market moves to secure their market share and uncover new channels of opportunities.

Salespeople often operate in silos and channeling field intelligence to executive management is a tall order, because most of the precious knowledge remains tacked in a salesperson's mind unless approached by a trusted party that value this unique knowledge and act on it.

Active field salespeople intelligence gathering should be encouraged and rewarded. There are two categories of field intelligence.

- New: Information, business models, new disruptive technologies, approaches, strategies, global entrant, new regulations, threats, and opportunities
- Known but evolving: technologies, new industry concepts, market breakthrough strategies, unique sales methodologies that are taking the market by storm

Questions to Ask.

- What are we currently doing that is not working? What do we need to improve or eliminate?
- What competitors are gaining ground quickly in our market?
- How can we differentiate our offering?

- How can we compete against lower-cost competitors?
- What level of product customization or offer customization will have a penetration impact
- How can we build an even stronger brand within specific ethnic markets?
- What reward system should we adapt to cement and grow our customer loyalty?
- How is the team morale? What market forces worry us the most?
- What opportunities are we neglecting in our market?
- What type of promotion should we leverage to drive new net business?
- What can we do to improve our sales force productivity?
- What idea or business concept can you share with me?

The key is to establish trust by joining the sales force in the field as often as possible. Not to criticize or penalize anyone, but rather to listen with humility and with the intention to improve sales professionalism and customer's experiences, while growing the company's profitability.

CRM Managers

I met Joe who was a newly-minted sales vice president. He was so proud of his CRM mastery. He was telling me that he had spent an enormous amount of time configuring the system and creating special reports for his sales managers to improve their salespeople's productivity and to monitor the following KPI's: pipeline management, margin assessment, products sales, win rate, activations and attrition. He was excited and proud of his accomplishment. He even sent the following directive to his regional reports. "Going forward, your daily activity should be logged into your CRM; if it's not logged in, it means it never occurred, and no justification shall be accepted."

He was managing his team through these reports. We had a conversation that went like this.

Me: How is your team pacing year-to-date?

Joe: We are seriously behind, and I don't know how to turn the ship around. The marketing team is not creating enough quality leads, our sales reps shy away from cold calling, and I don't blame them. The company has never had a solid training program that educate the sales reps on how to professionally call-in on new businesses. Marketing has recently created a business needs analysis template to help people structure the questioning process. Sales reps' feedback was anemic, and many believe that the templates were poorly designed and did not address clients' critical needs. Besides, our recent initiative to drive new net business felt flat as there was no economic initiative behind it.

Me: I see. It seems that your company enjoys a great brand name, has partnered with large reputable companies. Your CEO has opened your platform to several software developers, and you should get ahead based on your multiple existing competitive advantages.

Joe: I agree, except we are not. Our brand name has been tarnished since we initiated across-the-board cost-cutting policy, our customer services team was reduced drastically creating significant delays, frustrations, and service cancellations. Internal poor communication is the norm within the organization; it seems that everyone is working in silos, and most vital information is not shared or dissipated willingly. We have software's that launched to the market, and I only learned of their existence from customers who were browsing our website. Salespeople often become aware of a specific application only when asked by the customer. It seems insane that our company allowed web developers to create new apps and launch them into our POS platforms without warning or training the sales force that is supposed to position, educate, and sell these new products. The training department was reduced to a skeleton crew; they are overwhelmed and poorly trained. Hence, training sessions are rarely provided and often done in a rush mode with little or no incentive behind it.

Senior management is often overwhelmed; they are aware of most of the issues we encounter on a day-to-day basis. Unfortunately, most seem powerless to influence their cross-functional peers. It seems that every division either works in silos or works in total isolation from the rest.

Me: What are you doing about it? Do you see a resolution?

Joe: Honestly, I'm just focusing on my division, and I want to make sure that I'm doing everything to meet my quota or get close to it. In terms of resolution, we have voiced our concerns to our senior management. Nothing has been done so far, and I'm not even sure if they can influence our executive management.

Common Pitfalls

Joe's story is not unique, and most corporations take every opportunity to cut costs while hoping it won't affect revenue and margin. Drastically trimming back-office staff and support functional teams yields disappointing results as it affects customers experience and divert salespeople attention from selling. Reducing back-office staff and support functions seems to hurt revenue less than reducing the number of salespeople.

I understand that companies need to cut waste, but you cannot cut vital support systems and assume you are not going to affect negatively customers' needs and salespeople's morale. Customer perception about the company affects their buying behavior either positively or negatively. Drastic cuts forces salespeople to handle escalations and other functions that are best served with service professionals. The customer doesn't care about internal cuts, or company financial challenges. Customers are concerned about resolving their problems forcing the frontline sales reps to undertake support tasks, such as resolving technical issues, troubleshooting, and conducting staff training. These additional tasks reduce selling time, affect morale, as most salespeople are ill-equipped to handle technical complexity. I witnessed a situation where the sales manager became deeply involved in resolving a customer issue that lasted three days, forcing him to forgo other critical obligations related to his sales reps, business partners, and customers.

Cutting critical sales support staff may save money in the short run, but it often tarnishes the company brand. Unhappy customers tend to be extremely vocal on social media platforms; they usually provide negative online reviews that take tremendous effort to overcome.

A major B2B wholesale company in New York decided to cut its sales force and highly-paid back-office employees. The concept was to terminate one-third of the sales force and two-third of back office folks and increase the workload on the remaining employees.

This cost-cutting action affected the remaining salespeople who had to handle their business portfolio, new business acquisition, along with higher quota responsibility. Within months, droves of tenured, high-producing sales reps started leaving the company and joining their terminated partners who now worked for the competition. Additionally, experienced back-office employees were the highest paid and most affected with these terminations. Many took with them years of know-how that was impossible to replicate. The company even tried to rehire a few employees deemed dispensable. However, despite offering these few employees almost double of what they were making in the past, no one came back. The trust was broken and it was impossible to mend.

While it's necessary to cut costs, and eliminate redundancy, being surgical about it is vital. Some people are tough to replace. The key is to get to know your employee profile before you make any decisions; some people possess unique, vital knowledge and experiences that can resolve complex issues. Others may know how to attract profitable customers or larger accounts. Understanding your employees' economic and corporate value should be a cornerstone of your decision-making.

Inspect What You Expect

Sales management cannot be performed remotely, at least not for long-term. Sales managers who skip their coaching duties by managing from a distance or behind a desk won't achieve the results they are after.

Sales success requires steadfast, relentlessly dedicated salespeople who are equipped to win battles. Sales managers are responsible for equipping their salespeople with the right gear to win these battles.

Meeting often with your salespeople, customers, vendors, and industry experts allows for relationship building, feedback, and market intelligence gathering.

In the story above, the chief revenue-officer (CRO) spent most his time in front of a screen analyzing CRM reports. A quick visit with his field reps would have allowed him to understand local market dynamics and the forces that hinder his sales force's ability to sell at the expected level.

A leader cannot hide behind his job duties or his schedule busyness. Salespeople are the heart that drives the company's economy; at a minimum, the chief revenue-officer should have allocated a couple of hours for learning first hand from his salespeople, evaluating feedback, and making the necessary changes to affect performance.

CHAPTER 26: SUMMARY

- Productivity tools do not guarantee an uptick in output and performance. They are often more of tracking and measurement systems that organize information and data. They speed access to necessary information and delivery.
- Technology by itself cannot move the sales needle upward, only people can.
- Sales systems are not a strategy, they are just tools that facilitate selling.
- Some employees experience, and knowledge make them extremely valuable to the organization. Losing these pivotal people can potentially destroy the organization culture.
- Equipping your salespeople for battle and upgrading their weaponry continuously is the only way to stay relevant and profitable as a sales organization.

CHAPTER TWENTY-SEVEN: YOUR WORK TOOLS' EMPOWERING OR DISEMPOWERING ABILITY

Email Overload

Love it or hate it, email is a corporate communication necessity that works well. However, I have seen many sales managers whose entire day gets consumed with email responses. Receiving hundreds of emails a day may be the norm in some jobs, but how and when you choose to respond can mean the difference between being efficient or not.

Most organizations do not have an email protocol that manages salespeople and sales managers' inbox. A vice president I met gleefully stated that he averages over 500 incoming emails per day and at least half of them require urgent responses. Another senior vice president of sales said that he routinely has a backlog of two thousand or more emails. A regional vice president confessed that he deleted without reading all emails that are not directly sent to him. "If I'm just copied on an email, it's not an email worth reading. That's my way to cope with the flood of daily emails I receive," he says.

There are undoubtedly multiple books that educate one on the various techniques to control and manage your inbox. Checking your inbox once or twice a day is not a practical method for most sales managers. Sales managers and most vice-presidents of sales are required to review and approve multiple cross-functional requests, push pending deals forward, and pull strings to move agreements requiring finance, marketing or legal approvals. The above tasks require reading most incoming emails, and there lies the dilemma—it's time consuming, but it must be done. Keeping an email trail is another essential task; future escalations require the manager to retrieve the email to justify their actions and resolutions trails.

My conversation with a vice president of sales working for a Fortune 500 company in fintech went as follows:

Me: Fred, how do you manage your daily email inflow?

Fred: It's a significant challenge. I have so many priorities to manage, and I honestly receive way more email than I can potentially handle. Remember, I'm in the field with my salespeople trying to understand the market dynamics and eliminate constraints to help them sell more. Major issues requiring my attention is the norm in my business. However, I cannot afford not to look at my inbox every fifteen minutes even while with customers.

Administrative cross-functional approvals often require speedy response to move deals, and failure to respond promptly may delay the sale by another 24 hours. We are often reduced to the one-word answer to speed up the process. Due to an increase of email into my inbox, I have instructed my sales manager and salespeople to email or copy me only on vital issues. Internal cross-functional departments copy me on almost everything. It's truly impossible to be efficient under these circumstances.

To make things worse, our senior management has changed our internal policy requiring all vice presidents of sales to approve items that were historically handled by sales managers. Sales executives seem to mistrust the people who work the hardest. The current financial sales managers' approval tolerance was reduced to zero dollars, making our lives more miserable. Now I must approve financial email requests ranging from $1 to $1,000. I have sales managers who left the company where they were not empowered to approve customers' credits for less than $100. Smaller competitors have entrusted with budgetary decisions in the thousands of dollars. I believe these are lessons we should learn from and adopt.

Emails can be frustrating, but phone communications have almost vanished, and no one answers their phones anymore. Corporate email dilemma is real, but it can be dealt with through simple techniques of prioritization, delegation or elimination. What's puzzling is that most corporations do not realize the damage they are inflicting on their people's morale and consequently the organization's bottom line.

Email is becoming a costly distraction that wastes precious production time, energy, and effort.

Empower and Trust

1. People's empowerment and trust are vital to better employee morale and production. Research has demonstrated that empowered employees at work perform their jobs better, experience higher job satisfaction, and tend to be loyal to the company.
2. You cannot trust only a few people in the company and mistrust the majority of your employees that generate the revenue you depend on for survival, growth, and expansion.
3. Empower people to generate a sense of pride, loyalty, and belonging. Giving your employees information to improve performance is a start, but empowering your people with the right level of authority to make decisions and take appropriate action to resolve pending problems without getting approval from a higher-up is the definition of self-autonomy and mental independence.
4. You cannot expect people to become stronger and more independent by shackling their behavioral and mental independence. Human genius can manifest at all levels when

one is trusted and allowed freedom of thought and expression. Your corporate culture should exude employee trust and confidence.

Technical skills can be learned and training manuals can be created, however, true empowerment means freeing your employees to ask "why" to resolve hard problems. Everyone may agree on what success should look like, but getting there can occur through different paths. Empowering your employees comes down to the level of trust and freedom you grant them to achieve the company vision and mission. Hire intelligent people and let them use their creative problem solving capabilities and critical thinking to run the business more efficiently. Maintain a structure but allow enough flexibility to spur creativity, discussion, and cooperation.

Benefits of Trust and Empowerment

- Elimination of reoccurring problems at a larger scale. Solutions are identified and dissipated across the organization to benefit everyone.
- Every employee is empowered to own their problems and resolve it as if they were the CEO of the company. Collective decision-making is available on demand for complex issues.
- Customer retention increases dramatically when problems are quickly resolved through passionate, empowered employees.
- Employees are encouraged to get involved in causes bigger than themselves, providing a sense of self-worth. Employees morale goes up, and job satisfaction increases dramatically.
- Happy employees promote the company online and offline, which results in attracting a pipeline of healthy prospects who want to be part of a brand that cares about their employees, customers, and shareholders.

Centralized Decision-Making is Poor Management

- Employee genius dies when you are told through words, actions or gestures that you are paid for your mindless labor and that your mental power, passion, and desire to create a better world have no value for your employer. You cannot expect a garden to flourish without the presence of sun and water. Human empowerment and freedom is the sun and rain that allows creativity and innovation. Companies cannot preach the idea of going above and beyond serving others while using oppressive policies that belittle or ignore people's well-intentioned initiatives.

- Corporations struggle because of their own doing. Executive management pays lip service to the idea of employee empowerment, but at the same time, they take away their natural sense of responsibility, power, creativity, and self-autonomy. By disempowering and casting aside the mind power of most your employees, you create gaps of inequality that are not just demoralizing but poor business practices.

- Executive management's mental insecurities and power grips are evident in corporate culture. Incompetent executive managers embrace a cult of personality that exerts the ultimate control over all decision-making, depriving even mid-level managers and their people of decision-making. Some of these cult-like management groups believe that empowering others may backfire, hence the only way is to keep all checks and balances at their level.

- Centralized authority doesn't work, and it often leads to talent departures, low morale, and revenue loss.

Companies that continue to disempower their employees by continuously elevating decision-making to higher authorities are doomed to failure.

For example, a corporation that has a sales force of couple thousand people was empowering their account executive to use up to $100 in the form of customer credit to resolve issues where the client felt he was wrongly overcharged or subjected to business losses due to company negligence. The credit empowerment system worked well for over two years, and client retention reached a historical peak of 90% in the second year. Only two cases of mismanagement of these credits occurred during that period.

The executive management decided to remove the credit authority from the hands of the account executives and place it at the discretion of the 120 sales directors giving them additional responsibilities. Under pressure, some sales directors used them freely to improve customer retention and satisfaction, while others used them as a power tool or reward mechanism to increase sales reps' productivity. Consequently, customer retention dropped to 75%. Faced with this new problem, a decision was made by the executive team where all $100 credit voucher requests needed to be justified by filling out a questionnaire form that would be sent to the vice president and his senior vice president for collective evaluation and approval.

This process created a major backlog and much unnecessary frustration from all sides. Customer retention dropped to 60% within a few months. Finally, senior management decided to do away with the program, resulting in further erosion of customer retention. The latest customer retention survey reflected that only 45% of customers stayed with the company for more than one year.

This company paid a steep price because of lack of trust and disempowerment of its employees.

Multiple studies have shown that it costs on average five times as much to attract a new customer than to retain existing customers. The first business rule is to maintain the customer base you have and expand it by providing additional value. Loyal customers promote the company brand and serve as a magnet of trust to attract new customers. It's a well-established fact that 44% of companies focus more on customer acquisition and only 18% focus on retention. Only 40% of companies have an equal emphasis on customer acquisition and retention.

Steps to Win Your Employees' Hearts and Minds.

- Express your gratitude for working with talented people. Make it clear that you expect people's best every day, and that you are willing to recognize and reward exceptional performances.
- Align employee purpose with the company purpose. Recognize people for their good intentions and sacrifices, not just job performances. Don't limit people's decision-making to job authority. People should have the flexibility to make good decisions that generate customer satisfaction and retention. Job functions should not restrict people's potential. Good ideas, suggestions, and opinions should be shared, debated and acted upon to benefit everyone.
- Encourage initiative, cooperation among employees, and decentralized group decision-making. Applaud decision-making that improves processes and collective learning.
- Empower all your employees and hold them accountable to make sound decisions. Free up your management team's time to focus on high-value, high-profit projects, and initiatives. Simplify the production process and speed up the decision-making procedures. Listen to your employees' ideas, suggestion

and opinions and implement the recommendations that have the potential to improve the business.

- Identify emerging leaders and develop them for the long-term success of the organization
- Eliminate all redundant tasks, meetings, and low-value time-consuming activities that are recognized as a waste of time.

Executive Calendar and Revenue.

Tom was the head of sales and his calendar was overbooked. Some hours have multiple overlapping tentatively accepted appointments. Tom's schedule was public, and everyone could see color coded busy time frames as well as the few open time slots in his calendar. People tried to claim open calendar spots to discuss initiatives, projects, issues, and promotions. Tom had the privilege to accept or deny these requests. To be a thoughtful leader, he often tentatively took invitations even when they overlapped. The training folks needed Tom's time, and so did people from finance, marketing, deployment, legal and credit.

Tom's attention and input was on high demand. He had mandatory calls and meetings covering most of his calendar space. He was overwhelmed, with no time to unwind or take a rest. His day started at 6 am and ended around midnight. His Saturdays were the days he caught up with his boss and the executive team, and Sunday was the day where he prepared for his next week events. Besides that, he had a grueling travel schedule.

Two years ago, I had the following conversation with Tom.

Me: I have been observing you for the last few days. I cannot understand how you manage your hectic schedule. I'm impressed on how you effortlessly seem to transition during your conference calls from one complex topic to another.

Tom: (After a long reflective pause) I don't believe I do it well. I think that most executive managers are doing a poor job at handling crises. I certainly believe that most corporate managers cannot efficiently manage more than six conference calls per day. Successful partner conference calls require preparation, reflection, and planning—time I don't have. Frequently, I don't even recall the purpose of these calls. If I omit jotting down notes, chances are I will forget what initiatives we discussed and what actions we decided to implement. Many of these meetings are honestly a waste of energy and time.

However, as an executive manager, I must show that I'm involved and informed. I was discussing the subject with a peer of mine in the same industry. He stated that he pretends to listen, while often multi-tasking, and when asked for feedback, he will say that he lost communication for a brief period to force the host to recap the discussion. It's a sad reality, but executives do not necessarily have a better attention span or unique capabilities than we tend to believe.

Me: Why don't you deny the invite request, and accept only what you can handle?

Tom: I tried it in the past, but it's hard. People get frustrated if you keep rejecting their invites. Some reports elevate the importance of their meeting but send me an invite and when I don't show up, they make an excuse for me. I tentatively accept knowing that I won't be able to make the conference call. I must admit that I love to sometimes listen to calls when I'm not expected. You can learn a lot about your sales leaders and their reports when they don't expect you to be in the call. That is why I often accept their requests tentatively.

Me: Do you frequently conduct these anonymous listen-in calls?

Tom: Not really, but they are fun for sure.

Me: Do you feel pressured knowing that most people in the corporation have access to your calendar? Do you think that you should eliminate all white space?

Tom: Not at all, I have no obligation at all. My assistant manages my calendar and pings me on all critical meetings before she accepts or reschedules them.

Many sales executive actively engineer to fill in their calendar to show how hard they work and to validate their position. Busyness doesn't always reflect efficiency or effectiveness. Executives who allow themselves to be carried away by a multitude of conflicting demands, overlapping calendar requests, unmanageable projects and taxing travel schedules are not multitasking but rather fleeing their responsibility by allowing others to control their productive hours.

Tom was brutally honest with me. However, throughout my career, I've met many executives who were enjoying being extremely busy as it makes them feel important and vital to the organization survival. I recall a senior vice president of sales who stated, "I had a week vacation this summer, I went with my wife to Hawaii, and while enjoying the beach I kept looking at the phone every minute for work-related updates. No messages, half-hour later no messages, two hours later nothing. I panicked after four hours, and I checked my phone workability and WIFI reception. Once I established that my phone was working just fine, I called one of my vice-presidents to ensure that all was well. I acted like I was checking if they need something from me, but the reality is I panicked not hearing from anyone. I thought I was fired."

The story above reflects how many senior managers view their job. Their busyness is viewed as the reason why they have the job. They are the brains who get paid big bucks to solve big problems. As long as they are busy, they are safe, and silence means it's time to worry.

Being insanely busy and stressed makes executives feel important. They get energized based on their level of demand. The higher the demand, the more important one feels. Distractions, stretching beyond capacity, over committing makes executives feel good, necessary, and worthy of attention and admiration.

Have you seen how many people flock around the CEO, during company event parties? Important executives want to hang around him for the longest time possible. Middle-managers crave the limelight as well. Everyone wants to show that they are worthy of the CEO's time and attention. Salespeople love to take pictures with the big boss. CEOs love the attention as well; after all, they are human. Imagine a CEO going to a party where no one knows him, how would he feel if everyone is flocking to shake another celebrity's hand? We naturally love attention, we love the appearance of busyness because we innately crave power and attention, and we feel powerless when left alone.

Tom accepted those overlapping calendar schedules despite the fact that he know that he wouldn't attend. As it feed his unconscious ego and perceived worth. The busier he appeared, the more valuable he felt.

Tools Are Just That—Tools

You can spend a fortune on complex selling tools. However, tools cannot make a difference unless they are in the hand of a trained expert. In sales, the expertise is the adequately trained salesperson and the competent sale manager who help navigate unchartered territory looking for opportunities and challenges to overcome.

It takes mental power, audacity, and bravado to reflect on a hairy situation, knowing full well that you will find the answer no matter what. If there is an answer out there, you will find it, polish it, tweak it accordingly, and execute on it.

Power Management

In August 2005, hurricane Katrina hit Florida. hard All flights were grounded. Like thousands of other travelers, I was stuck at my hotel. I went to the only bar open to have a drink and watch the news.

As I sat at the bar, two gentlemen who sounded somewhat drunk and looked like corporate executives sat next to me. The TV sound was muted, forcing me to read the transcription. The conversation between the two gentlemen was loud and hard to ignore.

Gentleman A: Congratulations on your recent promotion. I'm truly happy for you; you finally caught up to me.

Gentleman B: Thanks, but I'm still debating if I should allow my reporting sales vice presidents full authority to manage their business as they see fit or grant them limited authority.

Gentleman A: Your promotion comes with a level of authority that should be managed and guarded carefully. If you allow your vice presidents to do what they want, you will soon find yourself answering to the boss on why you allow it to happen. You worked hard to get to this position, and you cannot squander this opportunity by being soft.

Gentleman B: So, you are saying I should limit their authority and decision-making and ensure that I'm informed on all issues before deciding to approve or deny any request?

Gentleman A: Your subordinates should know that you are extremely busy, even when you are not. Let me explain; having been in this position for a long time, you can learn a few things from me. First, act like you are busy on essential matters all the time, even if it's not the case. Your subordinates will respect you more if they know you are working extremely hard on more significant issues — bosses should act busy, even if they are not.

Second, never approve requests quickly, take your time. If you get your people used to speedy evaluations and approvals, they will expect it as the norm. Hence, when you are truly busy, you will have to deal with their incessant requests for rushed approval. Give yourself time to breathe, you will thank me later for this idea.

Third, never approve anything without asking at least a couple of questions, such as have you vetted this case through research and conversation with the relevant parties? Can you think of a way to minimize these types of requests? Why is this approval necessary? Fourth, ensure that your subordinates complete these tasks in a timely fashion, but know that you have more flexibility on the matter (remember you are busy!) Fifth, I know that we have an open corporate policy, however, never allow your employees to escalate anything over your head unless you authorize it.

Gentleman B: Wow, that's a lot to absorb, but thanks for sharing your practical wisdom.

For a moment, I couldn't believe what I was hearing from these gentlemen. I always believed that people get promoted on the job because of their smarts, hard work, and stellar integrity, not work pretense, subordinate limitation and oppression.

Job authority encompasses power that should be utilized to improve employees' life not to create disengagement or resentment.

Many senior managers are fast at blaming others and view employees as expendable hands for hire. Some executives have a legitimate hectic work schedule and heavy travel load, but many pretend to be busy by intentionally burying themselves in low-value activities. Many suffer from poor interpersonal skills and become more and more inaccessible. Some managers despise responding to their employees while traveling and often hide for days behind out-of-office messages, hoping that the problem will vanish or that you find an alternative solution on your own.

Years ago, I worked for a boss who traveled 70% of the time and often returned calls at odd hours or on weekends. After a quick apology, he expected you to be ready to recap the problem, tell him what actions you took and what do you expect from him, forcing you to be prepared at all times. To resolve this issue, I started creating copious notes on my iPhone the moment I left him a message.

Conversely, I worked for a boss who never answers his phone or emails after 5:00 pm or on weekends. He valued his family time and wouldn't make any sacrifice beyond specific working hours. The problem was we worked in an environment that was prone to issues that occurred at all hours, which required immediate attention because failure to respond was a recipe for disaster and major escalations.

I couldn't call my boss, knowing that he shut his phone and computers outside regular hours. Left with issue resolution after working hours, I started escalating urgent matters to his boss, but my direct boss gave me hell for going over his head. My boss was competent, but he was paranoid and a total control freak. It didn't take long before he realized his mistakes when I started shutting my phones and computer one hour later than his routine schedule. Customer service folks not able to reach my boss or me began seeking assistance from the executive management team at odd hours. A meeting ensued, where I was given authority to manage these crises without fear of repercussion or retaliation. My boss's inaccessibility gave me the ability to distinguish myself and show my commitment to the job. Senior executives took notice, and I was promoted to my boss position primarily because of my dedication to the job.

Lesson Learned

Using lessons from my experiences, past failures and others blunders. I often adopted strategies incorporating learned best practices and values that I believed in.

Identify bottleneck to accelerate. Despite the span of control that I had, I responded as quickly as possible to most employees requests. My purpose was simple; I needed to create a system that evaluated and approved all requests promptly. Collectively with the team, we identified all the bottlenecks and speed bumps that slowed the process of production, then we try to eliminate them. Then I delegated any task that someone else can perform better than the rest; we trusted these individuals judgment and empowered them to make the necessary decisions. I learned early in my career that real power is shared power.

Hence, I delegated the authority of approvals based on complexity and dollar value to multiple people within the organization, including non-managers, especially during surge times. We addressed how to manage these powers responsibly to ensure minimal impact. Surprisingly, I could hardly think of any significant incident that occurred by empowering these non-managers. People don't crave power. Instead, they desire recognition, trust, and the making of identity.

The concept of trust and verify sped up production, eliminated bottlenecks, elevated morale, streamlined the process, and resulted in an uptick of overall quality delivery and performances.

With power comes responsibility. Empowering people means sharing the burden of authority and governance with your employees to accelerate productivity and customer satisfaction. Titles do not matter; what matters is to empower people to move faster, make better decisions, resolve conflicts, and do what's right. Excellent communication and people's trust lead to more magnificent performances and stronger cultural cohesiveness.

CHAPTER 27: SUMMARY

- Corporate email overload is counterproductive, as it erodes performances and employee morale.

- Excessive corporate emails is a dilemma that forces the employee to be in reactive mode attending to emails that often add no value to the company's bottom line.
- Job authority is a power that should be used to empower employees, not to create resentment or dissatisfaction.
- Respect your employees' private time and private life. Productive employees are happy employees.

CHAPTER TWENTY-EIGHT: PRODUCTIVE TEAM MEETINGS PRINCIPLES

Sale team meetings are vital to build team cohesiveness, connect people, share best practices, discuss challenges, and celebrate success.

I have attended countless meetings. Some were inspirational, some were educational, and many were plain boring. Some were well organized, structured and well delivered, while others had no agenda, started late, went overtime, abruptly ended and lacked focus. I also attended unproductive meetings and energy-killing meetings where the leader had daily meetings that were truly painful to attend.

Meetings' Purpose

Most organizations rely on meetings to set direction, convey changes, announce new strategies and tactics, and disseminate information. Whether you are an entrepreneur or work for a company, you probably have attended several meetings; they are an essential part of communication in the job.

Disciplined meetings can add value to the organization; they are real work and should be part of productive work time not a downtime session. It's common to hear the leader stating, "the meeting is over, let's get to work." As if the meeting was a time to relax and kick back. A meeting that doesn't have a strict agenda and doesn't add true value should be eliminated.

Good meetings should have:

1. A clear purpose and goals
2. A structured agenda and a path to follow
3. Participant role and time frames

Meeting Principles

- **Respect employees' time**. Aim to accomplish twice as much in half the time required. Cut unnecessary information, send 24 hours in advance an email reflecting your questions along with the details you will cover during your meeting. Allow people to absorb information, reflect on vital areas of improvement and respond via email with their ideas and insight.
- **Time is money.** Stay focused on productivity, use only the necessary time. If you schedule one-hour meeting and you cover your agenda in half the time, free up your people quickly.
- **Ninety-minute rule.** Never exceed 90-minute meetings. People lose focus. Cover the essentials and lose the fat. Meeting are expensive and mentally draining, so keep them on track.
- **Stay the course.** It's natural that people will digress and get off topic. Stay in control and steer back the conversation to the topic by reminding people that you take your agenda and time frames seriously. Off-topic subjects can be discussed at a different time.
- **Seek outcome.** Meetings must have a purpose and an outcome when applicable. Set the right expectation ahead of time on what you are to accomplish and define the decision process to get your specified outcome.

- **Measure outcome.** The key is to convert meeting ideas into actions that add value to employees and the company. Send a summary of collected ideas, insight, and comments with the group. Draft a shared action plan and measure its progress and results. People love to see that their ideas, time, and energy are creating lasting value and improving lives.

- **Candor.** People naturally refrain from saying things that may be taken out of context or interpreted differently. Create an email inbox where employees can freely and anonymously respond without fear of repercussions or embarrassment. This strategy unshackles people's minds, and allow the company to benefit from ideas and insight they wouldn't normally have access to.

- **Get better.** Pay close attention to the way your meetings are conducted. Request frequent comments, ideas, and insight on how to improve your meetings. Eliminate what doesn't work, and incorporate new ideas and approaches. Anonymous feedback can improve the meeting efficacy and quality.

Some meetings may be simply informative while others seek some form of decision-making. Decision-making can vary from leader-driven, group-weighted or consensual through members' voting; the key is to set upfront expectations to eliminate time wasting. Define a decision path and stick to keeping your meeting focused without preventing employee's creativity or stifling peoples out-of-the-box thinking.

Meetings that Deliver Bad News

- ***Time it right.*** Reserve bad news meetings to the end of the day or a Friday afternoon. Bad news disrupts people's morale and impacts productivity. You want to be honest with your people, but you need to think ahead of time on how to frame the delivery of the message.

- ***Be direct.*** You don't have to sugarcoat the reality of the matter by withholding vital information. Salespeople are resilient; they can handle bad news and overcome it.
- ***Question handling***. Allow your salespeople to ask questions. Anticipate questions and think ahead of the best way to communicate your responses in an honest sensitive way.
- ***Next step.*** Bad news creates fear and anxieties. Explain what one should expect next, what kind of impact it will have on the affected people and what's your vision on how to deal with it now and in the future.
- ***Expectations.*** Define new expectations and the course of action going forward. People are creative; they can handle unimaginable hardship as long as they know they have a leader who has a vision toward a better future.

CHAPTER 28: SUMMARY

- Disciplined meetings add value to the organization; unplanned meeting are a waste of time.
- A meeting should always have an agenda. Meetings are work time and should be treated as such.
- Every meeting should have a purpose, a rigid time frame, a conclusion, and an outcome with follow-up.
- The leader should anticipate questions that may be asked and needs to prepare to deliver value.

PART VII: THE SALESPERSON'S CHALLENGES

"I have never worked a day in my life without selling. If I believe in something, I sell it, and I sell it hard. When I'm not selling, I'm hard at work planting seeds in the mind of my prospects to ensure a perpetual cycle of bountiful harvest." – Anthony Chaine

"Don't watch the clock; do what it does. Keep going." — Sam Levenson

"The most difficult thing is the decision to act, the rest is merely tenacity. The fears are paper tigers. You can do anything you decide to do. You can act to change and control your life; and the procedure, the process is its own reward." — Amelia Earhart

CHAPTER TWENTY-NINE: SELLING IS HARD

Whether you are a sales manager, a sales executive or a salesperson, you probably realized by now that sales require endurance, creativity, and tenacity. Selling can wear you out no matter how passionate you are about the profession.

Most salespeople harbor an inner desire to become part of the management team to acquire new experiences and express their leadership style and philosophy. Several studies reveal that most salespeople who aspire to become part of the management team possess a sincere desire to help other sales professionals by sharing the unique knowledge and experiences they acquired over the years.

Most successful salespeople confidently believe that the characteristics that allowed them to become successful as salespeople will enable them to become successful as managers. Becoming a great sales manager is indeed an idea worth pursuing.

Alternatively, other studies have demonstrated that many aspiring salespeople desire to join the rank of sales management to escape the daily grind of having to deal with rejections, setbacks, and the monotony of the selling profession. A survey conducted by a medical equipment manufacturer in Japan showed that even the most successful people who understand the value of rejection in the process of developing relationships with the customers stated they could not help but take customer rejection personally.

A top salesperson describes it this way: "While you intellectually understand that rejection cannot be taken personally, you cannot help it as a human being. Each rejection is like toxic waste, you can hide it deep into your mind, but you can never get rid of its toxicity seeping through your mind's cracks." Another salesperson puts it this way. "Rejections are like tiny wounds that hardened with time and leave scars that deepen with new injuries. Soon, your whole body is covered with depressing scars that remind you of the battles you went through and survived." A B2B salesperson describes rejections as the following. "Prospects' harsh or negative comments may be forgotten, but dismissive attitudes, demeaning gestures, and bad behaviors stay with you forever. Over time, they erode your enthusiasm, diminish your confidence, and slow your initiatives."

Sales success requires one to go through an unimaginable number of disappointments and heartbreaks before you catch a break. As a sales professional, you should accept that you will lose deals due to personal mistakes, company errors, buyer's remorse, uncontrollable events, stronger competition, and unpredictable external forces. The question is, how do you regain your equilibrium quickly to rebound back?

Long-Term Impact of Rejections.

Rejection tolerance. Salespeople tend to have a higher understanding of rejection, and most can handle a considerable amount of denials. It gets harder when one experiences a long period of rejections. High rejection intensity can be tolerated for a short period, but a long period of sales droughts can be demoralizing and discouraging.

Emotional tenderness. Have you ever sent promotional material at the request of a customer and never asked for a meeting? Have you ever provided a thorough demonstration about your products, answered your customer's questions with enthusiasm and vigor, but never asked for the order? Do you efficiently manage to develop trust and friendship with your customers, but never ask them to make a buying decision?

If you answer yes to any of these questions, chances are that your fear of rejection is alive and well. That is why you avoid asking for the sale or try to advance the deal for fear of losing the relationship. Salespeople who behave as such try unconsciously to prevent the pain of rejection by not asking for the sale, and hope that the customer will buy from them because they provide on-demand service without pressure. These salespeople see their approach as a differentiator factor.

Perceived Worth. Have you ever hesitated to call on corporate CEOs thinking they are too powerful to take a sales call? Do you play it safe and call on lower-ranking non-decision makers business employees?

If it's the case, you are not alone. Most salespeople avoid calling on the C-level decision makers because they believe.

1. They are shielded by gatekeepers.
2. They are too powerful, busy, and smart. Hence, they will be dismissive and hard to persuade.
3. They will blacklist you if you fail to impress them right away.

Winning Probability

Selling is a mind game. Your success depends on:

- ***Preparation.*** Show confidence, because each customer dialogue will have twists and zigzags along the way. You should expect comments, requests, and questions that will take you away from your path. The key is to stay in control and bring back the client conversation into your pre-planned path.

- ***Knowledge.*** Most customer dialogues are ongoing quizzes and evaluations. Your customers will pick quickly on the areas that reflect your lack of knowledge. You don't have to pretend to know what you don't know; research the subject matter after the meeting and get back to your customer. Your knowledge enhances your confidence, and the latter is derived from how you feel about yourself in general.
- ***Visualization.*** You've got to realize that selling is a mathematical probability game. You cannot predict your success rate, but you can improve your win probability by following a sales process and sharpening it to increase your winning odds.
- ***Decision-making.*** If you decide to call in daily into 50 prospects, you should not deviate from that goal. You should self-renew your commitment daily without the burden of past disappointment. Stay focused on your goals. What do you want to accomplish? Moreover, how are you going to achieve it?
- ***Act.*** Go all in, stay true to your goals, stay calm, collected, and confident no matter what the outcome is. Evaluate your options as you go, reflect and make the necessary adjustment throughout the day.
- ***Desire level.*** Keep the faith, stay faithful to your commitments, and firmly develop your conviction and desire to win. Refuse to go home until you accomplish your set desires.
- ***Confidence.*** Your knowledge, preparation, visualization, and action won't make a difference if you don't project a good dose of faith of your skills, your business solutions, and your ability to deliver the outcome you promised your customers.
- ***Persistence.*** You can be armed and ready for battle all you want. However, you won't win the war unless you are mentally

prepared to keep fighting, even when you lose your will and desire to continue. Persistence is what wins battles, not resources. Only the toughest win the sales war because they never give in or give up.

- ***Value Delivery***. Your value solution needs to fulfill your customer's needs and preferably go beyond to deliver a "wow factor" that becomes memorable long after the sales occurs. Your product and your services need to be far superior to your competitors to stay relevant and create loyal customers.

The Power of a Strong Mindset

Have you ever wondered why some salespeople can sell at a higher frequency than others? Why is it they can turn anything they touch into a fortune, while many others strive to survive?

A healthy mindset is a trait shared by top performers. It's the strength of mind that is derived from a combination of environmental awareness, heightened mental sensitivity, keen focus, strong resilience, and connectedness to your inner belief systems.

How to Build a Healthy Mindset?

- ***Reflection time.*** There is a time for action and hustle to execute your plan. However, it would help if you allocated time for introspection and adjustment. You cannot measure your progress while on the go, you can only evaluate your progress, ponder on new ideas and concepts during idle time. Eagles spot more prey when cruising at higher altitudes than when actively looking for prey. Some animals stay idle for extended periods before unexpectedly attacking a prey that is often not aware of their presence.

- ***Idle time.*** Allows you to clear your mind of mental chatter and noise to focus on planning your self-development and success path. Clarity happens when silence meet mental concentration.

- ***Channel the energy of negative thoughts.*** Top performers manage the power of negative thoughts as a source of abundant positive energy. It's natural and healthy to experience a variety of negative emotions and feelings through the day. These negative emotions can propel you from feeling sorry for yourself to a state of confidence where you push yourself to achieve significant progress. Make it a habit to start your day with a positive, powerful, and inspirational thoughts, but allow negative energy to broaden your perspective, strength your resolve, and infuse a dose of healthy paranoia into your day. Growth requires you to reframe your thinking and rework your inner-self-talk to achieve your true potential.

- ***Loser syndrome.*** Feeling lost or overwhelmed? No problem, it happens to the best of us. The key is to stay focused, work your priority list, commit to getting things done. The more successful you get, the more negativity and setbacks you will have to face. People by nature tend to doubt someone's success. It's harder sometimes to prove the legitimacy of your victory than to achieve it. The higher you fly away from the herd, the more negativity you will be subjected to. Focus like the pros on your inner motivational guidance, ignore all external judgment and noise that attempt to erode your self-confidence and bring you down. There will be a time when the haters will try to become your friends.

CHAPTER 29: SUMMARY

- Salespeople aspire to become part of the management leadership. Allow for internal upward mobility, coach and educate your people on what it takes to become a great sales leader.

- Salespeople must be resilient, gritty, and driven to survive and prosper in a competitive landscape.
- Building confidence takes practice, coaching, and training. Self-assurance and enthusiasm in sales is a transformative force that turns average individuals into great performers.
- A healthy mindset is a trait shared by top performers. Mindset recalibration and adjustments requires deep reflection, fluidity of thoughts and willingness to change and evolve.

CHAPTER THIRTY: PROFESSIONAL SELLING

Do You Believe in Your Products?

Selling is a rewarding and humbling experience. Whether you are a novice in sales or a veteran salesperson, nothing will prepare you for skepticism, mistrust, and disbelief that you will have to endure to make a sale. Your smarts and enthusiasm may not be enough sometimes to get an appointment. You can be a fanatic believer in your company's products and services, but your customer may not believe you, thinking you are just staging enthusiasm to win their business. The value you are trying to convey through your business solution may not be viewed the same way by your customer.

Selling is hard no matter how long you have been in the business. Ask field salespeople that sell a product to small-medium-business in the heat of summer or the bitter cold of winter how much they enjoy their job trying to make a presentation to super busy small retailers trying to serve hordes of customers.

Ask salespeople who are trying to solicit business in high-rise buildings in New York, being chased away by building managers even though they may have had a pre-set customer meeting to enter the building. Ask the B2B salesperson that try to meet the CTO or CMO that never has time to meet despite multiple attempts.

Selling is undoubtedly financially rewarding, it's liberating as you control your income and schedule, but it's also tough, humbling, emotionally draining, and mentally crippling sometimes. Believing in yourself first is the key to learn, adapt and conquer. The profession of selling forces you to get in touch with your inner strengths and weaknesses. Overcoming challenges forces you to bring your best game, improve, and learn continuously to win.

Believing

Should salespeople believe in themselves, their products/services, and their company to excel in sales? The answer is obvious: yes.

Professional selling is about trust and confidence, building good rapport and relationships with customers, and adapting to your audience's personality to connect at a deeper level.

Selling is a transfer of belief from the salesperson to the customer. Believing in yourself and the business solutions you are selling can compensate for the lack of skill. Customers are emotional; they either believe in your story or not. When they sense doubt, hesitation or trickery they back off from the deal.

Belief Myth

Proper training, coupled with a solid education and a good dose of personal curiosity, will give you a good grasp of the features, advantages, and benefits of your products. A good market study can allow you to understand your product's competitive strengths and gaps in comparison to your competitors.

Do you have to believe in selling?

If you don't believe to your very core in sales, you probably won't last long in the industry. Selling is an exchange of enthusiasm, energy, and trust. If you don't believe that you can genuinely help your customer achieve their goals, then you attempt in selling will sound shallow, phony, and unauthentic.

Do you have to believe in your products or service to sell?

You don't have to believe in your product or service to establish a great rapport and build a stable relationship with your customer. However, without an unshakeable faith in the value of your products, one cannot succeed in the long term. Phony selling is unethical selling.

Do you have to believe in yourself to sell?

You don't have to believe in yourself to deliver a rehearsed presentation. However, you will sound shaky, lacking confidence, and confused the moment you meet a shrewd business owner or a savvy corporate executive. I have witnessed few product demonstrations where the rookie salesperson, concealed well their nervousness and delivered acceptable presentation to the customer, but that's uncommon. You can sell anything to anyone with the proper training, a good dose of curiosity and practice.

Professional selling requires a strong belief in oneself and the business solutions you are recommending. Your convictions and strong belief is the fuel that powers your thinking, communication, and persuasion skills. It's the glue that builds genuine relationships and long-term success.

Genuine Belief is the Force that:

1. Keeps you interested in your customer
2. Allows you to ask impactful and significant questions
3. Permits deep listening to your customer needs and wants
4. Allows you to offer sincere recommendations
5. Helps your customer make good choices
6. Connects at a deep level with your customers

Selling is Believing.

If you are not genuinely passionate about helping people to better their businesses and life, then you may want to explore other field where your skills may be more suitable. Selling is all about caring and doing the right thing for your customer all the time. Your company hired you to grow its client base and revenue by helping its customers.

Sales is extremely tough, and you will get hit from many fronts every day. Some days you will have to move mountains to resolve all types of issues. You will get challenged, frustrated, ignored, and misunderstood more often than you can handle. Some days, you will feel helpless and hopeless, when your customer experience problems with a product you sold them and is now crippling their business operations.

You do your best, and despite your best efforts and pleading with your boss to escalate the issue for a quicker resolution, nothing works, the customer's incessant calls become unbearable, the tone changes, the language gets more colorful, threats amplify. You feel trapped, desperate, and alone. You want to resolve you customer's issue because you care and because it's your responsibility and duty.

No matter how successful you are in sales, you will have days where you want to quit, give it all up to start somewhere else fresh. A new start, a new beginning, sounds tempting sometimes where nothing works, but you know in your heart that it is the same anywhere you go. So, you keep going.

You wake up the next day, not too desperate to get to the office and start selling. You look at the phone, and you want to start selling. However, you remember what you just went through to resolve the customer's issue, and you hesitate. You want to sell, make money, create revenue and make your customer happy. However, customer support and management assistance are not adequate, and it brings your morale down. So, you keep yourself busy with non-revenue driven tasks that produce no tangible results but keep you busy.

Then, your fears, doubts, and self-loathing start slowing getting into your psych. You feel like you lost your passion and desire to press on and do your job. You make a few sales calls and pretend to be engaged. You may even sell enough to avoid your sales manager's close scrutiny. However, you know that's not professional selling or believing on you purpose. It's simply a short-term mental tactic to dodge your responsibilities and duty .

Issues will happen; some days it feels like you've got a tsunami of challenges that require your time, energy, and creativity. These storms are part of sales cycles, and you will occasionally have to go through rough times, before the calm returns.

Is it You or Your Business Solution?

When you joined the company, were you committed to success? Did you have the necessary level of conviction to do your job?

Most salespeople do. No one starts a job to fail or predict that the market will be extremely super-competitive, making it hard to get prospect's attention, or work in an organization that has poor customer service or management team.

It is easy to exhibit pessimistic views and tendencies when faced with significant challenges or when you are questioning the viability of the deal, the customer credibility, the company brand and credibility in the market or the quality of its cross-functional team or management.

Selling is tough and riddled with customers' debilitating issues, where you may find yourself to be the only destination for customers' frustration. Handling it professionally turns irritated customers into satisfied, loyal believers. Great customer trust and healthy relationships are built during hard times. By going above and beyond what's expected, and delivering a wow-factor you can demonstrate your professionalism and reliability when it matters the most.

Sales is about the salesperson first, products and services come second. Sales is about understanding, good communication, and a show of a good dose of empathy. Loyal customers are won in moments of need. Being present and fighting for your customer will improve your chances of building long-lasting, lucrative relationships.

CHAPTER 30: SUMMARY

- Believing in yourself, your purpose, and the value you add to your customers' lives is a must to become successful in sales.
- Believing with conviction is something that can be cultivated through deep reflection and selective exposure to testimonials from customers that benefited from the value of your business solution. A product that improves customers lives is worth selling.
- The sales profession can be tough. However, it's among the most rewarding jobs in the world, whether financially, personally or psychologically.
- Selling requires issue resolution skills. Your ability to navigate and seek assistance and cooperation from the organization's key-players to resolve hard-to-solve issues is key to your success.

PART VIII: BUSINESS ADAPTABILITY MECHANISMS

"Business adaptability means accepting continuous change and assimilating quickly to meet market demands, which lead to survival. To win, you will need to create the change and force your competitors to adapt to survive."— Anthony Chaine

"Adaptability enforces creativity, and creativity is adaptability."— Pearl Zhu

"It is not the strongest of the species that survives, nor the most intelligent. It is the one that is most adaptable to change." Charles Darwin

CHAPTER THIRTY-ONE: TRANSFORMATIVE FORCES THAT ARE IMPACTING SALES

The Internet Transformative Powers

The internet has eliminated the competitive informational advantage that salespeople use to leverage in the past to win new business. Historically, a salesperson would hold essential product information and share with the customer as he saw fit to influence decision-making. The internet has changed the way data dissipated and was controlled. It moved the information control from the grip of the salesperson to the customer. Today, the customer has access to a flood of information on almost any topic, but access to too much information can leave the buyer confused and in search of an expert salesperson to simplify these ambiguities.

The Transformative Power of the Internet

The internet is a transformative force that has changed the way we live, shop and interact with one another. The internet has facilitated the creation of breakthrough technologies comparable in magnitude to true innovations like the electricity, telephone or the automobile. Today, most people believe that companies that do not have a significant internet presence are doomed to failure. The internet has impacted the way we gather and share information, entertain ourselves, and communicate. The internet impact on business is substantial. From e-commerce to mobile-business, every facet of business is forced to adapt to survive.

The way companies had operated in the past is no longer the way customers interact, consume information, shop, or self-educate. Customer buying behavior is changing fast as it is influenced by social media, brand recognition, feedback, and review scoring. Customer's attention span is getting shorter. Most companies are spending more money to grab customer attention, drive a message or create awareness. It's getting harder to sell the old way, and today companies must reach out to the customer via multichannel with customized content that meets customers' needs and desires.

The internet allows businesses to reach directly to their customers via digital social marketing and traditional marketing. It lowered costs dramatically across the demand and supply chain. In the past, it took decades of evolution and natural progression for a business to reach the scale and maturity necessary to dominate a specific industry. Today, new e-business comers can disrupt major industries and dominate the space within a brief period, leaving well-established brands in the dust.

Amazon is a good example. Its founder Jeff Bezos started the company in July 1994 with the website launching publicly in 1996. Today, this company, which owes its existence to the internet, is the second company in history that reached a market value estimate exceeding a trillion dollars. Amazon's job is to connect the buyer with the seller using a website portal. People buy from Amazon primarily because of convenience, available options, and ease of returns.

Client Loyalty Is a Relic

In the past, companies that have done an excellent job advertising their products and educating their audience enjoyed immense loyalty that went on for decades. Ford Taurus lovers or Mustang drivers would never have shifted to a different brand. Harley Davidson die hard patrons would never consider another brand, even when it's an established brands like Indian motorcycles. Loyalty was everything when you loved a brand you stuck to it. Unconsciously, you became an extension of the brand and an unpaid promoter of the brand. It was natural to advertise the brand that you patronize and love. Being part of a brand name gave you a sense of belonging to a tribe and it gave you the right as a connoisseur to share your experience with your tribe, family, friends or anyone willing to listen. However, that was then!

Today's customers are looking for innovation, simplicity, transparency, ease-of-use as well as excellent customer experience. E-business has transformed local businesses to global competitors. Today, a company can generate a tribe of followers as well as industry influencers by simply being interactive over several social media platforms. A good example is how loyal customers follow, interact, review and promote brands like Apple, Tesla, and Virgin. They are not just users, they are fans.

The internet evolution continues to transform the way we do business all over the world. Companies like Facebook, Netflix, Alibaba, Dell, Google, and Amazon’s core businesses revolve around e-commerce; without the internet, these companies won’t exist.

Their websites act as smart billboards; you get updates on products, your curiosity gets whet, you spend more time on the site, you buy, chat, post reviews and comments. You become part of the interactive experience which cement your loyalty and elevates your buying confidence. Customers are no longer looking to buy a product and move on; they are looking to buy a product while being entertained and informed throughout the whole buying experience.

Lagging Business-to-Business

While many business leaders understand the importance and impact of e-business in terms of building brand awareness and attracting potential buyers, many have little or poor interactive marketing presence to drive new prospects.

B2B retailers using field sales reps to interact with business owners will become a rarity in the future. According to *Forrester*, B2B e-commerce sales will reach $1 trillion by 2020. This fundamental shift will require B2B retailers to evolve to meet the market demand to stay relevant.

Forrester reported that 75% of B2B buyers prefer to shop online when shopping products for work, but only 25% of these companies sell online. B2B business owners are working to bridge the gap. *Forrester* estimated that 1 million U.S. B2B salespeople, or about 20% of the sales force, will lose their jobs to self-service. This evolution of e-commerce to meet market demand will force many salespeople to find new careers. Technology has rendered several positions obsolete, like phone operators, elevator operators, gas pump attendants and tellers.

In specific industries, e-business may have a limited effect on growing the company's bottom line. That may be the case for large ticket transactions related to government and some types of B2B businesses. For example, Boeing won't sell Airbuses online. However, that is changing fast, as well, as most industries are increasingly adding large ticket items to their sites to attract unique buyers.

The internet, aka current social media, will have even more transformative powers to affect buyers and sellers alike. It has already shifted the power from sellers to the buyer by reducing the cost to switch along with the ability to make informed decisions based on product reviews, company reputation, customer services, and other critical factors that clients deem vital.

Today, a quick search online can provide a slew of potential options at the click of the mouse. However, too many choices can slow down the decision process. Hence, customers will steer toward the providers with a one-stop-shop options. The company's brand name, reputation, and credibility will play a significant role in the customer decision-making process.

Finally, the internet has broadened market reach, increased available choices, and reduced product costs. Today, a local business can have as much access to international clients as large players. While not every company can become a direct e-commerce global force, most companies can benefit from establishing a substantial presence online to reach a broader audience.

Today, the right marketing strategy can allow a company to customize its messages and content to influence customers' decision-making processes. Many businesses exist today only in a digital form. Giants like Amazon and Alibaba have adopted a business model that is purely digital, and we recently started seeing some of these giant e-commerce multinational starting to acquire physical retail stores to further promote their brands. Decades ago, digital success would have been something that could exist only in someone's imagination. Brick and mortar businesses will survive, however, most of these businesses will probably morph into a hybrid model serving both physical products to local customers while serving a global demand digitally.

CHAPTER 31: SUMMARY

- The internet has eliminated customer dependency on the salesperson to acquire products and services information.
- The internet has changed the way customers search, interact, buy, and surf the web. Social media has become the most dependable customer-to-customer trusted feedback source.
- An organization brand has become subject to its online reputation. Bad reviews can destroy a reputation that took years to build.

- Customer loyalty become a hard-fought daily battle. Your customer loyalty is an ever-shifting wave that requires the sales organization to stay agile in terms of innovation, product communication updates, and social interaction to keep the customer engaged, curious and happy.
- Business-to-business sales organizations will need to upgrade their customer experience models to stay relevant in a hyper-digital competitive landscape.

CHAPTER THIRTY-TWO: SPEED TO MARKET DOMINATION

Organizational speed is the outcome derived from purposeful internal actions and common sense policies. Everything is getting faster than ever before, including computers, cars, trains, airplanes, communication, and even Olympic athletes' performances. Competition is no longer generated in China, Germany or India. Today's most dangerous competition is generated by two guys working insane hours in their garage in a startup venture leveraging a variety of technological platforms that will devastate an entire industry and render many legacy companies' obsolete within few years. Within the span of fewer than eighteen months, YouTube went from a startup funded by Chad Hurley's personal credit cards to being sold to Google for $1.4 billion.

As of this writing, Uber was valued at more than $72 billion, more than forty times its value a few years ago. Groupon leaped from conception to $2.4 billion. Usage of technological advents and the speed of market evolution has fostered the right environment for an expansion of a new breed of organizations that are scaling at a record level, attracting investors and customers, and generating market value at a pace never conceived possible few years ago. Companies that relied in the past on size and longevity are no longer shielded from newer startups that are scalable, fast moving, and use smart, modern systems that allow them to gain a competitive edge. This is the age of billion-dollar start-ups, where the best and brightest companies compete at a breakneck speed. Today, the fastest win, as long as the organization keeps speed, efficiency, and innovation as a core foundation.

Organization speed defines the company's ability to seize opportunities, act against external threats, innovate, expand to new markets, learn, hire and retain talented people that thrive in a fast-paced environment.

Companies built around the idea of speed and innovation are dominating the market, e.g.: Amazon, Apple, Facebook, Google, and Tesla. These companies' ability to make fast decisions in terms of innovation and creativity to serve the market has propelled them to become global giants.

In contrast, companies like Blockbuster, Blackberry, Kodak and Myspace are either out of business or have changed what they do because of their inability to move fast enough to meet market demand.

Samsung's slogan "perpetual crisis" is a strong message that organizational growth happens when you stretch beyond your natural limits, break conventional thinking, and adapt to global changes and breakneck innovation speed. Apple is another company that moved with incredible speed to new business areas and dominated them from the start.

Fast Growth Dominates Slow Growth

Domino's Pizza realized that the biggest issue with home delivery pizza was by the time it arrived at its destination, it was cold. Hence, Domino's focus on one specific unique selling proposition to turn a regional player into a global brand. "Pizza delivered to your door in thirty minutes or it's free." Domino's realized that winning was all about speed, so it transformed its business model to exploit that opportunity. Domino's new concept was to serve its customers quality pizza fast and at the expected temperature. The business concept allowed Domino's local brand to become a global household name.

Historically, the business world was about the survival of the fittest; today's business is about the survival of the fastest. Speed matters in any race. Speed is required in decision-making, implementation, execution, delivery, getting a yes, getting funded, and gaining a competitive advantage.

Fast growth yields high returns, and it predicts the longevity of the company and the sustainability of its business model. Company growth depends on the following factors: market demand, rapid adoption, and capitalization. Companies that don’t increase their top line will stop growing and become either subject to acquisition or financial insolvency. Sales and profit-making are vital for survival. The CEO needs to be in competing mode at all times. He should be looking for ways to grow fast, take advantage of opportunities faster than his competitors, and predict market trends that could allow new growth and geographic expansions. Growth requires refocusing time and resources on faster-growing areas where the company has expertise, capabilities, and human assets needed for profitable growth.

Every CEO should be asking the following questions to evaluate and accelerate growth:

- What growth level do we need to achieve? Moreover, how fast do we need to acquire it?
- What markets are available to compete in?
- What risk would we incur in our core markets?
- What opportunities are available to allow us to create enough cash flow to sustain our business while investing in the new expansion?
- When should we act?

Throughout my career, I have seen major deals lost because of slower reaction, misalignment of priorities between cross-functional teams, disagreement among managers, and pure corporate rivalry. I have witnessed talented people leaving companies because they couldn't handle deliberate decision-making any more. Many got tired of internal corporate bickering, self-sabotaging, back-stabbing corporate game, and snail-pace decision-making, so they left.

Winning a deal is a laborious process. It takes a great deal of effort and ingenuity to win a contract. Losing a deal for frivolous reasons, like the deliberate slow reaction from a specific individual or manager, personal vendetta, internal rivalry or power shows is counterproductive and harmful to the salesperson and the organization. Many hard-earned deals die a slow death waiting for cross-functional team decision-making or painfully slow decision-making by some corporate managers that act like they are doing you a favor with each approved deal. Many senior managers pretend to be way too busy to move people's requests at an acceptable rate. Playing the power and ego game is alive and well in most organizations. Everyone knows the managers who are working and those who pretend to work, those who move things along because it's the essence of the job and those who create bottlenecks to exert control and stay relevant.

Deliberate Slow Decision-Making

I worked with a senior vice president who was known for his slow decision-making. It took a minimum of three emails of back and forth before he considered approving even the most insignificant request. He bragged about his management philosophy of checks and controls. He complained about division performance, but he never realized that he was asphyxiating the production velocity by his poor decision-making rationale.

Some managers either pretend to be perfectionists or are unable to make decisions fast enough because of fear of making mistakes or love of control. Routine decision-makings should be performed quickly. Decisions that require additional input and clarity should be handled with care and speed. Tough decisions should be worked on with a sense of urgency and priority because these are the decisions that have the most impact on revenue, policy, risk, and progress.

Slow decision-making costs organizations time, money, relationships, reputation and affects salespeople morale negatively.

It's mind boggling, the level of incompetence we see at the corporate senior management level sometimes. The sales manager must deal with intense pressure coming from the salesperson and often irate clients who have a business to run.

Selling is a marathon. The salesperson may be working a deal for an extended time, but the moment the customer signs the contract, the sprint begins. Smart companies work as a force of one to get everything done super fast to get customers up-and-running in record time. Slow companies ignore time, build frustration along the way, and by the time the business solution is delivered, customers are already tired of hearing weak excuses and apologies from everyone.

Slow Decision-making Disrupts Innovation and Creativity.

Blackberry was a leading cell phone manufacturer that dominated the business world a decade ago. However, because of lack of innovation and slow decision-making, they lost their competitive edge to other cell phone manufacturers that were more innovative, audacious, and agile decision makers.

Blockbuster's deliberate decision-making to not embrace online streaming contributed to its business demise. Seizing an opportunity has everything to do with timing and fast action. Good, fast decision-making encompasses risk, but it's better than deliberate hesitation, slow fact-gathering, and waiting for the perfect timing that may never come.

Unfortunately, most companies operate inefficiently because of broken systems and broken internal communication and alignment among cross-functional teams and managers. You would expect that senior managers should know the economic impact they have for slowing the process, but that's not always true. Slow decision-making leads to loss of financial opportunities, diminished employee morale, loss of trust in leadership, and weakness the brand positioning.

Jack was a regional vice president in a telecommunication company. He had two hundred salespeople reporting to him and he operated without an administrative assistant due to a recent cost-cutting strategy. When I met Jack in a local coffee shop for a chat, he looked exhausted and expressed that he was tired of his executive managers' decision-making horrible response time. He was contemplating moving to another smaller company where the decision-making pace was somewhat acceptable.

Me: What's going on, Jack? You seem like you have a lot on your mind.

Jack: I don't understand why today the development cycles of products and services is getting shorter, which is excellent as it gives us more opportunities to penetrate new markets. However, it seems that our underwriting department folks and finance managers are deliberately slowing the decision-making process. They are acting as the antithesis of speed. They are holding action hostage because they fear making mistakes.

Sales revolves around the speed of delivery. My people are working hard to win new B2B opportunities, and once they do their part and submit the contract, the process takes forever. It's demoralizing and mentally paralyzing.

Most of our business solutions require multiple approvals and assistance from a variety of cross-functional teams and support teams to deliver our proposed customized solution. However, when every department is slow to act, it makes our job near impossible. Senior managers are aware of the problem, but they are not doing much to change the behavior. I'd rather work for an organization that moves fast, even when things are not perfect.

Great organizations like Facebook are obsessed with speed. Mark Zuckerberg said "move fast and break things" and "if you never break anything, you're probably not moving fast enough". My salespeople's morale has shattered because, despite their best effort, they feel that their efforts are not appreciated by senior management.

Me: Are your executives aware of the situation?

Jack: The executive team knows of our challenges. However, I believe they don't know what to do to resolve this problem. It seems that sales is the only department that is working with a sense of urgency here. When we try to push these folks, we not only get pushed back, but we get lectured by mediocre people who are not doing their jobs. Senior managers are hard to reach; decision-making is painfully slow, often requiring too many unnecessary back-and-forth. It's just a quagmire. I honestly feel that the reason we are not advancing fast enough is that we are self-sabotaging.

Me: How do you propose to speed up the process?

Jim: We need to trust and verify. Making quick decisions is vital to moving forward. We need to streamline the whole process of decision-making. We cannot slow our pace and growth by creating walls every step of the way. Simplifying the current process is a necessity for our survival.

To remain competitive, relevant, and agile in this global market, organizations need to establish a decision-making process across the board. A right decision-making policy will prepare the organization to stay relevant and on the right path when faced with leadership turnover, operations changes, or shifts in the business model. Continuous education is required to ensure that all managers know how to resolve personal conflicts and external issues to advance the company best interest. A consistent and thoughtful approach should be the norm when making business decisions that affect the company, employees, and its customers. Everyone should be accountable for the quality, accuracy and speed of their decision-making.

Organization of Speed

Most organizations fail not because their products and services are poorly designed or have little market appeal to create enough revenue. They fail because of the aggregate poor decision-making of all its employees. People are the problem and the solution at the same time.

1. ***A conscious matrix of speed***. Developing an organization that is conscious of the value of speed across its departments and processes can eliminate stagnation, create a speed culture, and promote innovation.

2. ***Productivity speed must be measured.*** System and process bottlenecks need to be defined, studied, and improved upon. By monitoring progress and the impact of adopted changes, the company can determine the factors that contributed to its positive effects.

3. ***Employee collaboration***. Cooperation among the company's cross-functional teams is an essential element to productivity and success. Cross-departmental cooperation improves morale, speeds execution, and improves results.

4. ***Fast Thinkers.*** Some managers and employees tend to learn, think, and act faster than others. A quick salesperson may find it

hard to work for a slow manager. Salespeople who are used to communicating more quickly via text and emails may find it difficult to work with a manager who prefers a phone conversation. A faster employee needs to be put in a position where the speed of decision-making is paramount. Slower individuals need to work in areas that match their capabilities.

5. ***Rapid, but accurate decision-making***. The company should provide continuous training to develop individuals to make rapid but accurate decisions that impact company revenue production.

6. ***Cross-functional team sharing.*** An internal employee sharing system should be implemented to allow different individuals to share best practices and new information. Sharing discoveries that improve decision-making processes should be encouraged and rewarded accordingly.

7. ***The barrier to speed.*** By establishing a culture of speed, all employees should be educated in making speed a priority in everything they do. Each employee should become part of the solution by using their role to contribute to the organization speed.

8. ***Reduce manager's approval to a minimum***. Approvals slow the process of revenue generation. If approval is required, then you should reduce the time needed to get it to an acceptable minimum.

9. ***Benchmark your speed against your competitors.*** Your organization should gather data from your industry competitors and benchmark their decision-making time against yours. If it takes a week to get your business solution in the hand of your customer and your competitor does the same thing in one day, you have a problem that needs to be resolved fast. Your time should be equal to or less than your competitor's.

10. ***Reward for speed and accuracy.*** Customers expect both quality and speed. Reward your employee for achieving both components. Conduct internal contests that promote speed among cross-functional teams by measuring the positive impact that speed has on the company's bottom line.

11. ***Pair the slow with the fast.*** Slow managers need to be paired with faster peers to learn. Managers who refuse to adapt to the company requirements will need to be released of their duties.

12. ***Train for speed.*** The training department must develop courses, educational programs, and interactive systems to allow managers and employees to think and act fast.

Speed is all around us. In sales, the fastest eats the slowest. Salespeople move as fast as they realistically can to win new business. Customers expect fast delivery and excellent performance. Yet, despite all effort that goes into the process, some internal managers slow their decision-making process to avoid errors and mistakes. A cross-functional manager may worry that he may get blamed. That is why the company needs to educate these managers that a well-intentioned mistake is an opportunity to learn and get better and not something to worry about.

Fast companies are not necessarily the company with the best products, services or prices. These companies are fundamentally the most adaptable and most tolerant to risk. Risk leads to opportunities, and the latter leads to revenue growth and expansion.

CHAPTER 32: SUMMARY

- Speed and technological advents had made even the most traditional industries ripe for disruption.

- Imagination and innovation of entrepreneurs make it possible to take an idea from conception to billion-dollar start-up.

- Legacy organizations that capitalize on their size, longevity, and market dominance will be devastated by smart start-ups that rely on technological evolution, smarts, innovation, and social digital on-demand partnerships to dominate sectors that were deemed safe in the past.

- Internal obstacles created by human insecurities, inefficiencies, and political power will need to be eliminated. Employees and managers who act as a bottleneck to progress will need to change or be terminated. Humans run companies, and human behavior can slow or propel progress faster than any mechanical or technological platform can.

CHAPTER THIRTY-THREE: CUSTOMER-CENTERED SALES CHANNELS

Today's customers are more demanding than at any time of the history of humanity. Customers expect to buy a product that will perform as expected without glitches or issues; satisfactory quality is the minimum expected standard that any reasonable person would accept. Your product should meet or exceed the purpose specified and deliver the promised outcome. Customers have little tolerance for companies that provide products riddled with problems and do not live up to their promises.

Today's savvy customer demands exceptional end-to-end holistic customer experiences to earn their business. Customer loyalty is hard won as it requires infinite attention to details and follow-up.

Customers want products that perform as promised and deliver total satisfaction. Technological advent makes customer buying process, social interactions, and feedback gathering much easier than in the past. It's common nowadays that a customer performs product research online, reviews other customers' feedback and continues shopping and interacting with the company via mobile, social media or email. Some customers may even call customer service to acquire additional information that is not found on the web to finally purchase the product face-to-face from a sales rep in a department store. For example, a customer can visit the BestBuy website and browse their camera selections and prices, then read customers reviews on Amazon.com, compare prices using Google search, then buy it from bhphotovideo.com.

As technology advances in an exponential way, customer dependence and usage of various interactive multi-channels to communicate and buy become an expected way of life. Most customers in developed nations have several internet-connected devices. Even in remote areas of Africa and Asia, people have access to mobile phones with internet access. The evolution of technology is changing customers' buying behaviors, consumption of information, data usage and expectations .

The lines between shopping online, offline and virtual reality are shrinking rapidly. Faced with this new wave of customer buying behaviors, many companies changed their way of doing business to meet their customer's multi-channel demands. Now you can shop by connecting to the company portal, whether you are using a desktop, a laptop, a mobile phone, a tablet or an Apple watch. Staying connected with the customer via multiple channels is key to staying relevant.

Omnichannel Experience

Omnichannel is an integrated multichannel sales approach that provides the customer with a seamless, uninterrupted holistic shopping experience. Whether the customer starts their shopping on an e-commerce website and later accesses it on their mobile device, or calls by phone, or visits the company's retail store, the buyer experience would be the same. Just for clarification, omnichannel experiences will use multiple channels; however, not all multi-channel experiences are omnichannel. The difference is the depth of integration. To have an omnichannel experience, all your social media campaigns, mobile marketing campaigns, e-commerce, and physical location will need to be integrated to be an omni-experience.

You may have a fantastic e-commerce site, great interactive social media campaigns, and first-class mobile marketing reach. However, that wouldn't mean you have an omnichannel unless they together represent a seamless integration.

Many companies are moving toward an omnichannel experience, while most businesses are still in the early stages of creating multi-channel experiences. In retail, several large companies have accomplished significant progress towards establishing an excellent omnichannel foundation. However, in the B2B environment, most companies are still operating at an infancy level while trying to create a solid customer multi-channel experience. Establishing B2B omnichannel may take decades to become a reality. Most companies may have teams of marketers who handle their website, send updates, and news via company blogs, social media platforms like Facebook and Instagram and Twitter. However, a seamless customer experience requires an integrated omnichannel platform that delivers total customer satisfaction.

An omnichannel experience will provide the same continuous experience regardless of whether the customer uses the web, mobile, social media or a telesales agent. The advantage of an omnichannel experience resides on the transferred knowledge, history and transaction data, and communication between parties that will be accessible in an uninterrupted fashion, whether accessed via cloud or on premise.

A study conducted by Crate & Barrel revealed that many of its shoppers switch from their e-commerce website to their tablets or smartphones while researching a product or completing a purchase. Armed with this knowledge, the company added the capability to save one's research or browsing history to allow the customers to start where they left off on any other device or browser. Crate & Barrel allowed customers using its wedding and gift registry to manage its record through any devices. Customers can edit, shop online, and scan barcodes in the stores to add products and even make real-time purchases.

Disney has perfected its omnichannel experience. It all starts with their state-of-the-art mobile-responsive website, which allows you to book your trip. "My Disney Experience" is a virtual system that allows you to plan your entire trip, from the restaurants you want to dine at to securing your "Fast Pass" to experience Disney's rides. Disney's mobile app locates the attractions you want to experience as well as the estimated waiting time. Your Magic Band program is your room key but acts as a photo storage device, food ordering tool, and it has an embedded Fast Pass integration that keeps you on track to maximize your vacation time. Disney certainly has a holistic omnichannel experience, yet it continues to improve on it.

B2B Multi/ Omnichannel Experience

Many companies are working hard to create an omnichannel B2B experience for their customers. However, it is a daunting task. Some companies are experiencing different levels of success with their multi-channel experience. Some have websites that provide a one-stop-shop experience — providing pieces of information, insights, and the ability to shop online.

Most business owners state that their business-to-business buying experience doesn't match their business-to-consumer experience. Today's customers are looking for seamless experiences like the Amazon experience. Achieving this goal will require investing significant resources, but the company that managed to offer its customers this level of interactive shopping engagement will reap major economics and brand recognition gains.

B2B Challenges

Achieving an omnichannel experience in a B2B environment will require a mindset change. Some companies may not be willing to make all product information public. You probably won't see Boeing displaying all their product specifications online, and there is a reason behind this strategy. Companies want to protect specific business trades that could be emulated by competitors.

The government sells expensive military weaponry to other friendly sovereign nations, but not to hostile dictatorship regimes. These highly sought-after military weaponry will always be protected for national security reasons.

Complex product selling will continue to require interaction with specialized field sales experts. Standard information and common business solutions will be accessible online, but large complex tickets items will continue to require human interaction and validation.

B2B Omni-Channel Experience Value

Companies that have achieved a level of sophistication serving their B2B customer can enjoy multiple benefits such as:

1. Increased customer satisfaction and better buying experience
2. Increased awareness, customer's loyalty, and transparency
3. Increased revenue by selling additional products and services.
4. Improved efficiency and reduced cost through an automated quote-to-purchase process
5. One-stop-shop total experience, with 3D customized business solution visualizations
6. Broaden reach and market shares
7. Price and quote transparency
8. Omnichannel experience with smart marketing recommendations that enhance the customer shopping experience.

Seamless Shopping Transition.

Despite the complexity of B2B sales, companies should embrace the customer's right to shop according to preferences. Web channels are increasingly playing a role in transactional sells; this tool allows customers to evaluate available options and make their own decision without pressure. However, there will always be a place for human-to-human sales. The more significant the risk factor and the higher the price tag, the more the need of an expert voice to help explain the pros and cons, the why's and how's that allow one to make a confident decision. Professional salespeople will always act as catalysts and advisors when the financial risks are high, the probability of error is great and when the consequences are severe.

A Sales Force of One.

A giant payment company had segregated its field sales force from its telesales. Both divisions were selling the same products and services, and each division followed its separate aggressive marketing campaigns. Within few months, complaints from existing customers started piling up; many of these existing customers were furious over the sent generic proposals or calls from the telesales group offering products at a lower cost than what the customers had already paid for with their field sales reps. Many customers were requesting refunds based on the offers at hand, others were threatening lawsuits, posting negative online reviews, while some decided to stop supporting the business.

While, the company was desperate to create new revenue. It lacked a strategy and process standards. Allowing the telesales group to target indiscriminately the whole company's existing portfolio to up-sell and cross-sell additional products without pre-qualification was wrong. Rather than being surgical with the company clients, they aimlessly called and sent generic proposals to the whole company client database.

Chaos ensued, and it took a lot of resources and time to undo the damage.

Unleashing the telesales force to generate revenue without a plan was a poor endeavor and a desperate move doomed to failure. Under pressure and competing priorities, senior management failed to create a strategic plan that would have produced better communication and alignment between the field sales reps and the telesales force. Rather than creating unwarranted customer dissatisfaction, they could have created additional value that promoted customer satisfaction and loyalty.

Creating Synergy

Executive management struggled to maintain the situation at first but later decided to pair each field sales rep with a telesales rep strategically. All substantial opportunities were to be assigned to the field rep, and all leads below a certain revenue threshold were to be managed by the telesales rep. All cross-sells, and up-sells were to be worked by the telesales reps, and any significant upgrade that requires a field rep involvement would undergo a commission-split structure.

In exchange, the telesales rep served as a point of contact to handle small issues and administrative changes. This separation of duties freed the field salesperson to focus on more considerable opportunities, knowing that they had a telesales partner who assisted their customers based on need. This action increased customer satisfaction dramatically; additionally, by implementing a transparent buying process and pricing uniformity, the company improved its employee morale and job satisfaction.

The collaboration between the outside sales reps and telesales reps generated a productivity uptick of more than 15%. More importantly, customer dissatisfaction decreased by 50%, and customer retention increase by 24%. Proper strategy and sound communications can create a competitive edge. Internal friendly competition can be healthy. However, it should never be misguided, where it becomes a real rivalry.

CHAPTER 33: SUMMARY

- Today's customers are rightfully demanding, forcing companies to live up to their promises in terms of immediacy, personalization, authenticity, and findability.
- Customer shopping behaviors has evolved dramatically in the last decades. The companies that met their customer's demands flourished; those who refuse to change will lose customer patronage, see their revenue vanish and risk being irrelevant.
- As customers are more and more comfortable buying online most of their products, e-commerce will grow globally exponentially. The omnichannel experience will become the norm. Slower adopters organizations will be disrupted and may lose significant market shares.
- Strong marketing strategy and internal alignment among cross-functional teams will become the business norm. To subsist and grow revenue in a fast-evolving hyper-competitive environment, companies will have to become consumer-focused. Customer loyalty is a thing of the past, and evident valuable distinctions will become a consumer magnet. Aligning the company business model with customer demand at a rapid pace is key to profitability and continuity.

EPILOGUE- THE NEXT WAVE

Sales organizations need to reassess and reevaluate continuously the elements that slow down or stop sales progress. Whether human, technical or mechanical, every aspect of the business will need to be streamlined, simplified, and improved to increase productivity.

Ultimately, a sales organization's role is to translate the company's strategy and vision into reality by adding value beyond what's expected, increasing its competitive advantage, and creating a sustainable level of profitability to keep the company financial health. This is tough to accomplish as customers are more demanding and savvier than ever before.

Sales organizations around the globe and across industries are finding themselves struggling to meet customers' increasingly complex demands and challenges in an environment of exploding exponential competition. It's becoming harder to maintain a competitive edge and distinguish oneself from a sea of suppliers.

This struggle is forcing sales organizations to be more agile, creative, and innovative in their way of doing business. Old business models need to be continuously updated, upgraded and changed. Antiquated traditional selling methods and traditional organizational strategies no longer work with an empowered, smart customer base and highly-effective competitors. Customers are increasingly relying on sales consultants who can simplify complexity, explain abstract concepts, customize a business solution that deliver results, and act as growth partners and freelance consultants.

Across countries, industries, and specialization, we have witnessed the following:

1. Sales managers and sales professionals are increasingly more knowledgeable, skilled, creative, and more adept at connecting customer needs to the company strategic growth projections. These sales professionals' connect customized value solutions to return-on-investment and risk tolerance while proactively collaborating with the customers from beginning to finish by providing insight and perspective that are mutually beneficial.

2. The adoption of team collaborative selling has become a strategic competitive advantage that companies can leverage to attract customers and win greater market shares.

3. The evolution of the sales manager's role from a supervisor and sales enforcer to a coach and empowering agent contributed to the development of a higher caliber of sales professional.

4. Relationship building and value selling is becoming the foundation that links sales organizations interests with consumer's needs.

5. Sales organizations are increasingly aware that they need to free up their sales force and sales management teams from the burden of operations to focus on revenue generation.

Although some of the trends have been evolving over the last decades, the velocity of change has increased exponentially in the last few years. Sales organizations' survival depends on the company ability to simplify its sales processes, empower salespeople and managers, and remove obstacles that hinder productivity and slow output, creativity, and innovation.

The following are some challenges that sales organization will continue to face:

- ***Internet Impact.*** E-commerce customer usage and adoption will increase dramatically, and omnichannel capability will become the norm for any business desiring to stay relevant and gain an edge. Traditional face-to-face salespeople who relied on old playbook selling methods will become obsolete. However, true sales consultants who provide valuable business advice using collaborative analysis that inspires customers and drives their productivity to new heights will become highly in demand. Additionally, telesales and telemarketers relying on old scripted methods and old sales methods will experience a steep decline unless they adopt innovative technologies like screen-to-screen and on-demand audio-chat that solve customers' problems on the spot.

- ***Redesigning the salesforce.*** Sales reality has changed and continues to evolve at an incredible velocity. The salesforce sales methodology and approach of the past can no longer influence the evolved, super-digitally connected customer. The next effective sales professional will need to be an explainer-in-chief, a simplifier of complexity and collaborator who do not simply customize and implement business solutions, but provide intelligent, fresh perspectives derived from unique of experiences that resolve problems from multiple angles.

- ***Salespeople empowerment.*** Today's savvy customers are impatient and have a short attention span. They know what they want, and they want it now. Today's customers want a sales force that can make impactful decisions and speed up the buying and implementation process. Sales support success will require access to critical information, empowerment to make on-the-spot decisions to resolve customers issues, increase productivity and customer satisfaction.

- ***Global digitation***. The development of technology and the internet has allowed some sales organization to go nearly virtual. The company office space no longer defines customer reach, sales generation or market impact. Salespeople and sales teams are becoming increasingly virtual. Virtual offices are becoming the norm in many industries, while the progress of technology renders salespeople and sales managers more effective and self-sufficient. It has also created new challenges for the sales manager on how to coach their salespeople remotely.

- ***Self-directing teams and larger team span.*** Many sales organizations have allowed greater access to information, granted more decision-making authority and autonomy to their salespeople while in some cases eliminating the role of the sales manager. This concept may work in a specific less complicated industries, but it represents serious challenges when the product/services are sophisticated and require multi-level strategies to influence decision-makers in a long cycle sales. Larger team span generally affects the quality of team communication, feedback sharing, and coaching negatively.

- ***Impact of Globalization***. E-commerce, faster communication, and the growth of highly efficient transportation have turned a big world into a much smaller environment. Customers' expectation that varies widely across geographies is becoming more and more similar today. A customer using an iPhone in Beijing has probably the same expectations as a customer in New York, Sydney, or Johannesburg. Shared global business culture is increasingly becoming the norm. The barrier that separated and segregated social customs in the past are vanishing quickly and are being replaced with cultural similarities.

What distinguishes winning sales organizations from traditional sales organizations is the following:

- Clarity on the goals they seek to accomplish and the strategy of how to get it done
- Nimbleness in understanding internal bottlenecks and external forces that are slowing growth and company performance, and the organization ability to address these issues with urgency, care, and empathy
- Continuous experimentation with new practices to improve sales force performance while empowering and trusting both sales managers and salespeople.

Smart sales organizations have a clear vision, unshakable commitment to winning, a strong unwavering determination to evolve, and a desire to take risks to achieve the company sought-after goals. Additionally, smart sales organizations trust and encourage their salespeople to share their best practices with their peers and management executives to build a better culture that believes in the power of sharing and continuous holistic progress.

Sales professionals and sales organizations will need to evolve at breakneck speed to meet demand and stay relevant. Today's innovations are already part of the past, and leadership must continue to push mental and technological innovation to survive in an ever-complex competitive digital world where the power is in the hands of the customer.

www.ingramcontent.com/pod-product-compliance
Lightning Source LLC
Chambersburg PA
CBHW060818170526
45158CB00001B/18
* 9 7 8 1 0 8 5 9 9 8 7 7 2 *